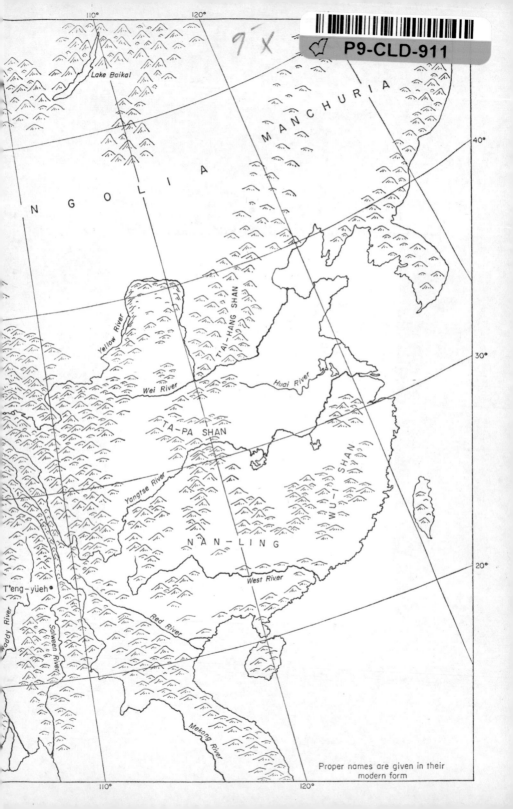

Proper names are given in their modern form

IMPERIAL CHINA

1. STREET SCENE IN K'AI-FENG, ABOUT 1100

From a roll painted by Chang Tse-tuan (about 1100), depicting life in the city on the afternoon of the spring festival. The roll measures 25 by 525 cm., and the original size of the part shown here is 25 by 19 cm. On the far side of the street there is a chemist's shop or clinic; the written prescriptions which are displayed on the walls include a cure for the after-effects of excessive drinking. Two women have brought a child for medical attention, and the expert's examination is in progress. Beside the shop there is a well, from which water is being drawn by bucket; on the opposite side of the street a crowd is listening to a story-teller. An itinerant [Buddhist priest?] is making his way along the street, followed by a mounted official and his attendants. The official holds a whip, and one of his servants a furled umbrella.

IMPERIAL CHINA

THE HISTORICAL BACKGROUND
TO THE MODERN AGE

MICHAEL LOEWE

FREDERICK A. PRAEGER, *Publishers*

NEW YORK . WASHINGTON

BOOKS THAT MATTER
Published in the United States of America in 1966
by Frederick A. Praeger, Inc., Publishers
111 Fourth Avenue, New York 3, N.Y.

All rights reserved

Printed in Great Britain

For
H.M.J.L. *and* E.V.L.

———

FOREWORD

Developments in politics, learning and education of the last few decades combine to prompt a new attempt to describe the principles of China's history in a single, short volume. Politically, China cannot for ever be excluded from the conference tables of the nations, and it can be expected that statesmen and others will acquire a growing interest in the political ambitions that are visible in China's past. While diplomats and journalists are paying greater attention to the Far East, the universities and schools of the west are becoming more accustomed to the view that a knowledge of oriental cultures is a practical asset rather than an exotic luxury, and that suggestions to arrange courses in these subjects should be welcomed rather than discouraged. In addition the last thirty years have witnessed the attempts of scholars to approach the history of China on the basis of the same academic criteria as those adopted for studies of the west, and results are now forthcoming from patient years spent in evaluating evidence, isolating problems and defining standards of consistency. Thanks to the production of detailed monographs which clarify specific problems or illustrate historical developments, it is becoming possible to set individual events and achievements in a more correct perspective; and the general statements that were made but a few years ago require constant revision in the light of new interpretation.

In the past, China's history has suffered from various types of misrepresentation. Some writers have overstressed the degree of cultural enlightenment and ignored the practical difficulties of everyday life. Others have fastened on the mystical aspects of the Chinese genius but failed to elaborate the rationalist elements of Chinese thought. In the political sphere, equal justice has not always been done to the classes of governors and subjects; and some historians have reviewed their evidence only in the light of a preconceived notion of human development.

In addition, disproportionate attention has been paid to different periods. Up to 1939, most western specialists concentrated their studies on the history of pre-imperial China (i.e. before 221 B.C.). Since 1945 the emphasis has very largely shifted to the events and developments

9

of about 1800 and later, i.e. the time when the west became intimately concerned in diplomatic and other relations with the Chinese. It seems that the compelling need at present is to consider the history of China in strictly realist terms, with due regard to the long period of time that is spanned, and in the full light of the evolutionary growth of the institutions of government, the organization of society and the use of economic resources.

This volume has been prepared for readers who possess no specialist knowledge of the Far East. It is intended partly for university students or sixth formers, partly for students of history who have specialized in a particular aspect of western culture, and who may wish to compare and contrast the achievements of the west with those of other civilizations. Recent researches have given us monographs on topics such as economic practice, social structure or the institutions of a particular Chinese empire; it is hoped that the following pages will give the western student the major historical context into which such detailed studies can be set. Finally, there exists no short account of China's past which is of immediate use to professional men and women who are principally concerned in the affairs of the twentieth century, who have no primary interest in the Far East, but who may find it increasingly desirable to make a brief study of China's past in order to understand contemporary events.

Scholars and historians will for many years be engaged on relatively minor problems which must be solved before major conclusions can be reached. Their task will for long be formidable, owing to the nature and abundance of the original sources and the large volume of publications forthcoming from oriental and western presses. The value of such research will be cumulative, and it will render obsolete some of the earlier attempts at synthesis or appraisal. The present stage of academic research permits a very general description of certain fundamental unities that have persisted in Chinese civilization, despite significant and wide variety in space, and the constant changes of a political, social and economic evolution. Such unities are seen conspicuously in China's cultural heritage, which may be cleft by intellectual and artistic differences as deep as those of Europe, but which has been consolidated by the use of a single written language throughout imperial history. For although only a small part of China's populations has been literate, that part has included those leading elements whose energies have moulded China's civilization. The written language has possessed sufficient strength and flexibility to resist the cultural onslaughts of both Buddhism and Christianity, and to outlast the up-heavals of foreign invasion and civil wars.

This book does not pretend to be a comprehensive history of im-perial China. I have attempted to give due weight to the growth of government, the influence of intellectual activities and the realities of daily life, as it is on the basis of such major considerations that the study of specialist interests in literature, philosophy, art and science may best proceed. The selection of facts, figures and examples that are given by way of illustration is necessarily subjective, and where pos-sible these are presented in tabular form, separately from the main discussion.

The chapters are arranged by topic, in the hope of clarifying the significant factors of Chinese history; and within each chapter, events and developments are treated chronologically. Although it has some-times been convenient to refer to events of the early, middle or late empires, precise definition of such terms should not be sought, and they are used without the overtones that are implied by expressions such as 'ancient' or 'mediaeval'. Between the earlier (e.g. Ch'in and Han), middle (e.g. Sui, T'ang and Sung) and later (e.g. Ming and Ch'ing) empires, there intervened many dynasties and long centuries which can be classified only at the peril of periodization; and it is no function of this book to formulate or to defend precise temporal dis-tinctions. Examples of Han, T'ang, Sung, Ming or Ch'ing practice are cited to illustrate stages in a long process of development, rather than as a means of crystallizing the concepts of a particular period. While I have endeavoured to avoid undue emphasis on a single dynastic era, I am conscious that I have written more on the earlier than the later periods. In general I have purposely avoided a consideration of the developments that occurred after about 1850, except as a means of stressing how radical were the changes introduced from then. For those changes were such that the history of modern China, of the nineteenth and twentieth centuries, must be considered in an entirely different way and within an entirely different framework from one best suited to the earlier ages.

Any historian will pose questions that remain unanswered in this volume, whose omissions are due to personal judgment, a desire for brevity and to the nature of Chinese history. While the sources provide a wealth of detail on matters of minor interest, e.g. the correct insignia or equipment for use in imperial carriages, owing to the lack of suitable information we can do little more than guess at the answers to major questions, such as the proportion of rural to urban inhabitants at a given time. Many fundamental problems are as yet unresolved; or the theories that have been advanced for their solution are too tentative for inclusion here (e.g. problems such as the ethnic origins of the Chinese); and the book will certainly be open to the criticism that some subjects such as religion, intellectual trends, popular risings, the arts or scientific development are omitted or treated inadequately.

I am also aware that some statements are repeated in two or more chapters. This has occurred for two reasons. It is not always possible to retain a clear-cut distinction between different aspects of Chinese history, e.g. social conditions derive partly from political arrangements, and cultural advances are intimately concerned with both. The division of subject matter between chapters is at times arbitrary, and it has sometimes been necessary to re-state a principle for the sake of a full understanding of a particular topic. The second reason for duplication lies in the hope that each chapter can be read independently.

I offer no new conclusion based on personal research nor do I claim that all statements and opinions rest directly on a personal study of the most primary material that is available. It will be seen from Chapter Ten that such a method would be neither possible nor reasonable for a summary of this nature. I have depended largely on the work of my colleague specialists, and have endeavoured to present or to interpret their conclusions without misrepresentation. Scholars will certainly know that problems have been oversimplified, overemphasized or omitted, and there will be many points in which research can provide correction. In these circumstances no specific acknowledgement is made to particular writers. I am deeply indebted to the great host of scholars, living and dead, eastern and western, whose individual and joint researches over two millenia have made this ephemeral summary possible.

My thanks are due to the following friends who have been kind enough to read part or all of the book in manuscript and to proffer helpful criticism and advice: H. Blakemore, M. Elvin, D. C. Lau, D. C. Twitchett, and P. van der Loon; and to J. Ch'en, P. Kratochvíl, Yim Lee, J. Needham, L. Picken and L. S. Yang for their help and guidance with specialist problems. I am also grateful to the following authors and publishers for permission to quote from their works: J. L. Cranmer-Byng, and Messrs Longmans, Green, from *An Embassy to China*; R. E. Latham, and Penguin Books, from *The Travels of Marco Polo*; J. Needham, and the Cambridge University Press, from *Heavenly Clock-*

work; E. H. Schafer, and the University of California Press, from *The Golden Peaches of Samarkand*; Teng Ssu-yü and J. K. Fairbank, and the Harvard University Press, from *China's Response to the West*.

A few maps have been included to illustrate geographical conditions or some of the administrative problems and their solution. They are not designed to show the full sequence of dynastic succession, or to exemplify situations that were necessarily typical or long-lasting. In principle, only those places that are mentioned in the text are named on the maps, but a few additions have been made for the purpose of definition. Plates and figures have been chosen to illustrate various aspects of China's cultural development; these are not necessarily described in detail elsewhere in the book.

In general I have used the Wade-Giles system of romanization for Chinese names, without the diacritical marks usually omitted today (see pp. 301 f). Places are usually cited by their modern rather than their ancient names (with the exception of Ch'ang-an, which I have retained in place of the more modern Sian), and hyphens have been placed between the elements of which they are formed. Exceptions have been made in the case of very well-known names (e.g. Peking and Yangtse, rather than the correct but pedantic Pei-ching and Yang-tzu), but the correct versions are kept in a few contexts, such as Table One, and in the index (e.g. references to Tientsin appear under that name; there is also an entry; *T'ien-chin*; *see Tientsin*). For purposes of clarity a further inconsistency has been retained in the use of the two dynastic titles *Tsin* and *Kin* (both names are rendered *Chin* in the Wade-Giles system). The terms B.C. and A.D. have been used as a convenient means of denoting dates, but they do not imply the acceptance or application of a Christian interpretation of history.

M. L.
Cambridge
January 1965

CONTENTS

CONTENTS

CONCLUSION 299

B

ILLUSTRATIONS

CHAPTER ONE

GEOGRAPHICAL IMPLICATIONS

I. CHINA AND HER NEIGHBOURS

The achievements of Chinese civilization can be distinguished from those of other peoples by the continued presence of a few significant characteristics which recur in many aspects of the Chinese way of life. Many of these features can be easily recognized and described, but a satisfactory analysis or definition often presents difficulty, if only because they are so comprehensive. For these features underlie the extension of political authority, the growth of different elements of society, the development of economic practice and the promotion of intellectual and artistic activities; and they have been subject throughout to the slowly evolving influences of human genius, wisdom and folly. For this reason the creations of Chinese civilization have changed perceptibly, if slowly, during the 3,000 years of Chinese history, and it is part of the historian's task to isolate those characteristic aspects of Chinese life that have stood the test of time and can be regarded as comparatively constant.

The sub-continent and the periphery
It might be expected that such constancy would lie revealed in the geographical conditions of China, but a clearcut distinction between China and her neighbours is not easy to frame. For Chinese civilization has arisen as a result of human activities of a particular sort, and these have not been confined within a well-defined area of the world's surface. Historians of China are concerned with a sub-continent, whose centres lie in the valleys of the Yellow River and the Yangtse, and a periphery with which the sub-continent imperceptibly merges. The peripheral areas comprise territories which have been known as Manchuria, Mongolia, Turkestan and Tibet. At times, large expanses in the interior of the sub-continent have been situated outside the control of Chinese authority; sometimes Chinese families have successfully implanted the features of their civilization in the hills of the periphery that

overlook the Chinese plains. In view of the large areas that are involved, the history of China is one of several races, coming from widely separated parts of the sub-continent and the periphery, and struggling to snatch a livelihood by varied means in different types of territory and climate.

Chinese history has been partly conditioned by the existence of natural barriers, which have isolated China from neighbouring civilizations, and of natural divisions within the sub-continent itself. At times these have proved to be sufficiently large to frustrate attempts at political unification and to prevent the full exercise of cultural intercourse. The following description will proceed by first observing the force and nature of the barriers formed at the periphery, and the conditions of economy that prevail there; and thereafter by examining the divisions that separate different parts of the sub-continent. Finally, an attempt will be made to review the varied means and results of China's production.

Access by sea
On the eastern and southern sides of China, the western seas of the Pacific Ocean long denied the inhabitants the means of access to the outer world. Coastal and more distant waters are subject to typhoons for many months of the year, and safe navigation demands skill and experience at all times. There are early references to isolated Chinese maritime expeditions, e.g. to the Japanese Islands (about 200 B.C.), to Korea (about 100 B.C., for military purposes) or to the Malayan peninsula (at the start of the Christian era, by traders), but effective or large-scale command of the seas was long discouraged by natural conditions. By the eighth and ninth centuries successful attempts to establish maritime trade-routes to Chinese ports had been made by Arab or other merchants from the Middle East; and although ocean-going junks were plying foreign waters with the help of the compass from the thirteenth century, it was not until the beginning of the fifteenth century that large fleets put to sea for commercial purposes at Chinese instigation.

The mountain ranges of the south-west
The south-western and western sides of China are dominated by the eastern end of the great massif which comprises the Hindu Kush, the Tibetan plateau and the Himalayan mountains. This major range lies athwart Asia from West to East, and its extremities stretch out to form the lower hills of southern China. But a change occurs at the eastern

22

edge of the main range; for here the hills come to an end with an escarp-
ment that runs from north to south (from 27–35 degrees north), with
the result that the lands to the east of the line 100–105 degrees east are
effectively separated from central Asia. The southern part of this north
to south line is met by a chain of hills that runs north-westward from
the coast of Vietnam; and the Chinese cultural area is brought to an
end in the highlands of Yün-nan. Farther to the north the Yellow
River and the Yangtse, which form dominant features in China's
geography, take their rise from the same mountain massif of central Asia.

The open borders of the north

The area of Chinese culture is bounded in the north by a series of
deserts that are themselves divided by mountain ranges. Here, however, the natural separation between China and other areas is by no
means as clear-cut as it is elsewhere. For although very great geographical differences can be discerned between the plains of north
China and the steppes of Mongolia, between the two there lie spacious
intermediate lands wherein the two types of terrain approximate to
each other more and more closely. In these intermediate lands Chinese
and non-Chinese can mingle more easily than elsewhere; they are
tempted to experiment with each other's way of life and to practise
compromise systems of economy that are acceptable to both parties.
It is in the north that China lies most open to penetration by the foreigner, and it is from the centre of her northern borders (c. 110 degrees
East, 40 degrees North) that the invading tribes of the north-east or
north-west have assembled to launch armed attacks into the heart of
China. Much of China's foreign policy has been preoccupied with the
problem of an undefended northern border.

Seclusion from the north-east

A long ridge of high country running from north to south forms the
eastern edge of the deserts which separate China on the northern side.
The ridge continues southward with a chain of hills which penetrates
deeply into China and forms an important feature in China's geography;
this chain is called the T'ai-hang shan, and runs parallel with the north
to south stretch of the Yellow River. To the north-eastern side of the
ridge there lies the area known sometimes as Manchuria, whence access
can be gained to the Korean peninsula, and thence to Japan. Manchuria
comprises the lands of origin of several peoples who have established
dynastic regimes in China.

Communities of non-Chinese races

The distinction drawn between China and her surrounding neighbours can be seen in ethnic as well as geographical terms. China itself has been largely populated in historic times by members of the Han race. Whatever its origins may be, this race can be clearly distinguished from the Mongol peoples of the north, the Tungus tribes of the north-east, or the Turkish and Tibetan groups from the north-west and west, whose natural habitat has been situated now within and now without the Chinese sphere of political influence. Southern communities, possibly of south-east Asian affinity, have infiltrated to the south and south-west, and Arab or other Middle Easterners made their way to the north-western and south-western parts of China from the ninth century or earlier. Societies formed of these peoples have lived and survived, sometimes in large numbers, in separate enclaves within China, surrounded by the Han Chinese population. Such alien communities have sometimes grown up with the encouragement, or at least the toleration, of the Chinese central authority; sometimes, and particularly in the regions south of the Yangtse, they have lived in areas whose remoteness has made them free from interference by a Chinese authority. Individual members of the non-Han races have at times played a major role in Chinese history, thanks to military fortune or commercial enterprise; and the presence of these foreign communities has added considerable enrichment and variety to China's cultural achievement.

The Chinese farmer and his neighbours

The different geographical conditions of East Asia have given rise to the development of different types of economy. The emergence of Chinese civilization can be traced to the growth of an agricultural way of life which developed from the neolithic ages (*c.* 2500 B.C.) onwards. At first, agriculture was practised in northern China in an extensive fashion over wide areas of land which were successively reclaimed from forest and stripped of undergrowth. Once the farmer had exhausted the capacity of the soil, he moved elsewhere to repeat the process in fresh woods. It was only at a later stage that more advanced techniques enabled the farmer to settle in a limited locality, and to work comparatively small fields intensively, with the help of irrigation and manures. But neither extensive nor intensive forms of agriculture could be practised without a supplementary means of livelihood, unless arable land was easily available. In much of China, mountains, jungle or marshland prevent the effective production of cereals; and in the areas that lie at the periphery, it has been impossible to develop a purely agricultural economy on a scale that could support the population adequately. The Chinese peasant forms a contrast with his neighbours of Manchuria, Mongolia, Central Asia or Tibet, whose way of life depends principally on other means of production, which are in turn supplemented by some agriculture.

Occupations in the north-east
Manchuria can be divided into three closely associated sub-regions according to economic practice. There is an area of farmland in the south, verging towards the fields of north-east China; on the west side steppe-land adjoins the similar territory of the eastern reaches of Mongolia, and the inhabitants are engaged in similar occupations; and in the east and north the main source of livelihood is to be found in the forests which have covered much of the landscape. Here the principal occupations are hunting, river fishing and lumber work.

The stockbreeders of Mongolia
On the steppes of Mongolia the characteristic way of life is that of the pastoral nomad. Settled habitation cannot be maintained owing to the nature of the ground and the climate, and the population is largely engaged in rearing horses, cattle, camels, sheep or yaks. All these types of animal are reared for specific purposes (e.g. camels are used on the caravan routes of central Asia), and each presents its own peculiar problems of maintenance and feeding.

The communities of the oases
Further west, in central Asia or Turkestan, yet different conditions prevail. The extensive lands east of the Pamirs, which have long been penetrated by Chinese traders, have been inhabited by small communities living in isolated settlements at the foothills of the mountain ranges. For historical reasons the strategic importance of these localities may be far greater than their intrinsic value or their meagre material resources would suggest. Usually the settlements have been made around the infrequent oases grudgingly provided by nature in a singularly intractable part of the world. Two series of oases skirt the ranges which surround the Taklamakan desert, in such a way that a northern and a southern trade-route can be formed by passing from one oasis to the next. These routes, which are sometimes known as the Silk Roads, converge near Kashgar at the western end of the desert;

and from this point communication can be made eventually with the Mediterranean world. There is in addition a further series of isolated communities settled on the northern side of the T'ien Shan range and facing towards central Asia. These communities are of a somewhat different nature from that of the settlements of the Silk Roads. But in each case a mixed form of economy is practised; while part of the effort is spent on agriculture, sheep, goats, cattle and horses are bred, principally for local use.

The Tibetan highlands
Finally a mixed economy of yet a different sort has been practised in the bleak heights of Tibet. Agriculture is not generally possible on the plateau itself and is restricted to its perimeter. At the same time a small degree of pastoral nomadism is practised in the uplands.

Chinese penetration to the periphery
It must again be stressed that, while it is correct for reasons of geography, race and economy, to draw a distinction between China and the areas just described, there have been times when large parts of the peripheral areas have been included within the Chinese empire. Owing to the distinctions described above and the lack of continuous Chinese dominion over these wide expanses, the term 'China Proper' is sometimes used to denote that part of the sub-continent which is surrounded by the areas named as Manchuria, Mongolia, Turkestan, and Tibet. However, at times of imperial expansion these have been claimed as Chinese territory. A map of China drawn in the eighteenth century might extend as far as Khabarovsk in the north-east and Kashgar and Yarkand in the north-west; and in the south-west, Chinese Yün-nan would be shown as adjoining Burma near T'eng-yüeh. Neither the peripheral areas nor their inhabitants can be dismissed as being irrelevant to the history of China; for these lands frequently formed the objects of dispute between the Chinese and their neighbours; and the occupations of the non-Chinese peoples have affected the Chinese way of life in greater or less degree.

II. THE DIVISIONS OF THE SUB-CONTINENT

The area in which Chinese culture and economic practice has grown and predominates can thus be distinguished from other parts of Asia wherein these features have spread, and where a Chinese way of life has been introduced to join existing practice. Within China itself there exist widely divergent practices, and the area is of sufficient size to warrant treatment as a sub-continent rather than a country. Not only are the occupations of the inhabitants considerably varied; the rivers and hills of the interior are so situated that they have frequently acted as isolating barriers of marked cultural, political and economic significance.

The principal rivers

There are three river systems which have exercised a profound influence on Chinese history, those of the Yellow River, the Yangtse and the Huai. In addition, those of the West River and the Red River are of lesser, but still far-reaching, importance. In all cases these rivers flow in a general easterly direction; they rise from the mountain massif that lies to the west of China and are constantly fed by tributaries that originate in China's own territory. Although these rivers have sometimes separated, or been used to separate, China into different regions, their potential use as a means of communication recurs throughout the development of the Chinese economy.

The Yellow River

Of these systems it is the Yellow River that features earliest in Chinese history, for it is in part of this river's valley that the first evidences of primitive civilizations are found. The course of the river, whose sources lie on the fringes of the Chinese cultural zone, is far from straight. Thanks to a series of three major bends, each of almost 90 degrees, the river encloses a large rectangle of territory, set roughly in a north to south direction and comprising in its north-western part the Ordos desertland. For some two-thirds of the period of Chinese history the southern part of this rectangle has played a decisive, strategic role in the fate of dynastic houses. For it is an area which forms a natural fortress, guarded by mountain ranges that run along its southern, eastern and (less forcefully) western sides, and approached by way of relatively few and easily defensible mountain passes. The capital cities of several dynasties have been situated in the southern part of this rectangle, which is watered by tributaries of the Yellow River. Of these, the Wei River has considerable historical significance.

It is also of some importance to note that the area is relatively well-placed for communication with central Asia. By *c.* 100 B.C. Chinese explorers had realized the possibility of reaching northern India by routes that led north-westward from here; and although it was known that some access to India could be obtained by means of a southern route (through the modern provinces of Yün-nan or Ssu-ch'uan),[1] it was appreciated that such a route was less secure or practical, and official support was reserved for the use of a northern route that led from Ch'ang-an (modern Sian) to Tun-huang and the Silk Roads.

The difficulties of the delta

At the south-eastern corner of this rectangle the Yellow River turns sharply and now flows towards the sea, in an easterly or north-easterly direction. The value of the river as a means of communication is somewhat limited. For much of its course it can be used by small craft of shallow draft only. Passage is impeded by a group of rocks which are set mid-stream about 100 miles west of Lo-yang and which have seriously prevented the transport of goods upstream. Of further significance is the irregular nature of the river's course further east. For the surrounding land is flat and subject to inundation, and the banks of the river have frequently been unable to contain the volume of water that flows from the central Asian hills. In addition the fall of silt from the upper to the lower courses sadly detracts from the river's use; passage by steam vessels is only possible for short stretches, and the use of junks is limited.

Owing to its repeated vagaries it is not always possible to determine the precise route taken by the lower reaches of the Yellow River in historical times. Whereas the records mention the major changes of course which have occurred, there is not always a clear statement regarding the less violent changes, whose effect has still been near to disastrous. The tale of flood, famine and distress, which pervades so many decades of Chinese history, bears witness to these difficulties and the effect of such disasters in human terms; but the references in Chinese writings cannot always be associated with events or catastrophes that can be defined in time and space.

The main features of the Yangtse

Like the Yellow River, the Yangtse rises in the lofty mountains that lie to the west of China. After an initial southerly course, the river turns sharply to the east and proceeds on its distance of over 1,000 miles to the coast. The Yangtse has been described as the world's most beautiful

[1] These provinces correspond in general with those of the Ch'ing Empire (see Map 8).

waterway, and its valley comprises a rich variety of scenery. In its upper reaches the river runs through a famous series of gorges; later the course is accompanied by several large lakes, beginning with the Tung-t'ing hu (measuring 56 miles by 75 miles at maximum), and the broad estuary is flanked by an expanse of low lying flats. A major tributary, the Han river, flows into the Yangtse from the north-west near the modern conurbation of Wu-han. Owing to its length, and the great volume of water that is carried, the level of the river is subject to considerable seasonal variation (e.g. at Hankow (one of the cities comprising Wu-han), the depth reaches 25 feet in summer but only 10 feet in winter) and navigation can be seriously affected. Whereas in summer vessels of 10,000 tons can proceed upstream to Hankow, at other seasons the depth is insufficient for ships of over 6,000 tons. Obstacles are formed by sandbanks lying in the main course of the river, but the large capacity of the lakes is sufficient to drain off an excess volume of water, and there is little danger of flooding. A long delta is formed at the mouth of the Yangtse, and with the continual deposit of sediment the shoreline is being continually prolonged, at the rate of about one mile in seventy years.

The enclave of Ssu-ch'uan and the lower valley of the Yangtse
The Upper Yangtse flows through a province whose modern name is Ssu-ch'uan, or *The Four Rivers*. The name derives from the tributaries which flow into the Yangtse in that area, having irrigated and enriched the large tracts of territory through which they have passed. Owing to its natural resources, the area became prominent in the early days of Chinese history and was playing an important economic role from the fifth century B.C. As access from here to the east is made by way of the Yangtse river only, the area has tended to be somewhat isolated from the rest of China. For Ssu-ch'uan lies west of a line of gorges which reach as far as I-ch'ang, and it is only in recent decades that it has been possible to build special steam-driven vessels which can maintain a regular service from there to Chungking. East of I-ch'ang vessels of 2,000 tons can use the river to Hankow and beyond.

While the Lower Yangtse valley has long possessed considerable natural resources, it is only comparatively recently that its full exploitation has come to play a major role in the development of the Chinese economy. This process may have been set in motion by the eighth or ninth centuries, but its full effect was not felt for some 400 years later.

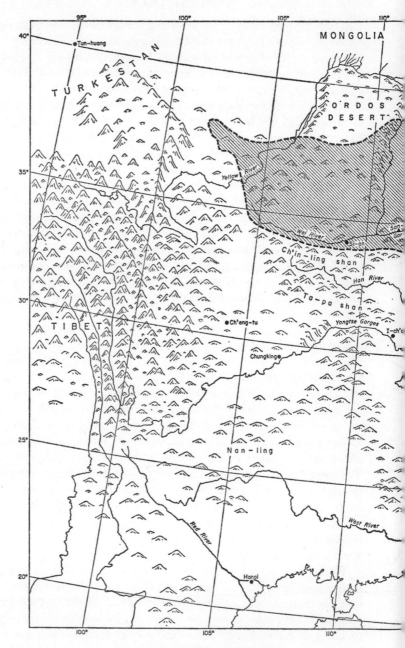

MAP 2. China's Natural Divisions

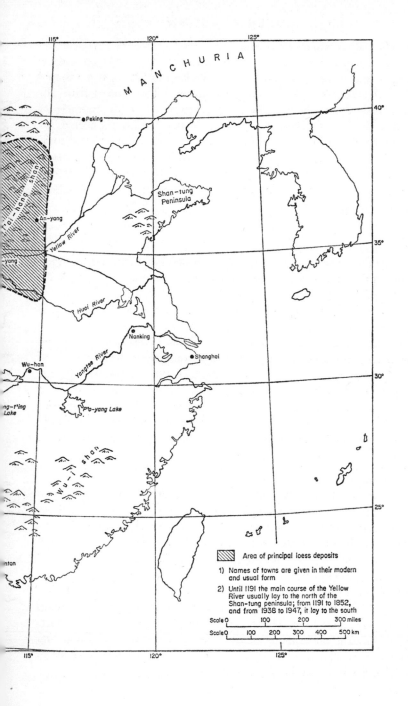

MANCHURIA

Peking

Shan-tung
Peninsula

An-yang

Yellow River

-yang

Huai River

Nanking

Wu-han

Yangtse River

Shanghai

ng-t'ing
Lake

P'o-yang Lake

s h a n

W u - i

nton

▨ Area of principal loess deposits

1) Names of towns are given in their modern
   and usual form

2) Until 1191 the main course of the Yellow
   River usually lay to the north of the
   Shan-tung peninsula; from 1191 to 1852,
   and from 1938 to 1947, it lay to the south

Scale 0   100   200   300 miles

Scale 0   100   200   300   400   500 km

The Huai River and its tributaries

The area lying between the lower reaches of the Yellow River and the Yangtse includes some of the most fertile land in China. It is watered by the Huai river and the many tributaries which join it from the north-west. Before the imperial era (i.e. before 221 B.C.) a number of small political units arose in the Huai valley, which supported the growth of some of China's earliest cities. The rich resources and commanding position of the area have sometimes rendered it a prizeground which has been contested by rival regimes based on the northern (i.e. Yellow River valley) or southern (i.e. Yangtse valley) parts of China.

The river systems of the south

Of the other many rivers of China, two deserve particular attention owing to their potential use for purposes of communication. The West River or Sikiang rises in the foothills of the central Asian massif and flows almost due east, reaching the sea near Canton. Similarly the Red River rises near the boundary of Yün-nan and Burma, and emerges near Hanoi. The territory through which these rivers pass is hilly and intractable, and communication is almost only by water. The use of these river systems to link the hinterland of the south-west with the seaboard ports was potentially of great value in the development of Chinese civilization. However, their significance is less conspicuous than that of the systems of the north, and may not have been fully appreciated by Chinese officials or documented by Chinese historians.

The mountain ranges and their effect

China can be regarded as a plain lying to the east of the central Asian massif, which is itself divided by numerous mountains. The last lines of the central Asian hills are mainly set in an easterly direction, forming the valleys in which the main river channels have been dug. Such ranges are seen in the Ch'in-ling-shan, the Ta-pa-shan, the Wu-i-shan and the Nan-ling. The two latter lines are so placed that they effectively bar the way from the interior to the coastal strips of the seaboard, which can thus be isolated from other parts of China. At times governments have been able to profit from the isolation of these parts by despatching undesirable elements to exile there. The Ch'in-ling and Ta-pa ranges are among the features that form the watersheds of the Wei, the Han and the Yangtse rivers.

GEOGRAPHICAL IMPLICATIONS

The plain of north China

Reference has been made above to the high ridge that runs south from Mongolia so as to form the T'ai-hang range of hills in China. These hills serve to divide north China into an eastern and a western part, that are linked by the channel of the Yellow River. The range affords protection to the western part, which was used as China's metropolitan area until the tenth century. The eastern part is watered by the Yellow River and is subject to considerable inundation. It forms the northern part of the Great Plain of north China, which stretches from the valley of the Huai river. The high ground which rises at the eastern end of the plain forms the Shantung peninsula, and it is from the points where these hills protrude that the Yellow River is likely to change its course. For the river has found a number of channels to lead to its mouth, sometimes on the northern, sometimes the southern side of the peninsula, and a major change of course from one side to the other takes place periodically. The crippling nature of the effect of such upheavals on the lives of the inhabitants can well be imagined.

Regional divisions and advantages: (a) the north-west

The cultural and political developments of China have been largely influenced by geographical features. The sub-continent has been split naturally into a number of units which have often existed independently of their neighbours, being provided with a natural means of defence or self-sufficient supplies of food. Three particular regions, the old metropolitan area, the Lower Yangtse and the Upper Yangtse, stand out conspicuously as playing important roles in this respect.

The natural protection afforded by hills and river to the metropolitan area has been noted above; its value has been thoroughly appreciated by statesmen and historians, who describe the region as the *kuan-chung*, or the area within the passes. Many of the campaigns fought to unite China under one authority were launched from here. The foundation of large cities to act as the seat of government soon resulted in a considerable increase of population, and the region soon came to depend on the conveyance of food from elsewhere. This has sometimes been supplied from the Great Plain, which has possessed plentiful arable lands and the resources of textile and mineral production, but has lacked the means of natural defence.

(b) The Lower Yangtse valley

While there have been some occasions when a political authority has

C

been able to rely on the resources of the Lower Yangtse (below Wu-han) valley to establish an independent regime, these attempts have not been as successful or their effects as far-reaching as those that have been based on other regions; the military advantages have not been as great as the economic resources, and other factors have discouraged the initiation of cultural or military advances from this area.

It is only from comparatively recent times, i.e. *c.* A.D. 1000, that the Lower Yangtse valley has played a major part in the economic development of a Chinese empire. The area has indeed been subject to intense cultivation for many centuries previously, and from *c.* 600 it had provided an imperial government that was seated in Ch'ang-an (modern Sian) with some of the supplies that it needed. But it is only from *c.* 1000 or even later that the Lower Yangtse valley should be regarded as a principal source on which an imperial government depended. The newly acquired importance of the area was due to political, economic and social causes. From about 1000 the full force of the movement of population from the north was being felt effectively as the cumulative result of some centuries' trend; and this trend was soon to be speeded and accentuated by the occupation of north China by non-Chinese masters. Meanwhile production was being increased in the south by means of scientific experiment and technological advances; a new strain of rice which had recently been introduced from Champa (in Indo-China) possessed the excellent qualities of resistance against drought and ripened early enough in the season to permit the cultivation of a second crop within the year. Moreover new means of irrigation were being developed; and there was growing up a section of the Chinese communities which possessed sufficient wealth and power to support such projects and to promote agricultural production on the basis of private initiative.

(c) *The isolated fortress of the west*
In the Upper Yangtse valley a safe enclave has sometimes been formed with the support of the abundant production of the region and a few major cities such as Ch'eng-tu or Chungking. Owing to the intervening lines of hills there is no easy access from here immediately to the metropolitan area, and the gorges of the Yangtse valley can obstruct communication with the east. A refugee regime that is fleeing in the face of invasion has sometimes found safe asylum in this region for long periods, and economic practices have sometimes survived independently here, long after they have been outmoded elsewhere in China.

GEOGRAPHICAL IMPLICATIONS

Problems of control and communication

Much of China's dynastic and political history is concerned with the efforts made by a master of one of these regions to gain control of other parts of the sub-continent. For the advantages of one particular region are often complemented by those of another, and the rivalries that have separated two or more regimes have sometimes been accentuated by the difficulties of communication. Broadly speaking, nature has provided China with more useful horizontal than vertical links. Governments have been forced to employ much of the manpower at their disposal on the tasks of remedying this deficiency; and as the territorial divisions of China's dynasties have been closely related to the conditions imposed by nature, from about A.D. 600 governments have been engaged in attempts to link the northern and southern areas by artificial routes. Further references will be made below to the significant connection between the efficiency of government, the control of manpower and the use of waterways (see pp. 36 f and 215 f).

III. VARIETIES OF PRODUCTION

Regional varieties of climate and staple product

Over 1,000 miles separate the extreme northern and southern, or the eastern and western points of China from each other, and it is only to be expected that this large area should be subject to widely differing climatic conditions. A total of eight zones can be distinguished on this basis, varying from a sub-arctic zone in Mongolia to a tropical type of the south. Similarly, the extent of natural water supplies and the need for artificial irrigation varies very considerably among the different regions. Immediate results of these differences are seen in the variable means and products of agriculture. The Yangtse valley is characterized by the production of rice, as nature has provided sufficient water for the wet cultivation of the paddy-field. In the north however, i.e. the valleys of the Yellow river and the Huai, the staple crops are wheat and millet; and it was the northern area which for long provided imperial governments with their supplies of grain. In the west (i.e. Ssu-ch'uan) terraced farming is a conspicuous feature of the landscape. Rice and rape-seed (a source of cooking oil) are grown, with wheat as a winter crop, and the area includes the sites of some of the earliest Chinese experiments at irrigation. In the sub-tropical and tropical conditions of the extreme south, where arable land is scarce, the intensive efforts of farmers have made it possible to raise as many as three rice

35

crops during the year; elsewhere several crops of different varieties are sometimes grown in rapid succession for harvesting during the same year. The greater part of China's tea is produced in the central area of the Yangtse valley. This plant has been cultivated in increasing quantity since the third century A.D. and has long constituted an important item of export from China.

Other crops, which have been introduced to China more recently from elsewhere, and which serve to supplement the traditional products, include *kao-liang* (a cereal grown in north China from the fourteenth century), maize (in north China from the sixteenth century) and sweet potatoes (used extensively in south China).

Loess
Varieties of soil have affected agricultural production very considerably, and the characteristic type which persists in the north-west and north is worthy of consideration. This is the so-called 'loess' region, where the soil consists of a fine, yellow silt, which has been blown and deposited for centuries by the winds of central Asia. Deep deposits of loess, sometimes ranging up to 300 feet, are found in the whole of the area bounded by the Wei river in the south, the T'ai-hang hills in the east and the Ordos and Gobi deserts of the north and the west; lesser deposits, still of considerable depth, are found further afield and extend as far as the Huai river valley. Loess has proved a fertile soil, as it is able to retain its mineral qualities and a sufficiency of moisture despite its light nature; but the light rainfall of the area may need to be supplemented artificially. In addition, loess type country is subject to severe erosion, with the result that the landscape is frequently cleft by deep vertical lanes. As a by-product of these conditions it becomes possible for the inhabitants to fashion their settlements in the caves that are naturally formed by the terraces of the earth's surface.

The control and supply of water
As a result of these geographical and climatic factors, agricultural production has often depended on the successful control and exploitation of China's supplies of water; and this has in turn resulted in major social and political consequences. In the loess territory, artificial waterways and means of leverage may be necessary. In areas such as the lower part of the Yellow River valleys, the abundant silt deposits that are brought down from the uplands of central Asia provide a constant source of enrichment for the soil, but they are often brought to the

2. COTTON-WEAVING

From the *Shou-i kuang-hsün*, an illustrated manual (published in 1808) describing the process of manufacturing cotton textiles, from planting the crop to dyeing the finished cloth. Original size of wood-cut 20 cm. by 14 cm. For the production of cotton in China, see p. 38.

farmer at the price of wide inundation. As the rate of rainfall is subject to great variation within the year, particularly in north China, constant care must be paid by the farmers to the provision of adequate supplies of water that can be used regularly. In the south, the successful cultivation of rice depends almost exclusively on the skilful manipulation of large volumes of water over wide areas of paddy-field. Conservation, irrigation and flood-control are matters of prime importance to a government and its people, and figure conspicuously in the economic and political struggles of the various regions of China.

Other products

China's economy has depended on a number of products other than the staple cereal crops. Sugar cane was cultivated in south China from before the imperial period, and techniques for hardening the product and reducing it to powder had been developed by the sixth century. In the succeeding five centuries the use of sugar spread widely, until the production of cane had become a regular secondary means of subsistence for many of the southern farmers.

Textiles designed for general use were long made from hemp, which has been produced in the north China plain from early times. Cotton goods had been imported to China from India and Persia from the second century B.C. The cultivation of cotton and manufacture of cloth was started by foreign communities in south China by at least the eleventh century, and techniques had been advanced considerably within two or three centuries. By the fifteenth century cotton production was general throughout China. The earliest Chinese writers who have been concerned with human welfare have looked idealistically to the universal growth of mulberry trees, so as to provide a more general supply of silk. This had been produced in east China from 1000 B.C. and earlier, and had spread thence to other parts. By the time of the T'ang and Sung empires (c. 600 to 1200) three main areas of silk production had been established. From the seventeenth century, the export of raw silk became more important than that of made-up goods.

Stockbreeding of horses or cattle has not been a common characteristic of the Chinese countryside, but few farms do not rear pigs and chickens. Sheep have been reared for their meat rather than their wool.

Minerals

Mineral resources include fairly extensive supplies of coal that are mainly situated in the modern provinces of Shansi, Shensi, Hopei,

Ssu-ch'uan, Kweichow and Kwangsi (see Map Eight), but these resources have not been exploited fully. Iron is found in many provinces,
but the main supplies of copper and precious or semi-precious metals
are derived from Ssu-ch'uan and Yün-nan. Rock-salt is mined in a
number of scattered localities. Ssu-ch'uan, eastern Manchuria and parts
of tropical China include rich sources of timber.

The population and its spread
More information regarding the extent and spread of the population is
provided in the Chinese histories than in those of any other people.
Nevertheless the information is highly sketchy and ill-balanced and
must be handled with considerable caution (see pp. 188 f). Despite the
need for reserve in drawing major inferences, it can still be shown that
the spread of the Chinese population has emphasized the natural
divisions of geography that are outlined above. Large areas have never
possessed sufficient means of supporting a dense population and have
therefore remained sparsely inhabited. The area of greatest concentration has been that of the Lower Yellow River valley and the Huai
River valley, which have been able to provide the necessary food for
large numbers and wherein large cities have developed from early
times. A second area of thick concentration is seen in the enclave of the
Upper Yangtse (Ssu-ch'uan); and, since the eleventh century, political
and economic factors have resulted in the considerable increase of the
population of the Lower Yangtse valley or the provinces further south.
An even more recent development, dating from the last century or so,
is seen in the emergence of a fourth area of density in the coastal belt
that stretches from Canton to Shanghai.

Cultural variety
The sub-continent of China has given rise to the growth of several
different cultures, but the degree of variety has sometimes been obscured, owing to paucity of information and historical treatment. The
sources on which historians depend were compiled almost exclusively
by men who represented the interests of political regimes seated in the
north. As some of these works were written apologetically, in order to
defend the authority of the north as against the claims of the south, a
tendency persists whereby the practices of the peoples of the Yellow
River valley are exalted to the detriment of those of other regions.
The growth of civilization is depicted as expanding from imperial
times (i.e. from 221 B.C.) in a southerly direction, and as providing an

IMPERIAL CHINA

ill-disciplined population of the backwoods with the benefits of a fully
cultured existence. Such a view is considerably oversimplified, and this
idealized account can be corrected in the light of recent evidence.
Several neolithic cultures are known to have existed in different parts
of China more or less simultaneously, and no claims can be made for
the superiority or seniority of a north-western, eastern or central type.
For more recent times (i.e. *c.* 1000 B.C. and later) archaeologists are
discovering the remnants of a southern type of culture in Hunan,
which possessed markedly different features from those of the northern
culture. However, it is the northern type that has long been accepted as
Chinese *par excellence*, and, thanks partly to the influence and reputation of the Chou kingdom, this type has proved dominant over its
southern neighbours. Owing to political preponderance and propaganda, it is not always possible for historians to analyse the constituent
elements of Chinese culture according to their different origins;
anthropologists and students of folk-lore may be able to evaluate their
evidences more satisfactorily, and may be able to arrive at a more
accurate degree of discrimination.

It is clearly no more possible to generalize significantly in regard to
China than it is in regard to other continents or major cultural areas. A
viable economy has been attained in the face of many variable factors
such as the proportion of workable to unworkable land; the uses to
which waterways can be put; the ease of access to mineral resources;
and the prevalence of different types of natural calamity. In these
circumstances the degree of cultural unity and continuity is perhaps
remarkable. Nevertheless a more accurate picture may perhaps be
drawn by regarding China as a sub-continent of peoples, whose
origins, occupations and reactions are accepted as variable, than as a
single nation, bound together by ties of overriding political and
economic unity.

TABLE ONE

THE PROVINCES OF IMPERIAL CHINA (see Map 8)

The following list shows the provinces that existed in the eighteenth and nineteenth centuries, when the Chinese empire was established over its greatest area[1].
Although China was not organized in provinces of this size and type until the
Yüan and Ming periods (see pp. 174f.), many of the earlier administrative divisions
were incorporated in this arrangement, which has been partly retained since 1911.

The names of provinces and cities are given in the Wade-Giles system of
romanization; more usual forms, and alternative names that have been used before or after the Ch'ing period, are given in brackets, e.g. Chi-nan (Tsinan), or

40

GEOGRAPHICAL IMPLICATIONS

Yün-nan (K'un-ming). Some of the names are not of Chinese derivation (e.g. Kokonor, Urumchi). The capital cities of major dynasties are shown in upper case.

Provinces	*Notable cities*
	(i) The interior: north of the Yangtse
An-hui (Anhwei)	Lu-chou (Ho-fei); Huai-ning (An-ch'ing).
Chiang-su (Kiangsu)	Chiang-ning (CHIEN-K'ANG, NANKING); Yang-chou; Su-chou (Soochow); Shanghai.
Chih-li[2] (Ho-pei)	PEI-CHING (PEKING, PEI-P'ING); T'ien-chin (Tientsin).
Ho-nan	LO-YANG; K'AI-FENG.
Hu-pei	Han-k'ou (Hankow); Wu-ch'ang; Han-yang.[3]
Kan-su[4]	Lan-chou; Tun-huang.
Shan-hsi (Shansi)	T'ai-yüan.
Shan-hsi (Shensi)	CH'ANG-AN (Sian); Yen-an.
Shan-tung	Chi-nan (Tsinan); Ch'ing-tao (Tsingtao).
Ssu-ch'uan (Szechwan)[5]	Ch'eng-tu; Ch'ung-ch'ing (Chungking).
	(ii) The interior: south of the Yangtse
Che-chiang (Chekiang)	Hang-chou (Hangchow; LIN-AN); Ning-po.
Chiang-hsi (Kiangsi)	Nan-ch'ang; Chiu-chiang (Kiukiang).
Fu-chien (Fukien)[6]	Fu-chou (Foochow); Hsia-men (Amoy).
Hu-nan	Ch'ang-sha; Heng-yang.
Kuang-hsi (Kwangsi)	Kuei-lin (Kweilin); Nan-ning.
Kuang-tung (Kwangtung)[7]	Kuang-chou (Kwangchow, Canton); Hsien-t'ou (Swatow).
Kuei-chou (Kweichow)	Kuei-yang (Kweiyang).
Yün-nan	Yün-nan (K'un-ming); Ta-li.
	(iii) Manchuria
Chi-lin (Kilin, Kirin)	Chi-lin; Ch'ang-ch'un.
Hei-lung-chiang (Heilungkiang)	Lung-chiang (Tsitsihar); Harbin.
Feng-t'ien (Liao-ning)	Feng-t'ien (Shen-yang, Mukden).
	(iv) Tibet
Ch'ing-hai (Kokonor)	
Hsi-tsang (Tibet)	Lhasa
	(v) Turkestan
Hsin-chiang (Sinkiang)	Ti-hua (Urumchi); Kashgar.

[1] The Ordos desert (modern province of Sui-yüan) which was not included in these units was sometimes comprised under imperial administration.

[2] Including parts of the later Jo-ho (Jehol) and Ch'a-ha-erh (Chahar) provinces.

[3] These three cities are collectively known as Wu-han.

[4] Including part of the later Ning-hsia province.

[5] Including the later Hsi-k'ang province.

[6] Included Taiwan (Formosa) from 1683 until its establishment as a separate province (1887).

[7] Included Hainan.

CHAPTER TWO

THE RISE AND FALL OF DYNASTIES

Difficulties of definition

Despite the varied attempts that have been made to do so, there is little practical value in dividing Chinese history into periods of time on a theoretical or conceptual basis. For the present purposes, major distinctions can be drawn on the basis of political development, between a pre-imperial age (before 221 B.C.), an imperial age (221 B.C. to 1911), and a post-imperial age (since 1911), but owing to the great developments that occurred within each of these periods, further sub-division is both convenient and necessary. For the imperial period, the difficulties of such a sub-division are similar to those of defining the territorial extent of Chinese empire. Certain periods, that are usually of short duration, can properly be characterized as those of particular dynasties, in so far as those dynastic houses were able at those times to influence contemporary government in a conspicuous and forceful manner. But such short periods merge with longer periods in which the same houses had been founded; or exercised a lesser or negligible influence; or fell into decline; and description in dynastic terms becomes controversial. Problems are raised by the simultaneous existence of several contemporary self-styled empires, and by their claims to acceptance or legitimacy; or by the selection of a particular point in time when a newly founded dynasty, native or alien, should cease to be regarded as a rebel usurper and should be acknowledged as possessing recognized authority.

Dynastic divisions and other criteria

Chinese historical method will be considered more fully below (see Chapter Ten). It will be seen that traditional practice has been to divide Chinese history into periods on the sole basis of the tenure of sovereignty by a particular family. However, dynastic divisions of this type are hardly satisfactory; the criterion itself is questionable, owing both to the nature of dynastic strength and the problem of selecting

42

one of several rival dynasties for the purpose; and the resulting divisions of time are very unequal, as they may range from one or two decades to three or four centuries. Although some Chinese historians have been aware of these shortcomings, the use of other criteria may present similar difficulty. The recent interpretations of Chinese history that depend on distinctions of social or economic maturity (i.e. the reliance of Chinese society on a system of slavery, feudalism or capitalism) have provoked lengthy discussions by experts but have provided scant practical assistance to students.

As elsewhere, so in China it is possible to take note of a few major events or processes which reveal the pace at which political, social or economic development has been achieved. However, such processes have often been drawn out over lengthy and irregular periods, and they can hardly be used as definitive indicators of historical periods. For clarity and simplicity, we are forced to fall back on dynastic divisions, with all their weaknesses and dangers. In the following chapters the terms early, middle and later empires are used purely as a matter of convenience, without necessarily implying that significant changes can be dated therein. Moreover, the terms are not used to cover the whole of the imperial period; i.e. the early empires are characterized by the Ch'in (221–207 B.C.) and part of the Han empires (202 B.C.–A.D. 220); the term middle empires refers usually to the Sui (589–617), T'ang (618–906) and Sung dynasties (960–1279), with some of their contemporaries; and the practices of the later empires are best exemplified under the Ming (1368–1643), or more usually the Ch'ing (1644–1911) houses.

I. THE EMERGENCE OF KINGDOMS

The golden ages of a mythical past
The traditional myths enshrined in Chinese literature have given rise to beliefs and misapprehensions that have been current for some 2,000 years. The beginnings of Chinese civilization have been traced to the work of godlike heroes, to men or supermen whose efforts have been rewarded by a mastery of natural obstacles and marked by successful feats of superhuman endurance. As a result the seeds of civilization have been sown, and there has been started the weary task of transforming uncouth communities into the polished societies of a cultured age. At the close of these initial stages there have existed several golden ages, in which mankind has basked under the full protection and perfect government of model sovereigns, whose saintly qualities have been blessed by every felicity that heaven and earth can vouchsafe.

43

Palaeolithic China

Unfortunately, archaeologists, pre-historians and historians cannot be so confident or specific. Evidence testifies to the activities of hominid or human beings in palaeolithic conditions, in the middle of the Pleistocene (i.e. about half-a-million years ago). Some of these men, including those whose remains are known as the type *Sinanthropus Pekinensis*, or Peking Man, lived in caves not far from Peking; they were able to walk erect, to control fire, and, possibly, to use their voices meaningfully. Other areas in which early evidence has been found include the Ordos, and there are signs of a human occupation of the Upper Yangtse valley in palaeolithic conditions. Both here and in the caves of Kwangsi, the evidence is of beings who existed after the time of Peking Man. Some of the early remains bear features that can be associated characteristically with the Mongoloid race, of which the Chinese peoples have been largely composed.

The neolithic cultures

The evidence of human activity between the palaeolithic and the much later, neolithic, periods is extremely scanty and unevenly spaced, and poses as many problems as the bare facts that it yields. Such evidence, however, is continually being confirmed or questioned as more recent finds come to light, and current theories are usually open to debate. Broadly speaking, at least three different neolithic cultures can be distinguished in the northern part of China (i.e. north of the Yangtse), each possessing its own characteristic features, and each being partially definable in territorial terms. These are the Yang-shao culture of central and north-western China, with its monochrome pottery; the painted ware culture that is associated with Kansu; and the Lung-shan culture of east China, distinguished by its thin black wares that are known to have been turned on a wheel. The relationship, if any, that existed between these three cultures is subject to dispute. That of Kansu is thought to have extended from *c.* 2200 B.C. to *c.* 1300, and to have overlapped the Yang-shao culture, which came to an end in *c.* 1500; and the stage reached at Lung-shan is thought to be later than that of Yang-shao. South of the Yangtse, evidence of distinct neolithic cultures have been found in a number of sites on the coasts of Chekiang and Kwangtung, and the use of the potter's wheel can be attested.

The bronzes and bones of the Shang-yin kingdom

The bronze age, which can be dated in China from the comparatively

44

late period of *c.* 1500 B.C., is sometimes taken as an intermediate period between pre-history and history. Early vessels and implements formed in this medium have long been known to Chinese historians and antiquaries, but it is only within the last sixty years that it has become possible to associate some of these magnificent artefacts with an area or period known to history; and considerable difficulties of interpretation still preclude precise or detailed definition.

Many of the bronzes can be associated with an early kingdom named Shang, and later known as Yin, which was situated in the Yellow River valley from *c.* 1500 to *c.* 1000 B.C. But perhaps the most important contribution to our knowledge of this early period lies in the recent discoveries of shells and bones that were used for purposes of divination, and which were inscribed with the earliest known form of Chinese writing. These fragments require skilful examination and evaluation by archaeologists and palaeographers, and can hardly be used as source material in which historians may seek the answers to their questions. For practical purposes Shang-yin China still remains within the province of the pre-historian rather than the historian.

The value of the inscriptions of Shang-yin
Specimens of the famous oracle shells and bones of Shang China can be inspected in a number of museums or libraries in Asia, Europe or America. The script that was used on these early documents is the direct ancestor of the modern form of written Chinese, and many modern characters are recognizable in their ancient garb (see Table Four). The inscriptions owe their origin to a religious faith in the power of augury, and it is clear that the earliest communities of China which acknowledged a central authority did so from religious as well as from political or social motives. The inscriptions have shed considerable light on the religious and secular practices of Shang-yin China and the way of life that was practised in a slowly emerging civilization.

Until the discovery of these fragments (from 1899), our knowledge of Shang-yin China was based almost exclusively on the references that occur in the *Shih-chi*, an historical text whose compilation was complete in *c.* 90 B.C. (see p. 281). The scant information and formal list of kings' names that appears there had become an object of profound distrust in the prevailing scepticism of the late nineteenth century but the new evidence of the shells and bones quickly served to dispel such suspicions. For the inscriptions refer by name to the kings and

45

their officials, and a remarkably high degree of corroboration exists between the two sets of reference. Thanks to the bones, a belief in the historical existence of the Shang kingdom has been firmly restored, and the authority of the *Shih-chi* has been dramatically vindicated.

The kingdom of Shang-yin

Much of the material evidence (e.g. tombs, remains of buildings, bronze vessels, treasure pits) of the Shang-yin kingdom has been found by archaeologists at sites that lie near the modern city of An-yang (Honan province). The kingdom was situated on the north bank of the Yellow River, but the extent of its authority can hardly be defined or conjectured. The position of king passed from one member of the family to another, and a system of fraternal succession was eventually replaced by one of direct transmission from father to son.

The Chou period and its reputation

The kingdom of Shang-yin came to an end *c.* 1000 B.C. or earlier, some few centuries before the use of iron had generally replaced that of bronze. According to Chinese tradition, which was formulated and crystallized at a much later period, there followed an age which has continually served as an ideal era in which the later imperial governments have sought inspiration for their institutions and customs. The accounts of this period (the Chou period: traditionally 1122 B.C. to 249 B.C.) include much that was framed for purposes of propaganda, with a view to ascribing an early origin to practices that were adopted at a much later stage of civilization. In this way, writers of, e.g. the first or second centuries A.D. could invest contemporary procedure of court or government with the authority of a hallowed tradition.

The absence of source material

But apart from this idealized view, there is little that would persuade a critical historian of the existence of political forms and practices on the scale that was envisaged retrospectively in the imperial age. Amongst the collections of literary pieces, both prose and poetry, that are alleged to originate from the Chou period, there have been included some extracts that may date from the ninth or eighth centuries, and many that were written by later hands. China's earliest chronicle is concerned with some of the events that occurred in east China between 722 and 481 B.C., and this terse account is accompanied by amplifications that may have existed but were probably not brought together

46

as a single compilation before 300 B.C. The many inscriptions that were skilfully made on the precious bronze vessels of the Chou period can be accepted as reliable evidence of particular practices or events, but their value as a source of historical information is strictly limited.

The establishment and decline of the Chou kingdom: the idealized view
It is probable that the Chou peoples made their way into China from the west and succeeded in defeating the last of the Shang kings in battle; they then proceeded to occupy his lands and to adopt the more advanced and more comfortable way of life of their vanquished enemy. The stages whereby this process was completed will probably never be known, despite the attribution of heroic achievements and just practices to the early leaders of the Chou peoples. Nevertheless the traditional account of Chou history, which may well include fictional elements, has exercised as profound an influence over later developments as the bare events themselves. For although that description of the Chou kingdom may be questionable, it has formed the background of the orthodox view of the Chinese empire or state, as this has been taught to successive generations of civil servants, statesmen and emperors.

The Chou house is envisaged, at its best, as the ruling authority of a fully organized empire, no less able to govern than the dynasties of the later ages. It is claimed in some of the writings of the early Chinese philosophers (i.e. fifth and fourth centuries) that the house of Chou had been invested by a beneficent Heaven with religious authority and moral qualities, and that it was only under the auspices of Heaven, a superhuman and supernatural being, that the house had been established. It was thus only the head of the Chou house who was entitled to bear the title of king. Chinese moralists from an early time claimed that the fortunes of Chou depended directly on the moral qualities of the presiding rulers and their servants, and even explained the dynastic history of Chou in such terms. It was believed that the early rulers had been saintly kings, fully justified in expelling the last, tyrannical ruler of Shang, and that their excellent government was operated over an increasingly wider area as the world became more civilized. At a later stage these saints were succeeded by men of lesser integrity and ability, whose temporal authority was brought into question. Their kingdom was invaded by foreigners; separatist revolts broke out among their own subjects; and finally the weakness of the king was so marked that Heaven ordained retreat, and the dynasty was forced to flee in the face

47

of danger and to find a more secure seat of authority further east (770 B.C.).

The traditional view of the early independent regimes
These 'separatist' tendencies are associated in the Chinese tradition with a feature of government that is said to have been adopted by the Chou kings at an early stage. This involved the bestowal of estates on the king's kinsmen or on those who otherwise enjoyed a dominant position in society. The estates were held on an hereditary basis; they carried certain administrative responsibilities, and the incumbents owed a few formal obligations of homage to the king of Chou. Chinese authors have explained that the greater the distance at which these estates lay from the centre, the more difficult it became for the central authority of the king to exercise effective leadership. Just as the quality of the royal house degenerated, so could the succeeding generations of the original estate holders shed their feelings of loyalty to the centre; and there set in a corrupt tendency towards the establishment of independent courts or regimes. In this way, dynastic events that occurred after 770 B.C. are traditionally regarded as a steady deterioration from a state of affairs that had originally been perfect. Centralized, beneficent rule over an extended area was replaced by a number of independent courts, each with its own practice of government, and each usurping the authority and title which was properly due to the Chou house only.

It is on this basis that the Chou period has often been described as feudal. Traditional historians divide the period of five centuries from 770 into two sub-periods, of which the first was marked by the existence of a comparatively large number of small pretenders, and a few attempts at a major dictatorship, and the second by the eventual establishment of seven major units into which the smaller units had been merged. The first of these periods (strictly speaking 722–481) is termed the 'Spring and Autumn period'; the second is traditionally described as that of the 'Warring States' or 'Warring Kingdoms' (480–222).

A realistic appraisal
This traditional interpretation of the history of some five centuries is somewhat negative, as it inevitably regards political events as unwarranted departures from a norm, and allows for no evolutionary progress of a political, social or economic nature. Thanks to archaeo-

48

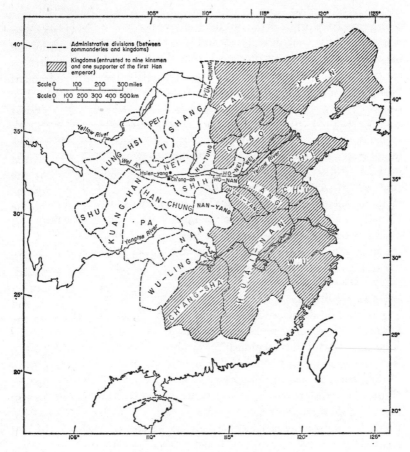

Administrative divisions (between commanderies and kingdoms)

Kingdoms (entrusted to nine kinsmen and one supporter of the first Han emperor)

Scale 0   100   200   300 miles

Scale 0   100 200 300 400 500 km

Yellow River

LUNG-HSI

PEI

SHANG

TI

YÜN-CHUNG

TAI

CHAO

YEN

Wei R.

NEI-

HO-TUNG

HO-NEI

CH'I

Hsien-yang

Ch'ang-an

SHIH

HO-NAN

LIANG

CH'U

KUANG-HAN

HAN-CHUNG

NAN-YANG

SHU

PA

N

HUAI-NAN

Yangtse River

WU-LING

CH'ANG-SHA

WU

MAP 3. The Han Empire (195 B.C.)

D

logical, anthropological and scholastic research, and a more critical appraisal of the slender literary evidence that is available, a different view can be taken. The establishment of the kingdom of Chou can be said to have derived from an eastward migration of a tribe or group which may have originated from the fringes of central Asia. The group was sufficiently well disciplined and organized to establish itself as masters of the fertile territory wherein the kingdom of Shang had existed; and its leaders were ready to appreciate the values of the Shang way of life. They therefore took over a number of features of the earlier regime, such as its practice of agriculture, its mastery of bronze and its system of writing; and a Chou kingdom became established on an hereditary basis. Possibly this kingdom extended further afield than its predecessor, but the area of its immediate administration was probably still somewhat restricted. Beyond its immediate confines lay lands which were recognized as being in the keeping of other leaders, including members of the displaced royal family of Shang, the king of Chou's own relatives, or warriors who had distinguished themselves during the successful advance of the Chou people to the east. As with the kingdom of Chou, the privileges and duties of these men were transmitted on an hereditary basis.

A feudal relationship?
The relationship between these leaders and the king of Chou is crucial, but unfortunately it is precisely in this respect that reliable information is lacking. Ideally the relationship has been viewed as that of servant and master; and it was believed that the estate holders stood possessed of their lands thanks to the bounty of the king himself. In this way a Chou overlordship has been portrayed in 'feudal' terms. However, there is little direct evidence to support the view that a defined contractual relationship existed as between a king and his vassal, or that a right to govern the outlying areas depended necessarily or exclusively on a grant of title and authority from an 'emperor'.

The formation of the seven warring kingdoms
It is from such a situation that there emerged the independent growth of a large number of separate units or 'states', beginning in the eighth century. Possibly these may have been originally formed of little more than the walled cities from which the exploitation of the surrounding lands could be organized and which afforded some degree of protection to the few inhabitants. In larger units, political development occurred

with the rise to prominence of professional advisers, scribes and over-
seers of labour. A growing degree of political maturity was doubtless
stimulated by other changes of a profound nature which were affecting
the general way of life of the Chinese in these centuries. The introduction and spread of iron tools, which can be dated from the
sixth century B.C. or perhaps earlier, led swiftly to the improvement
of agricultural techniques, the growth of cities and commerce, and a
more complex stage of civilization. Forms of political organization
were being forged which were capable of controlling large numbers of
manpower; small units were being integrated into larger 'states'; until,
by the fourth century, there existed seven major kingdoms, which
collectively occupied most of China north of the Yangtse. Smaller
units, including that of Chou, survived as buffers between these seven
major 'states' of Ch'i, Ch'in, Ch'u, Han, Wei, Chao and Yen. The
ruler of each of these had by now assumed the title of king, despite its
theoretical restriction to the house of Chou. Each of the seven kingdoms disposed of wider territory than that which had been under the
immediate control of the earlier kings of Chou; each enjoyed the use
of rich economic resources that could be exploited independently to
make the kingdom self-supporting; and some of the kings had erected
defensive walls or dykes as a means of protection against their hostile
neighbours.

The merger of smaller into greater political units in this way can be
regarded as an essential step in the evolution of a Chinese empire from
tribal groups, and it is only as part of that major process that the existence of the seven states can be properly explained or their importance
assessed. But it should be noted that this interpretation is at variance
with that of traditional Chinese historians, who explain the political
events of these five centuries as the break-up of an extensive dominion,
and as retrograde departures from an existing state of centralized rule.
Despite the full weight of Chinese scholarship, it is perhaps preferable
to suggest that the emergence of the seven states should be regarded as
part of the natural growth of larger and better organized units, that
occurred in the absence of an earlier scheme of effective central
authority.

The cultural influence of Chou

It is thus suggested that excessive importance has been attached to the
part played by the Chou kings in the development of Chinese political
history, and that the kingdom played a far smaller part in moulding

China's imperial unity than is often implied. However, despite the overdrawn picture that is presented by later Chinese writers, allowance must be made for the possibility that some of the practices and institutions of the Chou kingdom were incorporated in the later structure of empire. For it is known that some of the political arrangements of the seven states were taken over, and the same principle must be recognized in respect of the earlier kingdom of Chou. The difficulty of discriminating between elements of imperial governments that were truly a survival from Chou and those which were anachronistically ascribed thereto will long remain unresolved.

Moreover, due respect should be paid to the house of Chou in view of the cultural unity which it helped to impose on pre-imperial China. This influence may have been due in the first instance to the ties of kinship which existed between the royal house of Chou and some of the other leading families; and it is possible that the kings of Chou occupied a position of religious leadership which was respected by most prominent and ruling families. The original kingdom of Chou, founded some time before 1000 B.C., may not deserve its reputation as the supreme and only temporal authority entitled to obedience. Nonetheless the period of 800 years in which the kingdom existed is of extremely great importance as the formative age in which almost all aspects of Chinese civilization were developed, and in which barbarous practices gave way to the force of civilizing customs. The leaders of Chou may well deserve full credit for their steady contribution to this development.

II. THE FORMATION OF EMPIRE

221 B.C. is often taken as a turning point in Chinese history, as it was in this year that the first Chinese empire was brought into being. Henceforth the theory of government was based on the general recognition that a single imperial authority possessed the right to delegate authority for central and provincial administration, to direct the efforts of China's manpower and to co-ordinate the exploitation of her resources. These conditions did not apply to the practice of government before 221, and it cannot be assumed that they have been operative continuously thereafter.

The creation of the Ch'in empire from existing kingdoms
The events of 221 B.C. formed the culmination of a process which had been set in motion long before. For several centuries Ch'in had been

established as one of the major kingdoms of the Warring States period. The transformation of a kingdom into an empire took place after a long period of preparation and training, in which the population had been trained to shoulder the burdens of the State. Backed by efficient military force of a type unseen elsewhere, the government of Ch'in was able to expand its territory at the cost of its neighbours, and eventually to incorporate all their lands within its own realm. Ch'in's policy of territorial aggression had been inaugurated for over a century before its logical conclusion was reached in 221. The creation of empire was accomplished by taking over existing states, and owed part of its success to the existence of fully formed political units in six other parts of China. It was thus possible to plan and exercise a unified control from Ch'in's own centre, over areas already accustomed to some political organization. Having existed as a kingdom in the pre-imperial age and expanded to form an empire, Ch'in stands as a link between the two eras.

The structure of imperial government
Successful as the Ch'in house had been at the creation of Chinese empire and the initiation of its government, the dynasty itself barely survived the death of the first emperor, and ended in disruption after a mere fourteen years. An almost identical form of government was eventually adopted by its successor, the Han dynasty (202 B.C.—A.D. 220), and was practised for some four centuries, with a widely differing degree of intensity and with several periods of interregnum. By this means there was set the essential form of government which was to be practised in later centuries. A central administration, drawing authority directly from the emperor, was seated at the capital city, with its many constituent organs. A smaller, and less complex, replica of such a scheme of offices was practised in the provinces, under the authority of senior officials who were responsible to the centre. The establishment of government in newly acquired territory was comparatively simple, as no change of basic structure was necessary.

The character of the Ch'in and Han dispensations
Partly owing to the sequence of dynastic change, Chinese writers have long been used to denigrate the character of the Ch'in and to applaud the achievement of the Han regimes. It is frequently observed that Ch'in enforced a rigorous rule of oppression regardless of its subjects' will, whereas the Han governments made a continued attempt

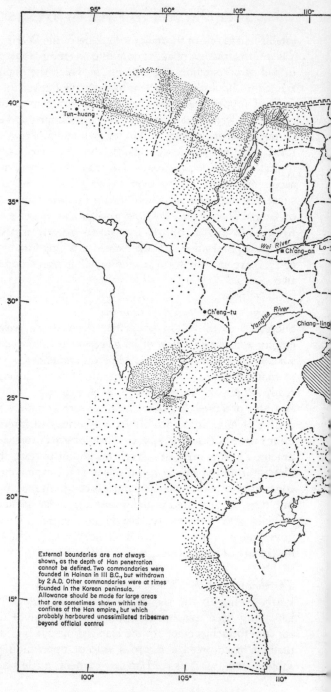

External boundaries are not always
shown, as the depth of Han penetration
cannot be defined. Two commandaries were
founded in Hainan in III B.C., but withdrawn
by 2 A.D. Other commandaries were at times
founded in the Korean peninsula.
Allowance should be made for large areas
that are sometimes shown within the
confines of the Han empire, but which
probably harboured unassimilated tribesmen
beyond official control

MAP 4. The Han Empire (A.D. 2)

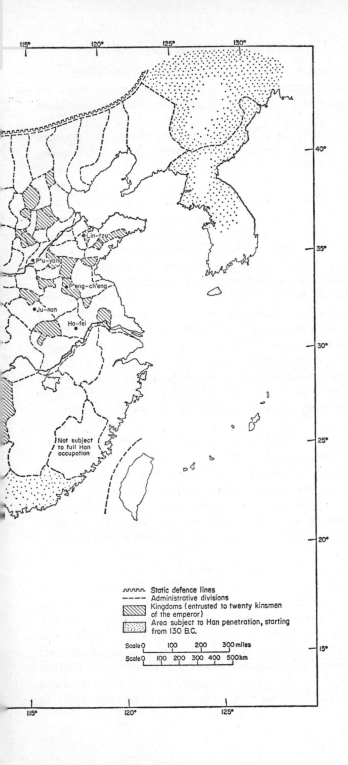

Static defence lines
Administrative divisions
Kingdoms (entrusted to twenty kinsmen
of the emperor)
Area subject to Han penetration, starting
from 130 B.C.

Scale 0   100   200   300 miles
Scale 0   100 200 300 400 500 km

to practise a benevolent administration in the interests of the community. As the documents on which these judgments are based are scanty and biased, there is some difficulty in distinguishing here between fact and prejudice.

The two regimes can in no event be compared closely, as they were established in somewhat different circumstances; and if a fair assessment is to be attempted, due account must be taken of the long period of seventy years in which Han empire and its rule were consolidated after the formal foundation of the dynasty. Good reason exists to show that the concept of government in Ch'in rested on the efficient implementation of the will of the emperor and his government, regardless of other interests. While empire was being forged there can have been little opportunity for the few officials to bypass the strict provisions of authority, in favour of a kinder or juster treatment of a particular subject of the emperor. By the time that the Han dynasty had been consolidated (c. 130 B.C.) government had become more intensive, and officials had longer experience of administration on which to draw; but there is no reason to believe that the Han official was encouraged, willing or able to exercise his discretionary powers with greater clemency or generosity than his predecessor. According to contemporary and later writers the decrees of the Han emperors were frequently directed to improving their own standards of behaviour, to ameliorating the lot of their subjects and to placating superhuman forces in the general interests of mankind. Despite such protestation, efficient Han government depended no less than that of Ch'in on the rigorous obedience of the subject to his master. It is only thanks to the partiality of the early chroniclers that emphasis has been placed on those aspects of Han administration that were conceived as a means of bringing welfare to the people, and that Han authority has normally been credited with aspirations to moral, enlightened and benevolent government.

The strength and weakness of the early empires
At their moments of strength, the early imperial governments of China were capable of directing much of the population that lived north of the Yangtse river, and of establishing official or military outposts that lay some 1,500 kilometres from the capital city (Ch'ang-an). Attempts were made to exploit China's natural resources and to initiate bold schemes so as to co-ordinate production. By these methods foodstuffs and textiles could be distributed or stored, and the necessary bases could be established for military undertakings and expansion. In

favourable circumstances of prosperity and stability, the institutions of the emperor would favour the general dissemination of cultural benefits, promote the cause of the individual intellectual, and attract men of talent to put their services at his disposal. At its weakest state, early imperial government was carried on in a capital city which was rent by faction or intrigue, and in a countryside which was subject to banditry or disaffection. As officialdom could not control or direct the efforts of a displaced population, natural products would lie wasted and the land would remain unexploited. Material goods would not be available to relieve distress, and manpower could not be mustered to prevent invasion. A weak regime would seek support from the populace by playing on popular superstition, but deviation from the orthodox doctrines of the court would meet with severe repression.

The significance of certain dynasties

To satisfy the demands of contemporary authorities, Chinese historians have tended to depict Chinese history as a succession of dynastic regimes, stretching steadily without interruption from the Chou to the Ch'ing periods. This result has been achieved largely by selecting certain dynasties and describing their rise and fall in terms of a continuous process, with scant reference to the degree of control that they actually exercised, or the simultaneous existence of several dynasties in different parts of the sub-continent. A total of some twenty-five[1] dynasties has been selected for designation as the competent governing authorities of China from 221 B.C. to 1911; and of these houses, a few (i.e. the Han, T'ang, Sung, Yüan, Ming and Ch'ing dynasties) have often been picked out as major dynasties whose effect is considered to be of wider and more permanent application than that of the others. As a result, a student's attention has tended to concentrate on these periods, for which more information is available and more research has been undertaken. But although this treatment is partly justified by an assessment of the depth and extension of authority of the dynasties in question, there have existed other regimes, whose duration may have been shorter than that of 'major' houses, but whose influence has been of equally great significance (e.g. the formation of dynastic unity, the extension of cultural influence, or the assimilation of non-Chinese peoples). The table of dynastic succession that is presented below (see Table Two) does not include all the regimes that have been established as empires within China. Some of those that appear on the list were con-

[1] Different criteria have been used for counting.

fined to a fraction of Chinese territory, and some, including two of the 'major' dynasties cited above, were founded by non-Chinese peoples who came from other parts of Asia.

The lack of imperial unity 220–589

The formal end of the Han dynasty, which is usually counted from 220, marks the end of the period of early empires. Despite several attempts to do so, until 589 effective imperial unity was never restored for long. The intervening centuries are known sometimes as the Age of Dispersal, or less suitably, as the Dark Ages. They were marked by the foundation of numerous dynasties, courts, or authorities which were based either in the northern or southern regions, and which were frequently engaged in fighting one another. In the north, these regimes were often founded by invading foreigners. At times, some of these small regimes succeeded in establishing themselves as masters of one of the major areas of production. However the period between the Han dynasty and the middle empires of the sixth century and later was neither negative nor retrogressive. It was a time of highly significant cultural development in which several intellectual and artistic traditions became crystallized, and of political reassessment in which local administrative experiment was tried out, and the way prepared for more universal application.

The fall of Lo-yang (311) and its consequences

Of greater historical significance than the formal end of the Han dynasty in 220 is that of the Western Tsin dynasty, whose capital city of Lo-yang fell to an alien conqueror in 311. By 317 an established Chinese court had been driven from its habitat to take refuge in the south (capital at Chien-yeh, the modern Nanking), and two complementary dynastic precedents were being set. A regime was claiming continuity of title and dynastic authority despite the abandonment of the original territory wherein it had been seated; and a regime which was established under alien masters was the first of many such dynasties to recruit the support of Chinese servants. The importance of these two principles was not consciously recognized in the fourth century, but their operation can be traced from 317 throughout the history of imperial succession.

Imperial kinsmen and commoner statesmen

Considerable confusion has sometimes been introduced into the understanding of Han and post-Han history by the unnecessary and irrele-

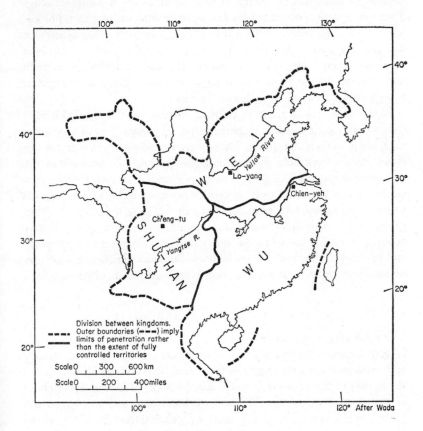

MAP 5. The Three Kingdoms (A.D. 221-263)

vant use of the term 'feudalism' to describe an aspect of the government of those years. Imperial government of this and subsequent ages has rested on the delegation of authority both to members of the imperial family by virtue of their family relationship, and to eminent soldiers or statesmen by virtue of their ability, experience or training. These groups were not mutually exclusive or antagonistic; each possessed different advantages which it could exploit; each could be used in different ways to further the schemes of a central authority. Members of either group were ready to answer the call of ambition or were liable to become the victims of intrigue; and each group could support its emperor with loyal and effective service.

In five centuries of growing political maturity and dynastic intrigue (200 B.C. to A.D. 300), some emperors reposed greater trust in their kinsmen, some in their statesmen. There were occasions when members of either group were able to dominate the palace, gain control of the armies or monopolize large provincial regions. A shrewd government could learn to make use of both groups as counter-checks against each other's ascendancy; but the exercise of a dominating influence by either group hardly warrants the classification of government as specifically feudal (i.e. on the basis of a contractual relationship between emperor and his vassal kinsmen), or exclusively bureaucratic (i.e. as a strictly hierarchic delegation of control from emperor to subordinate offices).

III. THE MIDDLE AND LATER EMPIRES

The value of past experience

Effective imperial unity, which had been lost during the third century and reaffirmed for a short period from 280, was next established under the houses of Sui (589–617) and T'ang (618–906; see Map Six). These dynasties were markedly different in achievement and character from their predecessors. Eight centuries of cultural development, social change and economic expansion separated the foundation of the Sui from that of the Ch'in empires. Whereas the Ch'in empire had possessed no precedent of imperial government on whose models it could call, the Sui and T'ang emperors had some idea of the success and failure of their predecessors and could acquaint themselves with their administrative practices and political accomplishments; and although centuries had intervened since imperial government had been fully practised, by the Sui and T'ang periods it was regarded as the norm to which successful rulers and statesmen should naturally aspire.

In addition, the limited experiments that had been tried during the fifth and sixth centuries with a view to organising the country's resources and mobilising its manpower could now be applied on a much wider scale with the backing of a full imperial system of bureaucracy.

The bureaucratic age

The empires of the seventh century and later are characterized by mature and complex government, and it is for just cause that the T'ang, and particularly the Sung, periods have been described as the age of bureaucracy. The administration was conducted in a far more intensive way than hitherto; civilians were brought into closer contact with the officials who governed them, and the activities of the private individual became more open to the scrutiny and interference of the official. New systems designed to make fuller use of the land, and to conscript the emperor's subjects to serve as labourers or soldiers more effectively than hitherto, demanded the supervision of an ever-increasing number of responsible officials with their junior clerks. And the process was cumulative. For with the support of a large civil service, a government could initiate large-scale schemes or enterprises which required yet closer supervision and yet more recruits to swell the ranks of the bureaucracy.

Moreover, it was during the T'ang and Sung periods that the civil service came to play its fullest part as the single profession which would attract the interest of educated men. The emerging bureaucratic class had every reason, and easy means, of perpetuating its own privi - leges. While the civil service could satisfy the urges of those men of integrity who sincerely wished to serve their emperor, sinecures could easily be found for ambitious men who merely sought the benefits of status and salary, or for the sons and clients of officials who already enjoyed the fruits of office.

The governments of T'ang and Sung China could boast that their institutions were more highly developed than those of any other parts of the world that they knew. The capital cities of Ch'ang-an, Lo-yang or K'ai-feng acted as models of an enlightened civilization which could be admired and copied by foreign visitors of the less forward lands; and many features of the T'ang system of government were adopted elsewhere in Asia with results that were not always as conspicuously successful as had been hoped.

Impracticalities and failure

This new degree of complexity could not be maintained successfully for long, partly owing to weaknesses that were inherent in the system. The organization of the government could easily become top-heavy and unmanageable. In theory the institutions of the state were comprehensive in scope, but their practical implementation frequently encountered grave difficulties. Although the form of the administration may have been designed to cover most contingencies, it demanded the active co-operation of efficient and honest executives, and it was assumed that loyal and sufficient support would always be forthcoming. Little count was taken of the potential ill-will, selfishness or corruption of local officials, on whom the ordinances of the state finally depended. Finally, rigid adherence to prescribed form could easily lead to anomalies, injustices or oppression, and a consequent breakdown of administration.

The practical effect of these weaknesses was felt little more than 100 years after the foundation of the T'ang dynasty, and from *c.* 770 it was to become clear that the economic and military needs of empire could not be supported by simple reliance on theory or an organization that existed solely on paper. By the ninth century central government had become largely ineffective, and a long period of warlordism heralded, accompanied and followed imperial collapse. China again became subject to invasion by non-Chinese peoples from the north-east and north-west, and large tracts of territory came once more under the rule of dynasties whose leaders had originated outside China.

The Sung dynasty of the south

Of the 'major' dynasties, the Sung suffered most at the hands of alien incursion (see Map Seven). Territory that had formerly been included within the sphere of Chinese empire became subject to occupation by the Hsi-hsia (also called Tangut) people in the north-west and by various Tungusic tribes in the north-east. Alien regimes which had acquired the form of Chinese empire in the north-east (Liao 907–1125 and Kin 1115–1234) extended their dominion into the Yellow River valley. K'ai-feng, the capital city of Sung (founded 960) was overtaken by invaders in 1126 and the court was forced to remove itself to a new seat of government, safely situated south of the Yangtse at Lin-an (modern name Hangchow). This event bears some resemblance to the fate that had overtaken the Tsin dynasty in the middle of the fourth century, but the economic and social changes that had occurred in the eight intervening centuries were such that the effects of the two migrations were very different.

Just as the Tsin dynasty is now known by two titles (i.e. Western Tsin, 280–316, and Eastern Tsin, 317–419), so too a distinction is made between the titles of the Northern and Southern Sung dynasties (i.e. 960–1126 and 1127–1279). In each case the line of imperial succession was maintained in the same family despite the removal to the south.

The year 1126 is also marked by the destruction of the imperial collections of books and other treasures that had been built up in the preceding centuries, when the art of printing was first being practised extensively. The losses that were incurred at this time had sadly affected the history of textual transmission in China. But although the move of 1126–7 reflects the military ineptitude of the Sung governments, it ushered in a new period of Chinese civilization which gave rise to new standards of cultural brilliance, commercial prosperity and artistic accomplishment. The material prosperity of China reached new heights during the T'ang and Sung empires, but its advantages were spread very unevenly among the population. Despite the endeavours of some governments, the control and use of resources was vested in a comparatively few wealthy individuals, families or institutions, and no effective means had been devised of harnessing and disposing the country's products in the major interests of the population.

The foreign dynasties

China's dynastic history since the twelfth century can possibly be regarded as a succession of alien houses, punctuated by the existence of only one native house (Ming 1368–1643) whose empire was established throughout the sub-continent. Such a view is perhaps extreme, and should not imply that for most of these centuries the actual government of China was taken out of Chinese hands.

Long before the Kin dynasty had captured K'ai-feng (1126) and established its dominion over the plain of north China, political and diplomatic initiative had rested with the leaders of the Tungusic peoples rather than the highly sophisticated, but politically weak, court of Sung statesmen. It was another foreign people, the Mongols, whose might extinguished the Kin dynasty and who replaced it with their own sovereign rule (the Yüan dynasty 1280–1367). The last native Chinese dynasty (Ming 1368–1643) was founded partly in protest against the regime of the foreigner, whose power was reasserted when the Manchus established the Ch'ing dynasty (1644–1910).

Of the alien houses, the Yüan and Ch'ing have probably exercised the most permanent effect on China's development. The degree to which conqueror and subject people have co-operated with each other or assimilated each other's ways has naturally varied very widely over the long period in question, and is still subject to full appraisal. A notable effect of the succession of dynasties which were founded from the north-east is seen in the new position where the capital city came to be situated. Before the Sung period governments of the north had mostly been settled either in Ch'ang-an or Lo-yang; from the time of the Liao dynasty the capital has usually been seated in Peking.

Achievements of the later dynasties

Under the Ming and Ch'ing dynasties, governments found it possible to enforce a greater degree of administrative power than hitherto and to centralize their powers more effectively. At times a reaction set in against the emphasis placed by the early and middle empires on civil achievement rather than military strength. It was appreciated that the alien houses of Liao, Kin and Yüan had been founded by warriors, and that the maintenance of imperial continuity could depend more on the use of armies than had been admitted. In addition the Ming and Ch'ing sovereigns themselves took steps to reclaim the prerogatives and powers of control which had for some centuries been wielded by their counsellors. Under the later dynasties, China was at times to acquire military strength on a scale hitherto unprecedented; and the force of Chinese arms was to be felt over wide areas extending deep into central Asia.

IV. DYNASTIC FAILURE

The breakdown of the traditional system

From its early beginnings in the third century B.C. until the end of the eighteenth century A.D. the form of imperial government was subject to constant development. The framework, however, remained basically unaltered, and the changes that were introduced were due mostly to internal evolution rather than external pressures. In many cases the reign of a dynastic house ended in a series of uprisings, which was finally resolved by the domination of one warlord over his rivals; and such a result could easily have come about in the middle of the nineteenth century. At this time the authority of the Ch'ing house was threatened, and all but destroyed, in a series of large-scale risings (including the T'ai-p'ing rebellion, c. 1850–1865) whose scars could still be discerned in Chinese cities some century after the event. In the meantime other causes had been at work which were to effect a radical transformation of the traditional concepts of society and government. By the middle of the nineteenth century the population had been increasing at a revolutionary pace (see p. 192 and Table Seven), but the statesmen of Peking could hardly envisage the dangers of the situation or the social and economic adjustments that would soon be necessary.

In addition, the impact of western civilization was being felt in a manner and degree that was totally unexpected. The nations of Europe and America were fast developing colonial, commercial and missionary interests which brought their representatives face to face with the men who operated the vast machine of an oriental empire. In the process of time these interests came into sharp conflict; while witnessing the rivalries of the western nations, Chinese commissioners and their central governments came to learn of totally strange forms of political theory and international behaviour. Westerners brought dramatic evidences of scientific achievements and technological skill which could well appeal to the fancy of Chinese authorities, unwilling as these were to provide the foreigner with an easy means of selling his wares. But despite the reluctance of the Chinese court to acknowledge the value of foreign nations, by the middle of the nineteenth century many of the actions of imperial government were the result of western stimulus. In the nineteenth century, the intervention of European troops helped to save the Ch'ing dynasty from collapse, and thanks to foreign enterprise the destiny of Chinese empire had come to depend on non-Chinese initiative. The coincidence of military defeat, political weakness and internal corruption was soon to end in the overthrow of China's last imperial dynasty.

Dynastic foundation and consolidation
Despite the newly emerging conditions of the last two centuries, the rise and fall of Ch'ing power bears many features that are characteristic of earlier houses. Although the history of each dynasty forms an individual case attended by its own peculiarities, sufficient similarities exist to permit a few general statements regarding the success and failure of dynastic rule.

Many of the earlier dynasties were centred in the north-western part of China whence they had been founded. The advantages of planning a campaign of conquest from the north-west have been demonstrated on several occasions in which a leader who has been so

E

situated has been able to overcome his rivals systematically and effectively. Conversely, attempts to establish imperial rule that were initiated from the south have rarely been successful. Comparatively recently empires have been founded from the north-east, and on such occasions they have been intimately associated with the place of origin of the conquering aliens. But whether they have been established by Chinese or other families, dynasties have usually been founded by the power of the horseman or swordsman; their leaders have been drawn from all ranks of society and have commanded obedience and support by reason of their personal qualities. Such leaders have duly been recognized as the first emperors of the new houses and have often been engaged almost exclusively with military problems and the completion of the tasks of conquest. In such circumstances the real work of imperial consolidation, i.e. the acquisition of the loyal support of Chinese professional administrators, the adoption or modification of existing institutions, and the foundation of a stable and prosperous economy, have been left to the second sovereign of the new dynasty.

Decline and disruption

Such consolidation has been effective for periods of a century or longer, and has then been followed by a loss of purpose at the centre, by decadence and corruption in high places. There have ensued long periods in which imperial unity has been preserved more in name than in reality. In the absence of a firm central control, powerful officials who govern wide regions have been free to practise government or to oppress the emperor's subjects in their own interests without challenge; and while the population has still been burdened by the impositions and restrictions of local officials, the central authority has been denied the resources that it expects from its provinces. Dynastic weakness has gathered pace, as popular distress gives rise to widespread banditry or rebellion. Ambitious men who are fortunate enough to command the obedience of loyal troops or high-ranking officials are tempted to exploit their opportunities to stage a *coup d'état* at the centre or to found a separatist regime in one of the more remote provinces.

Alien rule and its compromises

At such periods China is split into regions which lie at the mercy of rival warlords, until the time when one can prove his superiority over his fellows. When the cycle of dynastic foundation starts again, it may happen that the new leaders are men of different ethnic origin, and alien rule is established over the northern part, or the whole, of China. Such rule depends on the acceptance by both sides of a necessary compromise; the foreign conqueror must recognize that it is his conquered subjects who will organize his government and extract the produce from the soil; and the Chinese officials and farmers must look to their new masters to provide that degree of law and order which they themselves have failed to maintain.

The claim of continuity

The history of China's dynasties has been portrayed as an uninterrupted series of houses in which a single continuous line of legitimate rule can be traced. Such ideas of continuity cannot be accepted without grave reserve. When a new dynasty was founded, its initial authority derived from its own military strength, and not from an operative handover of the right and means to exercise dominion. Despite the pretensions inherent in the official Chinese histories, effective imperial rule has been practised for only a part of the period since its inception, and the existence of enthroned emperors for over two millenia does not imply that their officials were actively or continuously in control of their wide domains or numerous subjects.

Other implications of some of the writers on Chinese history may require revision. Long periods in which no single house has been recognized as dominant have sometimes been described in negative terms, as periods of transition in which Chinese institutions fell into disuse and government failed by default. But the assumption that such periods lacked historical significance cannot be justified. Although the absence of a fully centralized authority may have precluded the full exploitation of China's resources, the best use of her manpower or the upkeep of communications, it was precisely in these times that new institutions of government could be initiated, new experiments tried to promote prosperity, and local precedents set for later application on an imperial scale. Rather than view Chinese empire as a unity which lasted for two millenia with abnormal intervals of disruption, a more realistic approach would be to observe the existence of a large number of regimes which have exercised government in different parts of the sub-continent, and to admire with respect those successful attempts that have been made from time to time to forge a single polity of several constituent parts.

TABLE TWO: THE RISE AND FALL OF DYNASTIES

DYNASTIC SEQUENCES

The process of dynastic change usually lasted for several years, and diagrammatic representation is bound to be oversimplified and inaccurate. The divisions that are shown below should not be taken as rigid, and due allowance should be made for the simultaneous existence of several dynastic houses. The basis whereby dates are taken to mark the limits of dynasties is necessarily arbitrary. Where possible, the terminal dates of dynasties refer to the first (and incomplete) year of foundation and the last completed calendar year of dominion. Where possible, those regimes whose authority was generally restricted to the south (i.e. south of the Yangtse) are shown on the left side of the Table, and those confined to the north on the right. However, this distinction cannot be maintained accurately or consistently. Dynasties which were founded by non-Chinese families are shown in italics (in the case of the Five Dynasties, 907–59, three houses were not of Chinese origin).

THE PRE-IMPERIAL PERIOD

The divisions of the pre-imperial period are usually taken as follows (accurate dating is possible from 841 BC):

The Shang-Yin period: traditionally from 1766 to 1122.

The Chou period: this term applies somewhat loosely to the years ?1122–222. Sub-periods are sometimes entitled Western Chou (? 1122 to 771); Eastern Chou (770 to 256); the Spring and Autumn Period (722 to 481); the Warring States, or Kingdoms (480 to 222).

Ch'in 221–207 B.C.

Western Han 202 B.C.–8 A.D.

Hsin (Wang Mang) 9–23

Eastern Han 25–220

Wu 222–280	The three kingdoms Shu-Han 221–263	Wei 220–264
	Western Tsin 265–316	

Eastern Tsin 317–419	The sixteen kingdoms 304–439	
Sung 420–478	Northern Wei 386–534	
Ch'i 479–501		
Liang 502–556	Western Wei 535–556	Eastern Wei 534–550
Ch'en 557–588	North Chou 557–580	North Chi 550–577

Sui 589–617

T'ang 618–906

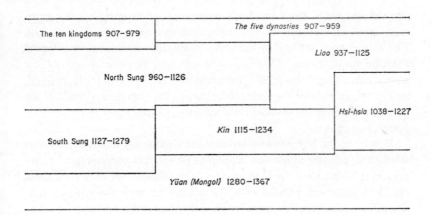

Sung 420 – 478

Ch'i 479 – 501

Northern Wei 386 – 534

Liang 502 – 556

Western Wei 535 – 556

Eastern Wei 534 – 550

Ch'en 557 – 588

North Chou 557 – 580

North Chi 550 – 577

Sui 589 – 617

T'ang 618 – 906

The ten kingdoms 907 – 979

The five dynasties 907 – 959

Liao 937 – 1125

North Sung 960 – 1126

Hsi-hsia 1038 – 1227

South Sung 1127 – 1279

Kin 1115 – 1234

Yüan (Mongol) 1280 – 1367

Ming 1368 – 1643

Ch'ing (Manchu) 1644 – 1910

CHAPTER THREE

THE BASIS AND PRACTICE OF IMPERIAL SOVEREIGNTY

No specific branch of philosophy corresponding with political science has been formulated as part of China's intellectual heritage, and until very recent times there has been little attempt to analyse the constituent parts or the nature of the state, such as is seen in Greek thought. For this reason, the use of the term 'state' in connection with China may be unjustifiable. The duties, needs and responsibilities of the rulers have long been tacitly assumed rather than explicitly defined, and in the absence of a written constitution the organs required for the conduct of government have resulted from natural growth rather than systematic design.

However, the lack of early attempts at written formulation need not imply that the statesmen and emperors of China's early empires were reluctant to mention their aims or the possible ways in which these could be achieved. Fundamental principles are repeatedly invoked in the writings or speeches of China's politicians, civil servants or pamphleteers; they recur in memorials presented to the throne by statesmen on their own initiative; in the advice tendered to the throne at the request of the sovereign; in the protests voiced against proposed schemes of government; and in the decrees drafted to publicize imperial decisions or policies. However, in many of these cases a principle may be cited for its formal value rather than for its immediate application to current problems of administration. Similarly, few Chinese accounts of historical events fail to refer to theories of imperial government, but the full logical implications are rarely specified or considered.

Owing to the uniform nature of the education whereby Chinese authors were trained, commonly accepted standards can be seen to persist in many of their writings. In the early, middle and later empires, education has been largely based on the study of certain texts which have been treated with canonical reverence. Some of these texts were written long before the idea of empire had been conceived; some were probably compiled during the Han period. In the course of time the interpretation of these texts has varied considerably, and different opinions have been accepted as orthodox. Nevertheless a permanent feature has been preserved largely unaltered in the remarks or actions which are ascribed to particular thinkers such as Confucius (see p. 75). These remarks include a number of assorted aphorisms, which sometimes refer to the qualities of the ideal sovereign, the successful rule of bygone golden ages, or the form and object of human government. They are quoted or misquoted, sometimes regardless of context, in many of the essays of the imperial age, and they are often utilized as political expedients. If a certain statesman can cite text A as authority for his proposals, we can be sure that his opponent will be equally well equipped with scriptural anecdote B that is sufficient to prevent their acceptance.

It is from such sources that an idea of Chinese political thinking has to be gained. The Chinese have from time to time misled themselves in this connection, by the constant reiteration of sayings which have been misunderstood or misapplied so as to suit contemporary circumstances. It is by no means easy to isolate basic principles and to assess their true significance in the obscurity that has resulted from the mingling of political motive and philosophical theory.

It is possible to discern three principal elements on which Chinese sovereignty has rested or has been shown to rest: religious belief, Confucian precept and authoritarian theory. It will be seen that although these three elements came into being in different circumstances and in order to satisfy different needs, their effect has been largely intermingled, and significant distinction cannot always be maintained.

I. RELIGIOUS MOTIVES

Divination and its evidences

It is largely owing to religious influences that reliable information regarding the kingdom of Shang has come to light. Some of the motives and practices of that era can be shown to persist in the ensuing three millenia of Chinese civilization, and it is unknown how far back they can be traced before the kingdom of Shang was formed. The inscribed shells and bones used in the process of consulting occult powers prove the existence of an established king, who was accustomed to worship and make appeal to those supernatural forces, which commanded a strength superior to his own. To what extent the king's position arose independently of religious practices (e.g. to provide leadership in war, to co-ordinate the erection of defences, etc.), or to what extent its attributes were derived from service to superhuman powers cannot be fully ascertained; but it is unlikely that the establishment of a king for practical purposes can be completely separated from his function of maintaining religious observances.

The consultation of oracles and communal leadership

The superior forces to whom this devotion was paid were uncontrollable in the sense that they disposed of powers which lay beyond the reach of human perception. At the same time they were by no means completely implacable, and many of the practices of the Shang and later periods were designed to prevent the catastrophes which could result from their wrath. Above all it was possible to consult these beings, by use of the shells and bones, and to request their advice through the medium of omens. Questions could be put regarding the major activities on which the survival or prosperity of the whole community depended, and the occult powers were frequently asked for advice regarding projects for hunting, agriculture or war.

The consultation of superhuman forces by use of oracular bones forms one of the significant features of Shang civilization, and implies some degree of political organization. The king, on whose behalf the oracle was often questioned, may have been in a position to voice the needs or hopes of the whole community. The priest, through whose agency the questions were put, enjoyed an unchallenged mystical authority. If the oracle's replies were to be respected, it might be necessary to persuade, or even to force, the community to take the necessary action; and there might arise the need to enforce obedience to authority. In this way religious aspirations may have had no small bearing on the growth of the powers of the recognized leader, or king, of Shang China.

The importance of writing

In addition, the urge to perpetuate the questions that had been addressed to the oracle served to stimulate the development of Chinese writing and to enhance the prestige and value of those who had mastered the technique. The scribes whose scratches are still preserved on fragments of shells may be regarded as the ancestors of the Chinese official. For they may also have been engaged as the compilers of lists used to enforce the king's will, and they may in time have performed some of the functions of a rudimentary civil service. It is not without significance that the Chinese characters used later to denote ministers of state or officials already appear, with slightly different meaning, on the oracular inscriptions of 1500 B.C.

The manufacture of bronze vessels and its implications
The connection between religious practice and political development can be traced in the succeeding centuries, although the concept of the supernatural may have been transformed and different means of consultation devised. In both the Shang and the Chou periods, the cult of these beings entailed the provision of costly ceremonial equipment which was made in the most valuable medium that was available, by the most skilful artists of the community. A religious motive lies behind the evolution of most of the types of bronze vessel that were fashioned in Shang and Chou China. The production of these masterpieces required the removal of labour from tasks that were of immediate productive benefit and its assignment to the manufacture of luxuries. It was also necessary for some authoritative voice to determine that the scarce quantity of bronze should be used for religious rather than military or agricultural purposes. Such decisions called for the obedience of the population to a recognized authority.

A further political result accrued from the manufacture of bronze vessels. The spiritual and material value of these objects clearly required an effective means of protection, and the organization of manpower to erect defensive works or to fight in their defence could only be attained by the acknowledgement of a leader's, or king's, right to employ his men for this purpose.

The spirits of nature and their worship
In these formative centuries, religious concepts comprised the cult of supernatural beings of many different types. Spirits were believed to be vested in local natural objects or particular sites of land; there were also greater spirits, controlling natural forces such as winds or rivers; and of more universal application than these, there were spirits who commanded the destinies of the crops or the fertility of the soil. These beings needed placation, if prosperity was to be assured; and a systematic or hierarchic worship required some form of leadership or organization among the worshippers, who were still living in a very rudimentary stage of social development.

73

The worship of ancestors and a supreme being

Two other types of religious impulse which became associated with the growth of acknowledged political leadership are seen in the cult of ancestor worship and the reverence for a supreme being whose powers transcended those of the lesser spirits. Ancestor worship derived from the reverence due to the senior members of the family or community and the continuing need to serve them whether they still existed to lead the family in the flesh or whether their souls had passed to a further realm whence they could influence the fortunes of their descendants. The supreme being was known in Shang times as *Ti*, or *Shang-ti*; and the Chou peoples transferred his reputed powers to their own object of veneration, *T'ien* or Heaven.

The means whereby these cults became associated with the establishment of earthly sovereignty were complex and partly inexplicable. A sign of the process may be seen in the use of the same titles to designate forms of sovereignty, and in the rites that have ever been performed by Chinese emperors. From the end of the third century B.C. or earlier the term *Ti* had become incorporated in the expression *Huang-ti*, the regular phrase that has been used to signify 'emperor'; and theorists who claim to follow Confucian thought have regularly depicted China's sovereign as the *T'ien-tzu*, or Son of Heaven. It should be noted that this expression occurs in literature that was composed a few centuries before Confucius' birth, and long before a Chinese empire had been formed.

The implications of the phrase *T'ien-tzu* have exercised a profound effect on the Chinese concept of sovereignty. In so far as he is regarded as Heaven's descendant, a sovereign is responsible for the conduct of the worship of *T'ien*, just as every dutiful son attends to the placation of his deceased ancestors' souls. At the same time, the ancestor of the sovereign was placed in a unique position, as he possessed powers that were superior to those of all other spirits. As the worship of *T'ien* as the supreme power was restricted to the sovereign alone, his position became confirmed as the authorized or legitimate leader of mankind; and he acted as their representative or intermediary in negotiating with this supreme being. These religious implications persisted throughout the evolution and practice of imperial sovereignty until the end of the nineteenth century, and as late as 1915 a pretender to Chinese empire was actively participating in the slaughter of animals as part of the ordained worship of Heaven.

Confucius and his followers

However, long before the nineteenth and twentieth centuries the earliest forms of sovereignty had been overlaid with moral concepts and political ideals. The realization that human society requires guidance and instruction, and that its endeavours must be co-ordinated in the common interest, was forcibly advanced and considerably extended by Confucius (551–479 B.C.) and the thinkers associated with his school.

Confucius' influence on the development of Chinese sovereignty has extended for some twenty-five centuries. However, with the passage of time a divergence has occurred between the teachings which can be properly ascribed to the master and those opinions that have been attributed to his genius by later theorists. The political demands of the pre-imperial age in which Confucius lived differed basically from those of later periods in which his sayings were amplified, utilized or abused. Distinctions must therefore be drawn between the developments of Confucian thought that took place at successive stages of Chinese political and intellectual sophistication, e.g. of the Han, T'ang, Sung and Ch'ing periods.

Moral values and training

One of the fundamental principles of Confucian thought is seen in its view of mankind. The most valuable attributes of human nature provide civilized man with a respect for ethical qualities and an urge to behave in a way that is justifiable. Such standards distinguish him from the savage or the beast; they can be attained by training and discipline, and are neither naturally transmitted as a birthright nor acquired by accident. It follows that education plays a role of paramount importance in the organization of a community, for it is by such means that individuals can be taught to pursue ends that are truly moral. It also follows that successful government can, and should, be achieved by inculcating moral precepts, rather than by enforcing the ordinances of authority.

Social relationships and obligations

It is in the light of this principle that human society can be classified. The quality and merits of an individual are of greater importance than the circumstances of his birth or environment. True nobility lies in moral integrity and ability to serve one's fellow men, and it is therefore

75

possible for any man, however humble his origins, to rise to the highest ranks of society. Social relationships can be defined in terms of the services and duties which a man is fitted or obliged to render, if he is to exert his human qualities to the utmost. Such relationships help to regulate the behaviour of members of a family or friends towards each other; and of more immediate concern to the growth of Chinese statecraft is their application to a sovereign's means of dealing with his subjects.

The saintly ruler

Ideally the sovereign is pictured as a holy or saintly ruler, who has been provided by Heaven (*T'ien*) so as to appear at the appropriate moment on earth. The connection between earthly government and the ordinances of Heaven is taken yet further with the assumption that the saintly ruler is responsible to Heaven for the welfare of his earthly charges. By practising the noble qualities with which he has been specially endowed he is capable of influencing their behaviour and leading them to the practice of charitable and just conduct. If he fails in these endeavours, he will be warned of his imperfections by Heaven, who will plague his government with natural disasters and rob his people of the prosperity they should expect. Untarnished Confucian thought makes it quite clear that the duty of the sovereign, or Son of Heaven, lies in ordering his government for the benefit of his subjects and not for the realization of his own personal ambitions. To achieve this end he is bound to recruit to his service the most able counsellors whom he can find; he must delegate administrative responsibility to their specialist care, and must listen with respect to the admonitions or criticisms that they proffer; and he must reward their services with suitable bounties.

The sovereign's counsellors

The advisers of a sovereign are sometimes portrayed in idealist or conventional terms; they are men of outstanding intellectual ability and unquestioned integrity, standing apart from the great majority of their fellow creatures. It is thanks to such qualities, and their pre-eminent talents, that they are entrusted with the cares of state; they are not entitled to the enjoyment of official privilege or emolument simply by virtue of birth or hereditary office. Their duties are to arrange for the extension of their sovereign's rule, and thereby of the benefits of Heaven's blessing to all mankind. In the first instance this is achieved by means of education and discipline, and the establishment of schools or promulgation of moral precepts has often figured as one of the earliest steps to be taken by a newly founded Chinese government. The sovereign's advisers are also in duty bound to provide for the material welfare of his subjects; they must ascertain the practical difficulties under which they labour and the causes of their privation or distress; and when they have brought popular grievances to light they must suggest a suitable remedy. In providing for the general and equable enjoyment of material resources a sovereign's advisers must prevent his indulgence in selfish luxuries. Their loyalty to their master is such that they will not hesitate to protest cogently, if they feel that his conduct endangers his position or his people's well-being.

The people of the earth
In the Confucian scheme government is thus invested in a sovereign and his advisers. Below, there remains the vast mass of the population, men who are essentially of poorer intellectual capacity but who can be directed so as to fulfil their obligations adequately and to behave in a manner that is commendable. These are the children of the earth, placed in the care of the sovereign so as to enjoy the benefits of his rule, such as security from uncivilized man or wild beast and material relief needed in famine. The main task of the majority of the population is the production of crops from the land which they till; and in return for the blessings of ordered government they are in duty bound to obey the commands of their sovereign or his servants.

Ethical aims
No notice of Confucius should omit a due appraisal of his efforts to improve the moral tone of contemporary society. In his day there survived religious practices of a superstitious, totemistic and possibly barbarous type; to Confucius belongs the credit for attempting to inform such practices with ethical motives and to eliminate their more inhuman characteristics; by this means it was hoped that religious practice would conform with a higher concept of the value of human beings. As part of this endeavour, Confucius drew attention to the duty of government to promote the moral improvement as well as the material welfare of its subjects.

Mo Tʐu and the use of men of talent
The need to encourage talent and to apply it to the needs of govern-

ment had appeared first as one of the principles of the *Mo-tzu*. This text represents the views of the philosopher Mo ti (also called Mo Tzu; *c.* 480–390) and his school, who was at wide variance with Confucius over a number of other questions. Mo ti's main doctrine had been concerned with the need to spread human happiness universally, without a narrow adherence to a set of defined social relationships and without incurring unnecessary extravagance. While rejecting the Confucian requisite of obedience to a rigorous code of behaviour, Mo ti shared common ground with the later authoritarian thinkers (see p. 79) in seeing the value of a disciplined and well co-ordinated society.

III. AUTHORITARIAN THEORY

The third main element on which political structures have rested can be described as authoritarian theory, which was formulated more explicitly and systematically than Confucian precept. While the writings of authoritarian theorists were often directed at the exposition of particular aspects or problems of statecraft, in the Confucian scheme the formation of government constituted but one of many considerations of human activities and qualities. In addition, the two types of thought were crystallized amid somewhat different political and social conditions. Confucius had first preached his message at a time when political units consisted of small communities with a comparatively primitive concept of organization. The authoritarian writers however lived some two centuries later (e.g. Shang Yang, from the fourth century); by this time political issues were being fought out on a far grander scale than previously. Sovereigns could dispose of a new strength whose implications were very different from those of their predecessors' parochial resources. A more systematic and co-ordinated degree of control had become necessary.

Government on behalf of the sovereign
Authoritarian theory was diametrically opposed to the concepts of the Confucian school in two respects. First, it was believed that government was exercised not on behalf of the community but in order to benefit the ruler. The true aims of sovereignty lay not in the provision of welfare, or the foundation of charitable undertakings, but in the aggrandizement and enrichment of the state. Any advantages which might accrue to the inhabitants as a result of such government were accidental rather than essential; and clearly there was little need to in-

voke religious impulses to support this theory. In the second place it was stressed that the aims of the state were best achieved by the ordered and co-ordinated efforts of the community; and the required measure of human discipline could be achieved by the imposition of orders and their enforced obedience, and not simply by the promulgation of ethical precepts. For the purposes of political power or organization there was no need to expound the value of moral ideals or the values of civilized existence.

The imposition of authority

Attention was drawn to three means whereby a successful ruler could establish and maintain his government: the impressive exercise of his personality; the expedient adoption of suitable methods of control and delegation; and the strict imposition of law. As the last of these three aspects of sovereignty came to be emphasized more than the other two, the authoritarian school has become generally known as the school of Legalists or Legists.

The personality of the sovereign is, ideally, such that he can bring a pervasive influence to bear on matters of state without active interference. His position is such that he should take no direct part in the formulation of policy or administration; for those matters are delegated to the specialist and executive officials whose different spheres of activity are clearly defined. Delegation of authority, however, requires that the best possible methods should be adopted to select the sovereign's advisers and their assistants. These men must be chosen on the basis of their proven qualities and their ability to make full use of their talents. The correct method of delegation includes the promise of liberal rewards, almost salaries, for services successfully rendered, and the threat of severe punishments in the case of failure or incompetence. Provided that these promises and threats are not solely vain boasts but are seen to be implemented in public, a sovereign can hope to attract to his court the most notable men of the day.

The laws of the state were envisaged as an objective code of behaviour requiring universal obedience by all members of society; and as with the rewards and punishments of the state, the population must entertain no doubts that the force of the law and its punishments will be brought to bear regularly and effectively.

Purposeful government

Notwithstanding the fundamental difference of theory on which Confucian and authoritarian thought rested, the two systems are found to be in agreement regarding a number of matters of practical statecraft. Both implied the existence of a sovereign supported by a fully authorized civil service. In neither case could a state be established without a rigid division of classes and a recognized hierarchy of authority; and both Confucian and Legalist philosophers permitted or encouraged the servants of the sovereign to impose burdens on the community and to exact their due measure of service. Both the extension of the sovereign's bounties to the needy and the enlargement of the state's supplies of grain depend on the attention paid by the government to agricultural production. The difference between the two systems of thought lies in the methods chosen to reach the ends. Whereas Confucian philosophers would appreciate the value of an individual's undertakings and the personal interest that he might retain in their success, Legalist thinkers would endeavour to eliminate the scope for private aspirations and to introduce a selfless unity of purpose in the working activities of the community.

IV. IMPERIAL SOVEREIGNTY AND PRACTICAL POLITICS

Imperial authority has derived from religious influences, Confucian philosophy and authoritarian statecraft. These concepts had been moulded in the pre-imperial age and had given rise to forms of polity or leadership which were not sufficiently well developed for the needs of full imperial government. In the imperial age a compromise was successfully reached between widely different theories, and the exercise of forceful government, with the loyal support of the population, constitutes a major political and intellectual achievement of the Chinese peoples.

Historically, religious influences were perhaps the first elements to give rise to kingship, but the attributes of kingship which arose from such observances can hardly be regarded as conscious objectives of Shang religion. From the sixth century B.C. the Confucian ideal of kingship came to be advocated, but neither Confucius nor his immediate disciples was able to persuade a contemporary ruler to translate those principles into practice. From the fourth century B.C. Legalist measures were being tried out in the kingdom of Ch'in with results that were to be far-reaching. For in due course Ch'in developed into the first Chinese empire (from 221 B.C.) which was organized and governed according to the same authoritarian principles of the Legalist school.

BASIS AND PRACTICE OF IMPERIAL SOVEREIGNTY

The compromise of Confucian and Legalist principles

The formative period of imperial authority was that of the Han dynasty, for it was then that a compromise was reached between the requirements of imperial government and the appeal of ethical humanism. The compromise was of sufficient value to affect the nature of imperial government throughout succeeding dynasties, and to colour many of its theoretical institutions and practical arrangements. It had been reached at a time when political thought and philosophical speculation were becoming increasingly more sophisticated while still retaining their vigour. The lessons of the failure of the Ch'in empire were still freshly in mind. It could not be forgotten that an authoritarian empire, despite its pretensions, had in fact depended on the strength and personality of an individual leader and had survived his death only to crumble into ruin. In the second century B.C. it was realized that political institutions needed to be strong enough to outlast the personal destiny of a sovereign; that such strength could not entirely be imposed from above; that it was not sufficient to enforce the rigid obedience of the populace to the orders of officials; and that the support of a written tradition was a useful, and perhaps necessary, adjunct to successful government. The new Han emperors had learnt the value of enshrining their powers in the canons of the past; their statesmen could appreciate the benefits of texts which advocated a society composed of different orders, each one with its defined duties and privileges.

The emergent political form permitted the rigorous exercise of executive and judicial powers, under the guise of establishing an administration that was designed for human welfare. Government was conducted under a continual appeal to the utterances of Confucius, but the structure of imperial Ch'in was retained with many of its ordinances. At the same time the claims to a humane philanthropic regime demanded the bitter denigration of the injustices and severities of the Ch'in empire. Elements of religious belief were utilized as a means of presenting the contemporary institution of imperial government in its full solemnity and authority. In this way ideal conditions were fostered for the formalized delegation of authority in established hierarchies, in accordance with the conclusions of both the Confucian and the Authoritarian schools.

The uses of sovereignty

Soon after the establishment of empire, imperial sovereignty became subject to the influences of its own creation, the civil service. While

F   81 the emperor had no means of maintaining his situation or conducting his business without the active support of his administrators, his statesmen and servants owed their powers, privileges and salaries to the institution of empire. The two elements of government soon became interdependent; according to the strength or weakness of the throne the position of the emperor could be raised or lowered; and in accordance with the ambitions of the civil service, the institution of sovereignty could be enhanced or manipulated so as to satisfy personal designs. In the course of some centuries of growing political maturity it became possible, expedient or necessary to emphasize particular aspects of sovereignty and to represent or utilize the institution in as favourable a way as was possible.

Han pretensions to benevolent government
Some of the documents whereby political decisions were reached or announced by Han emperors have been incorporated into the contemporary histories; and although it is difficult to discriminate here between the personal views of the emperor and those of the advisers who framed the documents, they shed valuable light on the opinions current at the time. It is understandable that those who professed the Confucian belief that government existed for the benefit of the governed would see no need to reiterate the practical claims that imperial authority was wont to make on a population, or its right to enforce the commands of the emperor. Rather would they be tempted to gloss over, or to omit reference to, the restrictions imposed by officialdom or the demands for service or payments that were presented to the public in the normal conduct of government. Han statesmen tend therefore to describe the ordinances of government in golden, idealist terms. Imperial decrees and memorials presented to the throne rarely refrain from emphasizing that imperial government exists to practise lovingkindness, and that Confucius and his followers advocated the voluntary adoption of conventions and disciplines in order to add value to personal, social and political relationships.

Propaganda designed to present imperial authority in a favourable light was taken a stage further in the depiction of the golden ages which had existed in the dim mists of antiquity. It was claimed that in those ideal times government had been vested in saintly rulers whose word had been law; whose inspiration had lain in the well-being of their subjects; and whose endeavours had been rewarded by active co-operation. Little reference is made in these documents to the harsher aspects of government, or to the need to enforce obedience, repress crime and dispense justice. Readers were intended to infer that the Han empire was a close imitation of a perfect system that had prevailed in those earlier days.

The spiritual powers of the emperor

Similarly religion, as well as history, was invoked to enhance the position of the emperor. Supreme authority for government rested in the sovereign, and it was in respect of his person that appeal was made to spiritual elements. The Han and subsequent emperors could not be viewed simply as the highest members of an hierarchic authority; for, as such, they would be subject to the same vicissitudes of fortune or weaknesses of character as their own servants or assistants. Emperors must be shown to possess innate qualities with which they are endowed for special reasons and which are intended to be exercised in their subjects' interests. Following Confucian and earlier teaching the emperor is referred to as the Son of Heaven. The supreme arbiter of power has solemnly entrusted him with the rule of the earth together with the necessary qualities and virtues. Only by exercising such powers correctly can he discharge his functions adequately.

The emperor as a scapegoat

Nevertheless the success of government may in the last resort depend on human failings or the tricks of nature, and the image of the emperor may suffer in consequence. Ideally, if the claims of statesmen and the pretensions of emperors are to be convincing, it must be shown that their powers are efficacious. If it is agreed by a community that the imposition of burdens on the population is due to the will of Heaven, it will be expected that the Son of Heaven and his assistants will thereby ensure the provision of material prosperity. But if the restrictions imposed by the emperor's officials fail to result in such benefits, the emperor's subjects are clearly entitled to question his claim to the powers wielded by his servants.

The annals of Chinese history abound with records of constantly recurring natural disasters, in the form of flood, drought, famine or plague. There can have been few periods when a government was not confronted with the need to explain the occurrence of such catastrophes at a time of allegedly Heaven-blest rule. It is on such occasions that the emperor himself may play the role of a scapegoat. Decrees are issued in his name in which he castigates himself for his shortcomings and the resultant punishments that have been visited on his people. By this device the strength of the institution is preserved at the cost of the reputation of the incumbent.

The institution as a political weapon
In this way the institution of the emperor could be used as a political tool. Decrees of the type mentioned form but one example of the conventions adopted by statesmen and historians, with results that are sometimes misleading or perplexing. However, at the time when such documents were drafted their true significance and their implicit dangers need not have escaped the notice of a sophisticated court. It was a short step from the self-depreciatory decree of an emperor to the impeachment of a politician who had successfully tendered his advice to the throne prior to the occurrence of a natural catastrophe. Or emperors could be shown to blame themselves for hearkening to ill-considered advice that had been offered by men now proved to be disloyal or depraved. Naturally Heaven had shown displeasure at such ill-considered steps, and could be expected to do so in case of similar events. The institution of imperial sovereignty was highly subject to manipulation so as to suit the outcome of political crisis.

Imperial sovereignty and dynastic change
Perhaps the classic case of the use of political jargon to overlay events which were difficult to justify is seen in the means whereby a change of dynasty is described. The statesmen who survived such changes and were willing to support a new regime, or the historians whose duty lay in recording such a change, were faced with the problem of discrediting an established order which had been originally founded with Heaven's blessing, and of creating the necessary authority for the establishment of its successor. As such change-overs were frequently brought about simply by military strength, the task was by no means easy. The solution adopted, so as to preserve the forms and decencies of the situation, has unfortunately given rise to basic misconceptions of Chinese dynastic history. The actual transfer of power from the last emperor of a dying regime to his conqueror is presented as an act of abdication based on motives that are traced to Confucian ethics. The mandate of Heaven is said to have been conveyed or transferred without interruption from one legitimate holder to the next. The new dynasty is said to be justified in the eyes of Heaven owing to the failure of its predecessor to maintain the correct standards of morality; the

old dynasty must therefore forfeit its right to Heaven's charge or mandate. By this means, first evolved to justify the Chou conquest of the Shang kingdom, the dynastic change is shown sometimes to have been brought about in response to popular movements or rebellions that are justified, and the authority of the new house is effectively upheld. If, on the contrary, a popular rising is suppressed and the authority of an existing regime remains unimpaired, the leaders of such abortive rebellions are castigated as lawless bandits, who dared to question the validity of Heaven's ordinances and who met the punishment that they richly deserved.

The persistence of imperial authority

The idea of imperial government which took shape during the Han period was to persist for some twenty centuries. In the succeeding dynasties or kingdoms which claimed sovereignty, whether of Chinese or alien origin, it was subjected to different pressures, with the result that the emphasis of authority was placed on different aspects of government. At times, forceful attempts were made to co-ordinate the economic output of China's peoples, at the insistence of authoritarian principles and at the cost of human values; more frequently, those elements of government which could be attributed to Confucian origin were stressed; and sometimes a regime would take particular steps to win popularity by exploiting religious emotions to their utmost point, even altering the protocol of the court in the process. Throughout such vicissitudes, and frequent dynastic changes, the idea of sovereignty has persisted, being practised on an hereditary basis. According to tradition there was a short interlude in the ninth century B.C., when a government based on 'Common concord' (*kung-ho*) had been operated, in the absence of a suitable occupant of the Chou throne. This form of government was always regarded as exceptional, and the term *kung-ho* does not recur until the twentieth century, when it was used to denote the newly introduced form of republican government.

V. THE SYSTEM OF IMPERIAL SUCCESSION

Nomination or inheritance

The direct transmission of sovereignty from father to son was not always conducted smoothly or without difficulty. According to Chinese tradition, some of the earliest sovereigns, whose rule had featured in the golden ages of remote antiquity, had selected men of proven qualities to be their successors, irrespective of any family ties. At a later stage of development the system was changed, by a hero known as Yü the Great, who left his title of sovereignty to his son and thereby introduced a system of hereditary transmission. It was in this way that the first of China's dynasties had been founded.[1] To sophisticated Confucian writers of the ninth century A.D., who were anxious to maintain a secure scheme of imperial government, each method possessed its advantages. The first made possible the choice of a man of outstanding personality to receive overall responsibility for mankind; the second meant that a sovereign's death would not necessarily be followed by chaos, dispute or civil war.

Problems of succession

In general an hereditary system commended itself to the Chinese as being superior, but its practice was subject to considerable complication. An emperor's court included a large establishment of women who received his favours. In theory only one was selected to be the recognized empress, and her eldest son was entitled to legitimate succession to the throne; the other women and their children enjoyed less favourable privileges. Difficulties arose if the properly constituted empress failed to produce a male heir; or if such an heir died, while other male children had been borne to some of the concubines. The situation was aggravated by political implications, if relatives of some of the less highly favoured women filled official positions in the government, or became the leaders of political factions. In such cases a political group could possibly pin its hopes to the reign of the next emperor, and thoughts of manipulating the imperial succession might easily arise. The Chinese solution permitted the preservation of correct form together with due attention to expediency. While the system of hereditary succession was maintained, it was possible and legitimate for an emperor to nominate, or be induced to nominate, a different woman to become his legal consort, and a different son to become his heir apparent. By these means the guardians of doctrinaire form were satisfied, and contenders for political power could look to the future for the realization of their ambitions.

---

[1] I.e. the Hsia dynasty. According to tradition this had preceded the Shang dynasty, but no archaeological or other evidence has yet been found to corroborate this account.

86

BASIS AND PRACTICE OF IMPERIAL SOVEREIGNTY

Changes from Han to T'ang

By the time of the re-establishment of imperial rule under the T'ang and Sung dynasties, political, social and economic conditions had changed basically from those of Han China, and the traditional Confucian ideology was being challenged by other doctrines. China was entering the age of the bureaucratic class, when officialdom had succeeded in establishing itself in an eminently favourable position that was at times independent of its imperial masters. From the first days of empire, statesmen had built up the economic structure of China on the principle that agricultural production must take priority over industrial or commercial undertakings. This principle had been common ground shared by Confucian and authoritarian writers, and formed an important part of the declared aims of government. However, already in the Han period it was becoming clear that artisans could earn more lucrative rewards than peasants, and that merchants could amass greater fortunes than farmers. By the middle empires these differences had widened, with the growth of material sophistication and the call for luxury goods. The importance of co-operative efforts and projects backed by capital was becoming increasingly clear, and Confucian theorists could no longer claim that the ideal state would rest on the unco-ordinated efforts of small farming communities.

The impact of Buddhism

Of similar importance was the discredit into which Confucian political thinking had fallen. This had followed not unnaturally from the manifest failure of dynasties, from the Han period onwards, to uphold an empire successfully or to conduct its affairs with the co-operation of its subjects or the support of honest officials. These failures had coincided with the centuries in which Buddhism was gaining a grip on the Chinese mind. This religion had been brought to China from India at about the beginning of the Christian era; it had gradually been accepted in the Chinese towns and countryside, and had sometimes been rewarded with the patronage of emperors at the short-lived courts set up between the Han and T'ang periods. The new religion was fostered in monasteries which came to possess considerable wealth and land, despite the distrust of material values embodied in the faith. Many Buddhist tenets came into sharp conflict with the basis of authoritarian sovereignty, and struck at the roots of the Confucian ideals of social and

87

political order. Amongst other principles, Buddhists believed in the value of individual merit, and a basic equality whereby all men, of whatever station, could practise the most noble ideals of conduct and attain the highest standards.

A world of difference lies between the Buddhist concept of merit and the path to its attainment, and the Confucian emphasis on the regulation of character. To the Buddhist, personality is developed so as to reach higher forms by means of spiritual or meditative processes, while to the Confucian, personal improvement is achieved by learning and acquiring higher standards of conduct. To the Buddhist, the desire to strive for enlightenment is of greater importance than the duties borne by members of a family or society towards each other, and the acceptance of eternal verities is of higher value than the obedience due to the temporal authorities of the material world; and the accidental circumstances of kinship, e.g. as a member of the imperial family, do not equip a man with the qualities of leadership or involve him in special relationships or obligations.

The strength of imperial structure

With the re-establishment of effective imperial sovereignty at the beginning of the seventh century there occurred a more serious confrontation of the Buddhist and imperial points of view than had yet been seen. With some exceptional periods a compromise was reached; the new bureaucratic structure of government remained solid and intact in principle, while tolerating the presence of Buddhist establishments, doctrines and observances. The victory of the official structure of empire was due both to ideological and material causes. It was clearly in the interests of the T'ang and Sung civil servants to perpetuate the political and social order which provided them with status, privilege and salaries; and although Buddhist establishments were developing in such a way that they too required expert leadership and administration, they could provide a far less certain means of advancement to men of ambition than the imperial institutions that rested on authoritarian theory and were clothed in Confucian garb. Some degree of contradiction may have been implied in the case of individual officials who had embraced the Buddhist faith but who yet chose to expend their energies on behalf of a kingdom of this world; but the Chinese have long shown a remarkable capacity for keeping different and even contradictory activities separate, and for serving a temporal and spiritual authority simultaneously.

The political failure of Buddhism

Nevertheless the structure of imperial government was subjected to some strain. Bitter protests were launched by reactionary thinkers, who blamed the degeneration of empire on the failure to adhere to traditional precepts; on the relaxation of demands for a single-minded devotion to the State; or on the extravagant attentions paid by emperor and court to the ceremonies of a new foreign cult. By the ninth century, Buddhist monasteries had accumulated rich assets, while the power of the central government was becoming more and more ineffective. Protests against the growing strength of the monasteries culminated in the persecution of the faith in the middle of the ninth century. Thereafter a Buddhist challenge to political authority and its economic resources did not recur. Intellectually, Buddhism was yet to play a highly important part in the re-interpretation of Confucian texts and in an attempt to reconcile ethical and metaphysical systems of thought. But the philosophers of the eleventh and twelfth centuries who were responsible for this reassessment were interested more with formulating speculative theory than with defining the scope of political authority, and the authoritarian-Confucian structure of government survived unimpaired.

The reassertion of sovereignty

Under the Ming and Ch'ing dynasties a reaction set in against the powers of the bureaucracy which had prospered so remarkably during the Sung and subsequent ages. One of the characteristic developments of the later empires was the endeavour to foster the power of the throne, by concentrating authority into the hands of the sovereign.

A divergence of interest between palace and civil service was no new phenomenon in Chinese history. It will be seen below (see pp. 154 and 165) that in the Han and T'ang periods various devices had been evolved to provide an emperor with an organ of personal government so as to offset the powers of the established bureaucracy. But such creations had successively suffered a similar fate. They had become merged with the bureaucracy itself, and had failed in the long run to provide emperors with an independent secretariat or executive control. The reassertion of imperial power during the Ming and Ch'ing periods derived partly from the energy and character of a few individual emperors, and was achieved sporadically by institutional changes which placed the throne in a more influential position over the executive organs of government.

A reaction against despotism

The Manchu conquest of 1644 produced a crisis of a type that had occurred frequently enough in Chinese history and which has been referred to obliquely above (p. 84), that of loyalty. How could those men who had placed their services at the disposal of a currently established dynasty face the fact of its conquest and replacement by another house? And in what circumstances would they be justified in transferring their loyalties and services to the new masters of China? The problem involved deeper matters than those of individual conscience, as it both struck at the basis of imperial sovereignty and threatened to deprive a government of its means of operation.

In these circumstances many Chinese civil servants were able to reconcile their consciences with the need to serve the new house, on the grounds that it had become the proper recipient of Heaven's Mandate, and that its conquest of its predecessor was justified by its predecessor's shortcomings. However, in 1644 the new regime had been founded by the blatant use of the sword, and the justification for serving an alien conqueror was not so easy to find. A few notable figures such as Huang Tsung-hsi (1610–95) refused to accept the legitimacy of the new house. In seeking to analyse the moral weaknesses and intellectual failures of the defunct Ming dynasty, they strove to reassert the Confucian principle that government should properly be conducted as a partnership between the governor and the subject, and to establish the means of limiting the arbitrary powers of despotism that an emperor or his henchmen might possess. It is hardly surprising that Huang Tsung-hsi's views were not acceptable to the contemporary masters of China, and any idea of the sovereignty of the people was still completely alien to Chinese thought. Nevertheless, Huang Tsung-hsi and his fellow critics succeeded in imparting a new emphasis to certain aspects of temporal authority, and the liberal reformers of the nineteenth century were glad to call on his view in their support.

The breakdown of imperial sovereignty

A far more serious challenge to the traditional idea of Chinese sovereignty came about in the nineteenth century, with changes of a radical and far-reaching nature. Alien political theories of a completely new type were brought to the attention of the Chinese as a result of the increasing activities of westerners in the Far East. Missionaries were preaching the Christian view of human nature and its dependence on divine grace. The European and American ideas of democracy that were being discussed rested on startling ideas, such as the right of a citizen to have a voice in his government, to control his political destiny or to limit the powers of a communal authority; and, somewhat later, the communist view of the state and society was being propagated. A further contrast could be seen in the western scheme of organizing government so that legislative, administrative and judicial functions are separated and placed under the control of different organs. It was learnt in China that some of the successful states of the west had come to distrust and dispense with monarchy. To their astonishment, Chinese statesmen were given a glimpse of foreign nations whose political maturity was as great or greater than their own, and the mere thought that non-Chinese could aspire to establish a successful regime without the blessing of Heaven was revolutionary. The dynastic weakness and military defeats of the nineteenth century have been followed by China's own revolutions of 1911 and 1949; and these have involved the complete rejection of the Chinese tradition in favour of foreign ideologies.

TABLE THREE

EARLY CHINESE PHILOSOPHERS

Many of the basic contributions to Chinese thought were formulated during the Spring and Autumn and Warring States periods (i.e. after 722 BC and before the establishment of empire). A number of works known to have been written at that time have since been lost, and some of the surviving texts, or parts thereof, cannot be accepted as authentic, or associated for certain with the philosophers whose names they now bear. Some of the texts consist of collected sayings of a philosopher, assembled by disciples or admirers posthumously, after lengthy intervals. The dates of the principal figures cannot always be supplied. The following list is restricted to those major thinkers whose works, or ascribed works, are easily available in translation. Only one version has been included here (for others, see the entries in C. O. Hucker: *China A critical bibliography*, University of Arizona Press, 1962). For critical appreciations or interpretations of select writers, see the titles listed on p. 305 below.

Name of thinker	Approximate dates BC	Associated writings and English versions
K'ung Ch'iu (i.e. Confucius)	551–479	Lun-yü (The Analects). A. Waley: *The Analects of Confucius*, London, 1938.
Meng K'o (i.e. Mencius)	390–305	Meng-tzu. Translated by J. Legge in volume 2 of *The Chinese Classics*, Second edition, Oxford, 1895.
Hsün Ch'ing	340–245	Hsün-tzu. B. Watson: *Hsün tzu, Basic Writings*, New York and London, 1963.

Name of thinker	*Approximate dates BC*	*Associated writings and English versions*
Shang Yang (also called Kung-sun Yang)	390–338	Shang-tzu. J. J. L. Duyvendak: *The Book of the Lord Shang*, London, 1928.
Han Fei	280–233	Han-fei-tzu. B. Watson: *Han Fei Tzu, Basic Writings*, New York and London, 1964.
? Lao Tzu	(contemporary of Confucius?)	Tao-te-ching. D. C. Lau, *Tao Te Ching*, London, 1963.
Chuang Chou	365–290	Chuang-tzu. H. Giles: *Chuang-tzu, Mystic Moralist and Social Reformer*, London, 1926.
? Lieh Yü-k'ou	legendary?	Lieh-tzu (compiled c. AD 300?). A. C. Graham: *The Book of Lieh-tzu*, London, 1961.
Mo ti	480–390	Mo-tzu. B. Watson: *Mo Tzu, Basic Writings*, New York and London, 1963.

CHAPTER FOUR

CULTURAL DEVELOPMENT

I. PRINCIPLES AND BEGINNINGS

Few visitors to the Far East fail to notice immediate differences between the Chinese and other varieties of civilization. But while many points of difference can be described, or even defined, in some detail, a satisfactory analysis of the basic causes which have given rise to different types of religious, artistic or philosophical development has proved notoriously difficult. In addition it is only comparatively recently that serious attempts have been made to study the frequency of communication between China and other parts of the world, and to estimate the influences exerted by one variety of civilization on another. The degree of originality which should be correctly ascribed to Chinese cultural forms and devices will long remain problematical.

The achievements of the élite

None the less certain material evidences of daily life in China show how the progress of human civilization can be assessed. Such evidences include achievements which concern the great multitude of the Chinese peoples, and are closely related to the development of social structure and economic needs. There are also other, more conspicuous, marks of progress which cannot necessarily be ascribed directly to such pressures, and which derive from the inspiration, effort and creation of a comparatively small, leisured class. Opinion will necessarily differ regarding which type of achievement can be more properly considered as characteristic of a civilization. The Chinese themselves have habitually shown their deepest pride at the accomplishments of their literary, artistic or intellectual élite, and have often overemphasized these at the cost of the more matter-of-fact practical advances in the daily work and lives of the great majority.

It is no part of this short study to provide a balanced guide to the achievements of the leisured élite throughout China's history. It is intended solely to sketch a few signs to the directions of cultural pro-

93

gress, and to attempt to discern the motives and means whereby Chinese culture has come to deserve a high place in any estimate of human endeavour.

Continuity

The continuity of Chinese civilization derives from a constancy of similar political and social conditions. Evolutionary changes can be traced during the last 3,000 years, but radical changes have been extremely rare. Economic pressures have constantly demanded the solution of much the same technical problems, and have resulted in a scientific and technological progress whose existence has not always been appreciated; in some ways the Chinese may have failed to take such progress to its logical conclusion; in other ways the degree of application has been more intense than, e.g. in Europe. The respect for a leisured class and for its material needs has possibly been accepted and satisfied more regularly than elsewhere, and contrasts sharply with the standards of China's neighbours of central Asia.

Continuity has rested on the stability of the social and political order despite the interruptions of bloody wars or the infiltration of foreign elements. The culture of the élite has derived from indigenous religious impulses and, more forcefully, from the official promotion of the Confucian cult. A further type of influence has been exerted by Buddhism, whose spread has been due more to individual and natural initiative than to a formal and sponsored support, despite certain periods when the religion enjoyed the full favours of court protection; and much of China's culture rests on Taoism.

Early painted wares and bronzes

The earliest signs of the enjoyment of leisure, if not of the presence of a leisured class, are seen in the painted wares of one of China's neolithic civilizations. The production of large vessels in pottery itself proclaims the achievement of cultural progress by men who had learnt the value and means of food storage in preference for immediate consumption or wastage. The addition of gaily patterned decoration to these vessels (c. 2000 B.C.) argues that man was not solely concerned with material needs, and could find some opportunity and leisure in which to satisfy other demands. With the further development of the new medium of bronze, the scope for such activities widened and was concerned with the religious impulses as well as the material livelihood of early communities. A greater human effort, in terms of co-ordinated manpower, was necessary for the manufacture of the

94

bronze vessels that are characteristic of the Shang-yin culture (*c.* 1500 B.C.), and this cannot have been achieved without an acknowledged response to artistic cravings, and a comparatively advanced degree of communal control. These early efforts have been richly repaid by the permanent value of the product.

The magnificent bronze vessels of Shang China were produced in the first instance for the performance of religious ceremonies. In addition the vessels probably constituted an object of material envy as well as spiritual veneration. For bronze itself was a valuable commodity, and the production of vessels was costly. Possession of such objects may well have been a cause of just pride on the part of a family, kingdom or group of priests. The objects also formed a valuable economic asset, in that they were a reserve store of precious metal for the use of a slowly emerging royal or priestly authority. For this reason, bronzes also attracted the attention of plunderers or neighbouring communities, as they could be melted down and transformed into military weapons or the equipment of horse and carriage. In this way cultural achievement was beginning to bring its own responsibilities, in the need to provide an effective defence for valuable objects. As such a need implied a greater degree of communal cohesion, and the assignment of manpower to tasks that were not immediately productive, the cumulative and inter-related processes of social organization, political development and economic evolution had been irrevocably inaugurated.

II. CONFUCIAN INFLUENCE AND IMPERIAL PATRONAGE

Confucius and his followers
The mainspring from which Chinese cultural developments have derived is the devotion to Confucian ideals, which have formed the background against which many aspects of communal activity must be set. However, a distinction must be drawn between Confucius' own influence and that of the men of later ages who fastened their opinions to his authority. The personal teachings of Confucius (551–479 B.C.) were extended by some of his disciples and applied to contemporary conditions of a China which had not yet been united as an empire; and during the different stages of the imperial period these sayings and the resultant texts were invested with an authority, supported by amplification and so utilized that they would suit the later systems of government and structure of society.

Similar reservations must be made in respect of the development of cultural achievements from Confucius' personal precepts. For the accretions of the centuries include much that would have surprised Confucius himself and his immediate disciples, and the claims that the cultural features of Han, T'ang, Ming or Ch'ing China could be attributed to the personal teachings of the sage cannot be readily sustained. The term Confucianism is used here solely as a matter of convenience, and denotes developments of very different periods which have been ascribed to the same origin.

The force of li

The social and political structure of China has been formed by a system of authoritarian government, modified by ethical or humanist principles that are described as Confucian. These can be briefly summarized as the insistence that man must take his appropriate place in the harmonious workings and arrangements of the universe; that individual human nature can be improved by education; and that government exists to serve the needs of the community. One of the means of achieving the desired ideals was conformity with a recognized order of procedure and behaviour which is termed *li*. The prescriptions of *li* were framed with meticulous attention to detail. They took full account of differences of social status and were concerned with a wide range of matters as diverse as the treatment of visitors at court or in the home, the burial rites for the dead, or the supervision of commerce and barter. *Li* was founded on defined ethical purposes and was possibly conceived as a means of weaning a maturing community from its earlier, and somewhat questionable, practices. Although *li* was not designed as a meaningless set of conventional rules, its veneration frequently resulted in an excessive attention to form and a disregard for matter or reality. At its best, *li* was conceived as a means of encouraging individuals to maintain their correct social stations and to discharge their full communal responsibilities, while striving to attain that higher and richer degree of culture which was the aim of the educated man.

The training of the élite

Chinese statesmen have repeatedly taken refuge in *li* in the face of the forceful pressures of economic distress or foreign invasion. It is partly thanks to the prescriptions of *li* that schools and academies have been founded at the Government's behest. Since the establishment of the Han empire, an increasingly deeper attention has been paid to education, so as to provide the State with the supply of civil servants that it has required. Education has produced the men who have formed the élite of imperial society, to whose efforts and initiative so much of Chinese cultural achievement is due. These men have been selected competitively for their profession after a rigorous educational discipline and severe tests of intellectual prowess and physical endurance. The system of examinations to which they were subjected was possibly inaugurated in the Han period, and was reshaped in more complex forms in the T'ang, and again in the Ch'ing dynasties. The syllabus required a diligent study of those texts in which authority was sought for the Confucian views, and therefore those in which the ordinances of *li* are prescribed; and examiners required a high standard of literary composition, in forms of prose and verse of a prearranged and sometimes highly artificial style.

The training of this leisured élite class has at times been highly demanding. As a result, the educated man has acquired an outstanding prestige among his fellow men, as well as the privileges and material benefits of the official post to which he has gained appointment. For scholar and author, civil servant and statesman have been one and the same person in China, trained in a characteristic way for a common purpose—the extension of the emperor's beneficent rule and the promotion of civilizing influences in Chinese life. These men were nurtured on basic texts that have come to be known as the Confucian Classics, and which include writings that may date from the tenth century B.C., material of the time of Confucius, and some texts of a far later period which have been incorporated and passed off as sacred. Throughout the imperial age these texts have continually demanded reassessment and reinterpretation, and have ever formed the favourite subject of Chinese scholastic criticism.

The Confucian Classics
The influence exercised by the Confucian Classics has been of a fundamentalist or scriptural nature. Originally (second century B.C.) five works were named as being suitable for specialist study at official behest and for their use as a moral discipline; but by the thirteenth century the canon had come to include thirteen separate texts. These comprised the anthologies of songs (i.e. *The Book of Songs*, or *The Odes*) and royal documents (i.e. *The Book of Documents* or *History*: see p. 278) and an early chronicle (*The Spring and Autumn Annals*: see p. 279) all of which Confucius was believed to have edited, and the sayings which were attributed to him personally (*The Analects*). There

were in addition the commentaries or amplifications of *The Spring and Autumn Annals* (see p. 279); three compendia of ceremonial or conventional behaviour (i.e. of *Li*); a textbook of divination (*The Book of Changes*); an explanatory list of difficult expressions occurring in these texts (The *Erh-ya*); the sayings attributed to Mencius; and a set of maxims used in the elementary stages of education (*The Book of Filial Piety*). In the Sung period, four of these works (The *Analects*, *Mencius*, and two short extracts from the works on ceremonial) were selected as representing the quintessence of Confucian doctrine, and have found perhaps the first place in Chinese literature as *The Four Books*. Few children who were taught to read and write in China between 1300 and 1900 were relieved of the compulsion to commit these four texts to memory.

The didactic character of Chinese writings

The large volume of Chinese literature composed by the scholar-officials of the imperial age owes its origin and inspiration to the ideals of Confucianism. A great deal of Chinese writing has been directed to moral purposes, to illustrate historical precedent, to express ethical judgment or to ease the practical work of the emperor's government. The composition of literature for its intrinsic value, whether in the form of descriptive prose or lyrical poetry, was a comparatively late development (from about the fifth century), and was followed in due course by the appearance of fiction and lighter forms of writing. It was only from the eighth or ninth centuries that conditions were ripe for the emergence of a popular literature (e.g. fiction and drama) as a medium of entertainment.

Literature and cultural unity

In this context it must be stressed that literacy has always been a rare and highly prized acquisition in China, and the greater part of the population has long existed beyond the immediate reach of these cultural benefits. In the absence of statistics, only a rough estimate can be given for the extent of illiteracy during the imperial age; at times it must have amounted to well over 80 per cent of the population.

But the natural pride which the Chinese man of letters has come to possess has in turn acted as a unifying factor and promoted the continuity of Chinese culture. The qualifications whereby the official and statesman have been distinguished from other men have remained of the same type and have derived from a study of the same literature throughout imperial history. For this reason officials of the middle or later empires have been able to evaluate the opinions or tracts of their contemporaries on the same intellectual terms as those of their predecessors of some few centuries. It has been possible for the Chinese to claim an identity of culture that extends beyond long divisions of time and place, and to contrast this quality with the inferior situation of the less-favoured peoples who live beyond the pale of civilization.

The patronage of the palace

As the most exalted personages in the structure of Confucian society and authoritarian government, the emperor and his court came to acquire a cultural no less than a political importance. The Son of Heaven must not only perform his duties as such, he must be shown to be doing so and to be acting in a manner worthy of his responsibilities. He must be provided with the symbols of his status, in the form of a court attended by loyal servants. His way of life must be the most luxurious in the empire, enriched by elegant luxuries fashioned for gracious living; and he should be shown to enjoy the benefit of material presents that his subjects from distant lands submit for his delectation. Imperial palaces must be built and decorated by the most skilful craftsmen and artists of the empire; they must be adorned with precious jewels and splendid furnishings; they must be equipped with libraries of universal and unique value; and the court must form a focal point for the meeting of the most renowned poets, painters and scholars of the world.

The burden of a non-productive class

The palaces of China have thus acted as official patrons of the arts and have stimulated the creative efforts of a cultured society. The existence of a non-productive class to serve the courts has imposed a corresponding burden on the productive members of the population, whose efforts have been necessary for the sustenance of the élite. Such demands have possibly contributed to cultural developments of a different type. Administrative arrangements have become necessary to convey the produce of China's farms to the homes of the officials or to the large number of craftsmen engaged in the upkeep of the palace; and an addiction to the extravagances of town life has in turn required the support of yet greater agricultural effort and a more frequent import of costly luxuries. The culture of the court may in this way have served to stimulate greater production, brisker trade and faster transport.

III. BUDDHISM AND TAOISM

The second major spur to cultural development is seen in the propagation of Buddhism and the prosperous growth of its establishments. Owing to its foreign origins, and its points of conflict with Confucian doctrine, the religion has at times been subject to the criticism of Chinese reactionaries (see p. 89). In contrast with the Confucian cult, whose fortunes have largely been bound up with those of the established systems of society and government, Buddhism has often thrived by means of personal appeal and private benefaction. Like Confucianism, it has not only been the means of promoting the culture of the élite; it has also favoured the improvement of material conditions.

The arrival of Buddhism in China

The birth of Buddhism is traced to the teachings of Gautama, who lived in Northern India much about the time when Confucius was instructing pupils in Eastern China. After a protracted period of propagation, the faith was eventually conveyed overland to China, at about the beginning of the Christian era. Very little can be said for certain regarding the circumstances in which this alien concept of human activity and values was received, or the first impacts which it made either on the beliefs of the intellectuals or the prevalent superstitions of the populace. That it took some time for Buddhism to gain understanding, respect and support is only natural; for its priests spoke a strange language, and the sincerity or strength of their message could hardly be immediately apparent. Although some Buddhist missionaries may have reached China from as early as 100 B.C., it is from the fourth or fifth centuries A.D. or later that the religion plays an active part as an integral element of China's cultural development.

The elimination of suffering

While the full implications of Buddhist doctrine are too complex for adequate description here, a few outstanding elements of the faith must be mentioned in brief summary. Human nobility is seen to depend on the appreciation of values that are eternal and which can be achieved alike by beggar or king. Human existence is but a single stage in a hierarchy, and can be followed by rebirth in a higher or lower form, according to the individual's conduct or merit during his human span. It is open to all men to strive towards higher forms of existence; and human suffering, which is no more than a transient emergency resulting from human failure, can be eliminated only if human desires are forsworn.

The appeal of the faith

The social and political conditions of the third and succeeding centuries favoured the acceptance of these beliefs both in the minds of the intellectuals and among the Chinese populace. In these years officials had seen that the structure of the Confucian state was by no means always able to uphold the rule of an emperor, and that it did not necessarily result in ordered government, loyal co-operation or material wellbeing. Officials anxious to avoid the dangers of political intrigue were ready to seek asylum in the calm of the monastery, where spiritual peace could be found without the burden of civil responsibility. In the popular view, officialdom had failed to bring relief in time of famine, but the monastery could supply medical or other help to the needy; and whereas the representative of temporal power—the official— made his appearance only to exact his dues, the Buddhist priest would visit lonely families to relieve or terminate human suffering. The peasant toiled in the fields to extract his livelihood and to procure the dues which he owed to his civil masters; and it was the priest and his monastery who could bring pageantry and colour of religious ceremony to an existence that was otherwise monotonous and drab.

The growth of monasteries

Like Confucianism, Buddhism stimulated the growth of a nonproductive class of people, which included the priests, monks and nuns on whose devotion the monasteries depended. At times (e.g. in the ninth century) the State suffered a serious loss of manpower in this way, and monastic institutions could be criticized for providing a refuge to those who sought to evade their statutory obligations. Similarly, the monastery provided attractions which could lure men of talent away from serving the Confucian offices. In addition, Buddhism required the services of skilled artists and craftsmen, to design and decorate their splendid buildings; gold and other precious metals were needed for the many statues which were erected in each temple; and scholars or clerks were required in large numbers to prepare the many copies of scriptures and liturgies. While didactic prose has constituted one of the most permanent contributions made by Confucianism to Chinese culture, the richly ornamented temple remains as a vivid heritage of the Buddhist impact (for a description of an early Buddhist temple see p. 232).

But Chinese society was compensated for these losses. Once established, Buddhist foundations contributed to advances in material undertakings. They could provide large sums of capital for investment in major productive projects, or they could pay for equipment whose price lay beyond the purse of the individual farmers. Watermills were run under the auspices of the monks; or the reclamation of unused land for cultivation was undertaken by the labour assembled by an abbot.

Links with Asia and India

Finally, the Buddhist stimulus to cultural advance is seen in the exchanges that resulted from journeys of pilgrimage. Travellers from North India had brought the faith to China and had continued with their missionary activities in the succeeding centuries. Similarly, Chinese devotees sometimes answered a call to brave the hardships and dangers of travel, and made their way through the deserts of central Asia, to seek scriptures, treasures or doctrines for the enrichment of their religion. The exploration of routes whereby Chinese made contact with their brethren of Asia and India was partly due to the energy and willpower of Buddhist missionaries and pilgrims.

The early texts of Taoism

Further stimulus to cultural progress was provided by the very different types of intellectual, emotional and religious activity that are associated with the term *Taoism*. The foundation of these cults is traditionally ascribed to two mystics, who are known as Lao Tzu and Chuang Tzu, and who are said to have lived in the sixth and fourth centuries B.C. However, it is by no means certain that Lao Tzu was an historical personage. An extant text entitled the *Tao-te-ching* consists of a collection of sayings which are ascribed to Lao Tzu, but which are probably better regarded as a collection made from a number of different, and later, sources. Together with the *Chuang-tzu*, these writings voice the natural protests of mystics against a growing conception of wordly values. The inherent weakness of human emotion and the subjective nature of human judgment are stressed throughout these works, whose message contrasts significantly with the political and social ideas of the authoritarian or Confucian writers of that age.

Popular Taoism

Just as Confucius was adopted by later thinkers as the authority on whom their own sophisticated ideas could be fastened, so too Lao Tzu and Chuang Tzu formed ideal personages to whom other, and totally different, ideas could be ascribed. Highly complex results have followed from this process, and considerable confusion has come about between superstitious, religious and naturalist approaches to cosmic and human problems. For many types of thought have been fathered on to Lao Tzu and denoted by the single term *Taoism*.

Most of the intellectual or emotional movements that are associated with Taoism were developed during or after the break-up of the Han empire. Popular leaders ready to exploit the superstitious tendencies of the public have sought to practice magical powers as part of the cult of Lao Tzu; more reputable teachers fashioned a Taoist religious movement and drew some of their teaching from the *Tao-te-ching*.

Taoist naturalism and alchemy

Perhaps of greater importance has been the part played by some Taoist groups in observing and seeking to explain the phenomena of nature. Such activities derived from a genuine desire to solve the problems inherent in the cosmic order, and the adoption of a rational approach to these matters forms a sharp contrast with the attitude of some other sections of the Chinese intellectual world. The scientific searches of the Taoist naturalists could well have led to a geniune study of the problems of physics and chemistry. At the same time other elements of the Taoist cult were trying to demonstrate their magical powers by producing drugs that would ensure a man the gift of immortality, or by examining processes to manufacture gold for his personal enrichment.

A further contrast is seen with the school of *Yin-yang* theorists which had been emerging from at least the fourth century B.C. This school may have started from a genuine attempt to explain the principles of cosmic creation and destruction. Its founders had tried to do so in terms of a cyclical interaction of the five material elements of the material world (water, fire, wood, metal, earth) with the two natural and complementary forces of *Yin* (female, passive, dark) and *Yang* (male, active, light). By Han times, however, *Yin-yang* theory had degenerated and become, at its worst, a tool for political or demagogic manipulation. It had departed far from a path that might have led to rational, scientific investigation.

Taoist religion and established government

Important and conspicuous developments of Taoism have been seen in religious or quasi-religious activities. Leadership of this type of cult could sometimes be linked with popular superstition and could be utilized for political purposes. As a result, established governments, usurpers claiming authority or leaders of rebel bands have sometimes been at pains to associate themselves with Taoist practices. Usually, however, the established authority of empire frowned on the cults, as both their origins and their practices were at strange variance with the forms and ordinances of a disciplined society.

Taoist religion gave rise to a small leisured class of priests, masters of ceremonies and other practitioners, equipped with their temples and texts, and perpetuating conventions and disciplines whereby the arts of meditation or experiment in magic could be effected. And, as with Buddhism, these establishments sometimes provided a refuge to those seeking to avoid the cares and responsibilities of contemporary politics.

IV. THE PACE OF CULTURAL PROGRESS

Owing to its long continuity, Chinese culture has sometimes been credited with earlier origins than it actually possesses. For in comparison with the civilizations of the Middle East, that of China is young. While the use of copper was known in Egypt by about 4500 B.C., in the Far East the bronze age must be placed at c. 1500. Similarly, an iron age is dated in Europe from c. 900 B.C., but for China the corresponding date is c. 600. However, civilization emerged considerably earlier in China than in other parts of the Far East and has influenced other indigenous developments in a characteristic way. Few features of life in China's neighbouring countries such as Japan, Korea or Vietnam fail to reflect the marks of Chinese culture.

Cultural innovation during political disunity

The relationship between cultural growth and the fortunes of empire is of some importance, and a cycle of development can sometimes be discerned. Often the genius of the Chinese peoples has been most noticeably revealed in the experiments undertaken at times when there was no single effective central authority. In the absence of an united empire, individual initiative has acquired a greater freedom; and it has been possible for a localized court or government to try out new methods of administration or production.

3. THE QUEEN MOTHER OF THE WEST

The worship of the Queen Mother of the West as a means of achieving immortality had been practised long before the imperial period, and remained popular during the Han dynasty and later. On this embossed brick (from Hsin-fan *hsien*, Ssu-ch'uan; original size 46 by 41 cm.; to be dated within the range of A.D. 100 to 200), the goddess is shown seated on a creature formed of a tiger's head and dragon's tail; to her right is seen the three-legged crow who acted as her food-gatherer; to her left a hare holds a branch of the magical plant which is capable of imparting longevity. According to one tradition, the hare possessed the necessary skill to compound the drug of immortality; and the crow and hare possibly symbolize the sun and the moon. The dancing toad in the centre recalls the tale of Heng-ngo, a woman who stole the drug and ran away to the moon, there to be transformed into a toad. The goddess is attended by a lance-holder, in human form, and the fabulous winged fox, whose tail is split into nine branches. According to one explanation of the scene, a worshipper is making obeisance and praying; the robed couple who are seated, or kneeling, on the opposite side of the table, are his ancestors who have already achieved immortality.

4. DOMESTIC BANQUET (eleventh to twelfth century)
Wall-painting from the antechamber of tomb No. 1, Pai-sha, Honan. The tomb contained the remains of a man and a woman, and was built with a gateway, two chambers and connecting passages. The structure was mainly of brick, and was highly decorated throughout; a date in 1099 is mentioned in an inscription found inside the tomb.

Plate 4 shows the painting (original dimensions unstated) that appeared on the west wall of the antechamber; the two occupants of the tomb are seen seated and enjoying a banquet. The dominant colouring is ox-blood, with the man's robes in indigo.

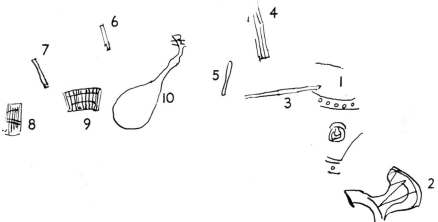

5. AN ORCHESTRA (eleventh to twelfth century)
(*continued from caption to Plate 4*)
Facing them on the east wall, the artists have depicted an orchestra of eleven
members, who are engaged in entertaining their master and mistress (dominant colour terra-cotta, with robes in red and blue). The instruments can be
identified as follows: 1 Barrel-shaped nailed drum; 2 Hour-glass shaped
cord-braced drum; 3 Transverse flute; 4 Clappers; 5, 6 and 7 Double
reed-pipes of cylindrical bore; 8 Mouth-organ, with long, tea-pot like spout;
9 Set of twelve Pan-pipes; 10 Five-stringed bent-necked lute, with large
triangular plectrum. A dancer separates the orchestra into two groups.

6. THE CONDUCT OF JUSTICE

From the *Chung-i Shui-hu chuan ch'a-t'u*, a set of illustrations to an heroic
novel of the thirteenth century (*Shui-hu chuan*), rendered into English as 'All
men are Brothers' (by Pearl Buck, New York, 1937). The wood-cut shown
here (original size 21 by 14 cm.) was made for inclusion in an edition of
about 1600, and probably represents contemporary practice. The scene por-
trays an incident from Chapter 74 of the novel. Li K'uei has come across the
robes and insignia of a magistrate and proceeds to hold a mock court trial.
One of the real magistrate's subordinates is punished for lack of courage
by being forced to wear the wooden collar (cangue) of convicted criminals,
and is shown leaving the court after judicial proceedings.

CULTURAL DEVELOPMENT

A rich variety of cultural innovation can be dated to periods such as the Warring States (480–222 B.C.) or the Five Dynasties (907–959). In the first of these periods the philosophical ideas of the Chinese were first defined; successful experiments were made to build canals and dykes, and to fortify cities; and a system of coinage became widespread in the sub-continent. In the centuries of disunion that intervened between the Han (202–220) and T'ang (618–906) dynasties, new forms of literature took shape, and the masters of sculpture, painting and calligraphy created new models; and during the Five Dynasties (907–59) the art of printing emerged from obscurity, and new monetary systems were evolved.

Achievements during political strength

A second stage of development is reached with the establishment and consolidation of a powerful dynasty, backed by the loyal support of competent servants, and able to make greater use of China's material resources. In such circumstances, experiments that have been tried locally can be applied on a wider scale and implemented with the full force of imperial organization. Effective imperial government can provide the financial backing needed for such projects and can order its manifold servants to supervise their completion. But frequently, the natural force of initiative was cramped by the heavy hand of official formalism. For in the earlier stages, during political disunity, schemes of technical or cultural advance (e.g. systems for irrigation, or the foundation of schools) could be initiated by the very men who had evolved them and who were fired with a personal enthusiasm for their success; but in the ensuing stages of fuller implementation, such schemes would be operated by men who were acting under orders, and who were possibly prejudiced against innovation; and regional differences could easily be obliterated in a dull uniformity of an empire.

None the less the cultural successes of empire were of striking significance. It became possible for the Ch'in, Sui and Yüan dynasties to dispose a sufficiently great force of manpower to build roads and canals which radically changed the face of China, and which remained effective in the succeeding Han, T'ang, Ming and Ch'ing periods. Similarly, the emperors and courts of those dynasties were able to patronize the arts to an extent that was impossible in the smaller states or at less stable times; and it was during the 'major' dynasties that artistic traditions were established and educational institutions consolidated.

The dispersal of talent

With the decay of imperial authority a new stage begins. The simultaneous emergence of regional courts once more permits the extension of patronage to scholarship and the arts from several centres. The bureaucratic organization required by an empire may be set up by several pretenders to imperial rule, with the result that there are more sinecures for the employment of talented men than at a time of single dynastic rule. There are thus more opportunities for the occupation of a leisured class in their cultural pursuits while drawing official salaries; and there may be greater opportunities for such men to make the acquaintance of human and natural conditions of far-flung regions. Alternately intellectuals may flee from a court at the time of a political coup, so as to devote their remaining days and energies to Buddhist or Taoist activities. In this way, imperial collapse has sometimes led to cultural dispersal, refreshment and enrichment.

The cultural uniformity of Han

Characteristic features of particular periods can best be considered with these major tendencies in view. In the few centuries immediately prior to the unification of Ch'in (221 B.C.), there was a distinct possibility that two or more independent cultures would arise in China, either in the Yellow River valley or in the Huai and Yangtse areas. Artefacts (e.g. carved wood, lacquered bowls and boxes) which have been found in the southern regions and which can be dated in this period are of a completely different character from that of the contemporary material found in the north. The styles of decoration betray different cultural, and perhaps ethnic, origins and bear features which are not apparent in the material of Han China or later. For with the political unification of Ch'in and Han, cultural uniformity was imposed on a far greater scale than hitherto. The political centre was situated in the north and political control was exercised therefrom. As this control was extended into the southern recesses of the sub-continent, independent cultural trends came to be stunted or discouraged. Although indigenous developments may have survived in the hills, marshes and fastnesses of southern China, it was the northerner whose influence became dominant, if only because he had evolved an efficient system of writing and had become a more efficient organizer than his southern neighbour of the Yangtse Valley and beyond.

CULTURAL DEVELOPMENT

Divergence and unification

From the Han period it becomes possible to think in terms of a single Chinese culture. Political conditions favoured the steady dissemination of new techniques and manufactures, and visitors to museums may perhaps be forgiven for dismissing much of the output of the Han potters as unimaginative examples of mass production. While the political and social instability of the fourth, fifth and sixth centuries favoured the growth of independent scholastic and artistic traditions, the masters of the newly reunified Sui and T'ang empires looked to cultural unity as a means of supporting their temporal powers. An example of their policy is seen in the treatment of the texts of the Confucian canon. The T'ang government ordered the preparation of a new edition, with the intention of reconciling the divergent views of the preceding centuries; and the new, officially inspired, interpretation became required reading for those entering official life.

The brilliance of Sung China

During the Sung period (960–1279) Chinese cultural achievements reached new heights, owing to official stimulus, private initiative and historical circumstance. The civil service was now greatly expanded, with more posts, more sinecures and new degrees of complexity; economic practice was changing almost beyond recognition and favoured the enterprises of individual merchants and manufacturers; and in 1126 the imperial house and court was forced by foreign pressure to remove its seat to a new capital city across the Yangtse (i.e. Lin-an, the modern Hangchow). With this move there was started a new era of cultural brilliance; inventive genius was applied in areas which had hitherto been situated at the edge of Chinese government, where civilized administration had hardly permeated. In the prevailing administrative weakness, cultural advances prospered as in times of political disunion. Emperor and court set new standards of gracious living and provided an inspiring degree of literary and artistic patronage; and economic conditions favoured the extension of material progress, with the help of new appliances of technology.

In the intellectual field, political dissatisfaction or disappointment led to a reassessment of the traditional schemes of Confucianism, and their realignment in metaphysical terms with some of the highly advanced and abstruse doctrines of Buddhism. The result of that reassessment, which occupied some of the ablest minds of the Southern Sung period, is known as Neo-Confucianism and was to dominate the Chinese mind for some four centuries.

The Ch'ing period

The consolidation of effective empire under the Ch'ing dynasty (from 1644) affected cultural developments in much the same way as had the foundation of the Han and T'ang empires. There followed a period of reaffirmation, of steady application and of compromise between the different innovations of the preceding decades. But the Ch'ing dynasty was also to meet a cultural challenge of new dimensions, which resulted from the more frequent contacts made with the non-Chinese world of the west. From the sixteenth century, members of the Jesuit and other orders had been reaching the Chinese capital in increasingly large numbers. Quite apart from missionary activities, their scientific skills and manifold gifts had earned them a high reputation and the gratitude of the imperial court they served. At the same time, examples of the material and technological achievements of the western world were being conveyed to China in increasingly large volume by merchant adventurers; and these were followed in due course by diplomats, who strove to ease the path of commercial activity and official intercourse. In 1793–4 Lord Macartney brought as presents to the Ch'ing emperor porcelains made in Derbyshire, lustres, pieces of clockwork, with a celestial and a terrestrial globe. Some of these symbols of British products were greatly admired, and by the nineteenth century the palaces of Peking could boast possession of many a glittering and fashionable product of Europe's craftsmen and decorators.

Of greater significance in the history of Chinese culture was the challenge with which the traditional Chinese conception of the state and society was being confronted. The old ideals had been strengthened by the new methods of criticism and the new academic standards that had been set by the Chinese scholars of the eighteenth and nineteenth centuries. But the Confucian view of man and his qualities no longer remained unquestioned by those who were gaining acquaintance with the personal religion and highly rationalist philosophies of the western world. This radical change coincided with a period of dynastic decline and rebellion, and was to result in the revolution which overcame Chinese thought in the second half of the nineteenth century.

Artistic innovation and decline

A further rhythm of action and reaction can sometimes be observed in the progress of culture, independently of political implications. This is noticeable both in the history of Chinese literature and in the evolution of new art forms, e.g. ceramic or lacquer wares. The first stage is one of bold technical experiment and individual creativeness; new forms of prose and poetry are tried, or daring innovations made by craftsmen in their chosen medium. Initially these works of genius may be exemplified in models that are somewhat coarse, and it is only in the succeeding decades that a more general practice results in more refined products. In such periods China has created her most beautiful and lasting monuments to human genius; emotion is expressed quietly and in a controlled, restrained manner, with the full freshness of the creative artist. But there follows a stage of decadence, in which imitation takes the place of inspiration. Artists, in word or plastic medium, strive and struggle to reproduce decorative complexity or excrescence with little sense of context or proportion; and a lack of artistic integrity results in products that seem stale or artificial. Finally a reaction sets in to free the literary and artistic world from such inhibitions. A movement is initiated to restore a taste for the rugged models of the past. Emotion is expressed by direct simplicity rather than forced elegance, and once again the balance is regained between the claims of form and matter.

Science and technology

While research is still in progress, no final judgment can be made regarding the pace of China's scientific and technological development. There are however a few outstanding principles whose operation can be observed. While the whole emphasis of Confucian thought has been directed to the achievement and value, actual or potential, of the individual man, it is thanks to Taoism that Chinese minds have been turned towards a study of nature and the sciences of physics and chemistry. By the end of the second century A.D. notable discoveries had been made in science, either thanks to Taoist or other influences, but these were possibly not so conspicuous as those of contemporary Greek thought. But whereas a period of retrenchment or obscurity set in for Europe during the so-called Dark Ages, in China there followed some centuries of the steady application of scientific knowledge and principle to the practical problems of everyday life. Thanks to the continuation of this tradition, the new techniques that were discovered in China during the T'ang and Sung periods were applied in Asia several centuries earlier than in Europe with conspicuous results. But from the fifteenth century the situation is reversed, owing to the prominent strides that were taken so dramatically and effectively in European thought. During the Ming and Ch'ing periods, the pace of scientific advance in China lagged far behind the prevailing tendencies of post-renaissance Europe.

More attention is now being paid to the potential exchanges of thought and experience between technologists of the East and the West. Despite the fundamentally different outlook of the Chinese and the Western scientists, many Chinese ideas have probably affected European thought and practice in ways that have not yet been fully appreciated.

V. PAPER, PRINTING AND CLOCKWORK

All general assessments of China's history will place a different emphasis on individual features of her cultural heritage and will fasten on different achievements as the most notable examples of her civilization. Luckily an increasing number of monographs enables a general reader to pursue the study of particular topics (e.g. poetry, ceramics, painting) and to set the predilections of specialists or enthusiasts in their wider context. Quite apart from the literary and artistic manifestations of human genius, the products of Chinese culture demonstrate technical qualities that are unknown elsewhere and derive from the early evolution of expert technological methods. The products of the master-craftsmen who designed and executed the bronzes of the Shang era; the calligraphic models that flowed from the brushes of master-scribes of the fourth century; the landscape paintings or delicate celadons of the Sung period; or the bolder porcelains of the Ming factories can all be quoted as examples of technical achievement that are without parallel in contemporary civilizations elsewhere.

The three examples of Chinese genius that have been chosen for brief discussion here have been selected both for their intrinsic interest and on account of the circumstances of their origin. They derive mostly from the urges of religion, Confucian statecraft and Buddhist devotion that have been described above, and have contributed nobly to the distinctive nature of Chinese civilization.

Paper and its precedents

Traditionally the Chinese claimed that paper was invented, and the invention brought to the notice of the throne, in A.D. 105, and the date can be accepted as a general indication. Before paper had been made from the pulp of bark and fabrics, documents had been drawn up on silken rolls or narrow strips of wood, that were bound together for consecutive reading. Neither of these media was entirely satisfactory; wooden documents were bulky and difficult to handle, and sections of the text could become displaced only too easily, once the strips had been disarranged. Silk, however, was an expensive commodity, and is a material which can be destroyed too readily. By the second century both the administrative requirements of Chinese officialdom and the production of literary work had increased the quantity of written material beyond all thought. In the centuries that followed, the Buddhist church demanded that more and more monasteries should possess their own copies of the scriptures, and individual worshippers may have needed copies of the magical chants that were reverently recited during religious ceremonies. The evolution of paper came about at a time well suited to satisfy these voluminous needs, and its more general use coincided with the growing literary accomplishments of the Han to T'ang age.

The beginnings of block-printing

The precise time and circumstances in which the art of block-printing was discovered will probably never be known. It may well be that some unnamed pioneer stumbled upon the process accidentally; and as he did not realize or could not exploit its full significance, his name has been denied the immortal fame that it has deserved. In about A.D. 175 a series of some fifty stone tablets were erected in the capital city. They bore an authoritative text of the books of Confucian lore, specially engraved to provide posterity with a permanent, unquestionable copy of the texts for consultation. Scholars may have been encouraged to make copies of these texts by taking squeezes or rubbings from the stones; in this way the inscriptions could be reproduced, either on silk or on the new medium of paper.

Some centuries before 175 the principle of using a matrix to produce identical copies of a written or painted device had been seen in the seals that were used by emperors and officials to give their mark of authentification to documents of state. But whereas such seals had been cut in reverse (i.e. in mirror fashion), so that the stamped image made by the seal could be read in the correct way, the stone tablets of 175 had been cut so as to present an observer with straight text, to be read at sight directly from the stone.

Printing proper can be said to have started when the principle of the seal was adopted for the production of texts, i.e. when wooden boards were engraved with columns of characters in mirror-fashion, not so as to be readable at sight, but deliberately to speed the process of reproducing copies. The earliest surviving examples of block-printing come in fact not from China but from Japan, where the technique had been imported at an early stage. These consist of narrow strips of Buddhist texts, printed in very large numbers at the command of the Japanese court (c. 770). The earliest surviving examples of Chinese printing dates from 868, but by that time the art was already considerably well advanced and skilfully executed.[1]

Early uses of print

The technique and practice of block-cutting was developed in the tenth century, in a somewhat isolated part of south-west China, during a period of political disunity. Some of the earliest texts to be printed were Buddhist scriptures, illustrated with figures used for liturgical purposes. At a later stage the state took official cognisance of the art, and presses were established and operated by the government. Confucian influence is seen in the choice of texts—inevitably the Classical Books—that were selected for printing. In addition the presses were soon being used to fulfil one of the purposes of imperial government, the dissemination of a correctly regulated calendar.

Private enterprise and initiative is seen in the use of the presses to produce bills of exchange needed for the transfer of sums of money. By the Sung period the government had taken over this project, and official banknotes were being printed for the state. Experiments in the use of movable type (i.e. single types cast or carved for each character, which were assembled to form the text as necessary) were also made by at least one pioneer of the Sung period, but this method of printing was not adopted for general use until the Ming age; and the use of wooden blocks continued until the last century.

Su Sung's clock

As part of their routine work of administration, military officers of the Han empire were obliged to maintain daily records of the work of their men, together with registers of the signals they received or the patrols they despatched. In such reports the operative or significant information sometimes consisted in the timing of a particular event, and this was

[1] Early examples of Chinese and Japanese printing are usually exhibited in the *British Museum.*

expressed in terms of one of the twelve hours of the day and night and its subdivisions of seven or eight parts. Sundials were certainly used at this comparatively early stage of Chinese culture, and the existence of other devices that were worked by water can be attested from literary references; but perhaps the most conspicuous example of Chinese astronomy and horology is the masterpiece of Su Sung, which was completed in about 1090. It is singularly fortunate that, in addition to supervising the construction and erection of the device, Su Sung compiled a detailed description of the mechanism, and with the help of his text and illustrative diagrams—perpetuated in print in 1172— it has been possible to reconstruct his clockwork today. Su Sung's records, which are almost tantamount to an engineer's specification, have recently been studied by Dr Needham, who summarizes the achievement as follows:[1]

> Su Sung's 'clock' was, in fact, a great astronomical clock-tower more than 30 feet high, surmounted by a huge bronze power-driven armillary sphere for observation, and containing, in a chamber within, an automatically rotated celestial globe with which the observed places of the heavenly bodies could be compared. On the front of the tower was a pagoda structure with five storeys, each having a door through which mannikins and jacks appeared ringing bells and gongs and holding tablets to indicate the hours and other special times of the day and night. Inside the tower was the motive source, a great scoop-wheel using water and turning all the shafts working the various devices. The wheel was checked by an escapement consisting of a sort of weighbridge which prevented the fall of a scoop until full, and a trip-lever and parallel linkage system which arrested the forward motion of the wheel at a further point and allowed it to settle back and bring the next scoop into position on the weighbridge. One must imagine this giant structure going off at full-cock every quarter of an hour with a great sound of creaking and splashing, clanging and ringing; it must have been impressive, and we know that it was actually built and made to work for many years before being carried away into exile.

It is significant that Su Sung's work was undertaken as a result of an imperial order, and that his career was that of a civil servant. While no direct statement survives regarding the motives which inspired the

[1] Joseph Needham, Wang Ling and Derek J. de Solla Price, *Heavenly Clockwork*, Cambridge, 1960, p. 3.

erection of his structure, it can be surmised that these were not unconnected with the state's need to maintain accurate astronomical calculations, if only for the regulation of the calendar. It has also been suggested that accurate time-keeping played an essential role in the determination or selection of the imperial heir. (See Needham *et. al.*, *op. cit.*, p. 170.)

VI. THE CHINESE WRITTEN LANGUAGE

No account of Chinese cultural development can ignore the significance of the Chinese script in moulding and perpetuating cultural unity. The overriding influence of written Chinese could perhaps be compared with that of Latin, had the use of Latin persisted among Europe's statesmen, churchmen, professional men, businessmen and men of letters as the normal means of communication that was in use until the middle of the nineteenth century.

The continuity of Chinese writing
An essential continuity can be traced from the writings that were scratched on the oracle shells and bones of the Shang period to the characters that appear in newspapers of the twentieth century. Already in the Shang period the principal means whereby characters were created had been evolved, although the actual number of those in use (about 2000) was very much smaller than, say, in the second century A.D. Furthermore, despite the lapse of 3000 years, the modern forms of many characters are very closely related to those of the earliest examples of writing (e.g. the modern forms 雨 (rain) and 鳥 (long-tailed bird) appeared as 雨 and 鳥).

Bones, bronze, wood and silk
The changes that have occurred in the interval have been partly due to the introduction of new media for writing and to the purposeful enactment of governments. Comparatively simple forms of characters were used for the writings that were engraved, and sometimes painted with a brush, on the bones. Complex elaborations, which were by no means standard, became possible and fashionable when inscriptions which conveyed authority, recorded royal actions or acted as title deeds to property, were cast as integral parts of bronze vessels (Chou

period). A further change, which included a reversion to a more simple type, came about as wooden or bamboo strips came into normal use for preparing the administrative records required by a more sophisticated government (from the fourth century B.C.). By the time of the Ch'in unification (221 B.C.), a yet greater degree of sophistication had been attained; silk was being used for luxury writing, in addition to the more regular use of wood for utilitarian needs.

Writing and the task of government

Political motives may now have played a part in the development of Chinese writing. According to Chinese tradition, the authoritarian government of Ch'in forcibly introduced the use of a standard form of the characters, as a means of eliminating any contacts that the scholastic world might retain with the ethical writings of earlier, and possibly anti-Ch'in, protagonists of Confucian thought. It is perhaps more likely that the new imperial government exploited the recent acceptance of wood, or silk, together with the brush (known from much earlier times) as convenient implements of writing; and that its purpose was to publicize a simple form of writing which would be easier for clerks to master and which could be used to speed the processes of administration. Early in the Han period further means were found to simplify and standardize the characters. The forms that were adopted c. 200 B.C. have remained essentially unchanged, and have been used for manuscript material of wood, silk or paper; for commemorative inscriptions carved in stone; and for books printed on paper. Very recently the western pencil or ball-point pen has replaced the brush. Again an attempt has been made to simplify many of the existing characters and to reduce the number that are in current use, so that more Chinese can be taught to read; and political motives have once more favoured a break with the literary traditions of the past. The modern (post 1949) experiments at substituting a romanized script in place of the characters must be considered with these developments and motives in mind.

The evolution of Chinese characters

The letters of a western alphabet merely indicate distinctions of sound. Although a similar purpose may have been present in the process of developing Chinese characters, the earliest forms were created to symbolize individual material objects or actions, or simple abstract concepts. Owing partly to the means whereby characters were evolved and partly to the changes of pronunciation of the intervening centuries, there is no immediate means today of determining at sight the correct pronunciation of a given character; and in any case this may vary in different parts of China, in accordance with local dialect.

Chinese scholars have isolated six methods whereby characters have been created or their use determined (for examples, see Table Four). Some simple characters, which bear the meanings of animate or inanimate objects are derived from pictograms, as can be seen even from the formalized versions that are used in modern print (e.g. 人 月 and 木, which denote man, moon and tree respectively). Others are simple ideograms, often expressing a spatial relationship. Thirdly, elements of these types are combined together to form logical compounds in which two or more ideas are juxtaposed to suggest the derived meaning (see the examples in Table Four for two ways in which this principle applies). The fourth method whereby characters have been formed allows for the combination of two elements in one of two ways: (a) in the course of time, an existing character of a simple type (i.e. a pictogram) may have acquired a number of very similar or derived meanings, and it may have become necessary to add some mark of distinction for purposes of clarity. In these cases a second element, with a clearly understood general meaning, was placed alongside the original character, so as to define its particular usage; (b) one of the elements is formed by an existing character, which was originally evolved to symbolize a meaning; but as it has subsequently become intimately associated with a sound-value, it can also serve as a means of indicating the pronunciation of a character which is being artificially created; a second element is chosen to give a broad idea of the meaning of the character, and so as to distinguish it from those others which possess a similar sound-value.

Two final methods whereby characters are utilized allow for them to bear secondary meanings, either by a conventional extension of ideas, or as direct loans. By such means, existing characters are used to express notions which may be highly abstract or complicated, and for which characters were not formed in their own right.

The accretion of newly formed characters
Compounds formed by the fourth method described above can be coined very easily, and it has been estimated that as much as nine-

tenths of the vocabulary of modern written Chinese has been evolved in this way. Many such additions were made during the formative years of cultural development of the Han period and succeeding centuries. At this time the written language was required not only to serve the needs of a speedily growing literary activity, but also to satisfy the requirements of Buddhist priests and monks, who were engaged in translating texts from Sanskrit and providing phonetic renderings in Chinese of the names and formulae that the faithful needed to chant. Much more recently it has been necessary to increase the Chinese written vocabulary so as to permit the inclusion of the technical nomenclature of western science. The single characters used to designate the 103 elements of chemistry will be mostly found to include a phonetic and a semantic part.

Stylistic differences

The continuity and identity of Chinese writing has served as a means of linking educated Chinese, whether they live in Canton or Manchuria, in Hunan or Fukien. For although these men may converse in dialects which are incomprehensible to each other, they have been trained to signify their meaning in writing by use of the same set of symbols, whose semantic value is constant, whatever their pronunciation (cf. the use of the symbols **I, II, III**, or **1, 2, 3** etc., in Europe, with unchangeable meanings but variable pronunciation in e.g. England, Germany and Italy).

However, the degree or nature of this continuity is sometimes overemphasized or misunderstood, as can perhaps be illustrated by analogy. Very great stylistic differences separate the Greek language of the Homeric poems from that written by Aristotle; and this again is very different from that of Patristic literature. Ability to read the Greek of any one of these styles need not necessarily imply familiarity with the others. Similar conditions apply to Chinese, whose literature comprises substantially different sections such as the 'classical' texts of the Chou period and later; the didactic prose of the historians and philosophers; the lyrical works of poets and mystics; or the corpus of the Buddhist Canon. While authors of the same age understand each other's prose easily enough, in extreme cases, the continuity of the Chinese form of writing may mean no more, even to an educated Chinese, than the ability to study an unfamiliar branch of literature; it need not ensure that different branches are immediately comprehensible to the one reader.

Despite these reservations, it should be reiterated that the written Chinese language has played a major role in shaping and disseminating cultural developments. The comparative difficulty of mastering the script, which is often severely overrated, may have acted as a deterrent to foreigners, and may thus have tended to isolate Chinese from other civilizations. In its defence, let it be remarked that by written Chinese, a poet or prose-writer can combine a richness of expression with an economy of words, an artist can match his painting with the delights of calligraphy; and it is through the medium of written Chinese that new measures of political organization, social and educational develop-ment, and economic advance were brought to those neighbouring countries of China which had failed to evolve their own native script.

TABLE FOUR

THE DEVELOPMENT OF CHINESE CHARACTERS:
FOUR PRINCIPLES

(Chinese scholars have long debated the precise significance of the principles whereby characters have been used by extension or as loans; in view of the complexity of the problems that are involved, no examples of these usages are included below.)

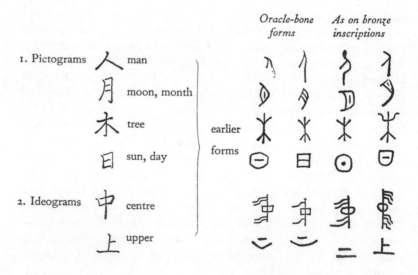

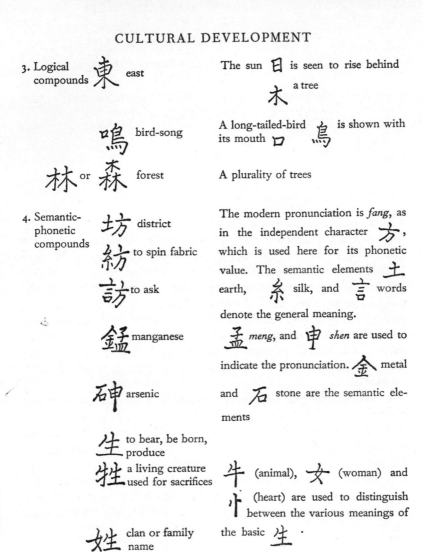

3. Logical compounds

東 east — The sun 日 is seen to rise behind a tree 木

鳴 bird-song — A long-tailed-bird is shown with its mouth 口 鳥

林 or 森 forest — A plurality of trees

4. Semantic-phonetic compounds

坊 district
紡 to spin fabric
訪 to ask

The modern pronunciation is *fang*, as in the independent character 方, which is used here for its phonetic value. The semantic elements 土 earth, 糸 silk, and 言 words denote the general meaning.

錳 manganese

砷 arsenic

孟 *meng*, and 申 *shen* are used to indicate the pronunciation. 金 metal and 石 stone are the semantic elements

生 to bear, be born, produce
牲 a living creature used for sacrifices

牛 (animal), 女 (woman) and 忄 (heart) are used to distinguish between the various meanings of the basic 生 .

姓 clan or family name
性 human disposition

CHAPTER FIVE

SOCIAL DISTINCTIONS

I. BASIC CONCEPTS AND THE PRE-IMPERIAL AGE

The classes of governor and governed

The existence of different classes, each with an accepted place in the community of the Chinese empires, is an implicit principle in the Confucian concept of human society and the authoritarian means of ordering its successful government. Reference to some classes, e.g. the officials, or an élite, has been made above, in connection with the practice of imperial sovereignty and China's cultural development; but despite the essential place of privilege in the social structure of the empire, it is difficult to define precise social distinctions, owing both to the nature of the source material and the Chinese distaste for analytical method.

In general there has been only one aspect of social status of which historians and philosophers have shown themselves aware, the distinction between a class of governors and one of governed. Although the overwhelming majority of the Chinese peoples has always belonged to the second category, there is little information regarding the finer distinctions which have informed this society. Historians have themselves been members of the governing class and have unfortunately tended to treat the governed class as if it were a single homogeneous unit.

The Chinese attitude

Chinese writings, then, are rarely concerned with differences in the reactions expressed by the many different sections of this great community, in accordance with their particular interests, occupations or status. It is only for the governors that extreme care is taken to make due allowance for the appropriate differences of grade and privilege. Major distinctions such as those of master and slave, feudal lord and his dependant, or aristocrat and commoner are not adopted as hard and fast criteria in traditional literature; and although historical phenomena

120

have more recently been explained in these or similar terms, the traditional Chinese view of privilege is by no means so sharply defined, and is not wholly concerned with a relationship between social status and political consequence. As Chinese writings have consisted more of conscious attempts at historical description than sociological analysis, they have tended to ignore questions that are implicit in the concept of 'class-structure'. In accordance with both Confucian and authoritarian principles, the relationships that are assumed to exist between different sections of the community are based on the acknowledgement of certain rights and duties; there is no need to provide an explicit description of a social hierarchy, provided that due attention is paid to the maintenance of such rights and the observance of such duties.

Distinctions of birth, wealth and occupation
Social distinctions had already acquired some definite and permanent attributes before the imperial age. They arose by virtue of religious or tribal qualities, or as a result of economic expedient, or thanks to political or professional training. Men, or groups of men, had begun to form classes owing to the circumstances of kinship in which they were born; the land or wealth which they possessed; and the occupation for which they were educated or suited. These three criteria cannot however be neatly separated. Even in the Shang period there had come into existence a privileged class of priests or diviners, whose distinction lay both in their religious significance and their occupational skill. Similarly, the value of kinship was already associated with that of wealth, as can be seen in the system of hereditary succession that was adopted by the royal houses of Shang and Chou, who constituted some of the greatest contemporary landowners. Qualifications of all three types had become causes of envy and pride long before the third century B.C. and had already been recognized as such.

Historical summary
In the pre-imperial age, birth and wealth emerged first as the most important criteria for determining privileged status. The third criterion, of occupation, proved its value in the course of the political development of the Warring Kingdoms (fifth to third centuries), and arose partly owing to the need to preserve privileges of kinship and wealth intact. The landowning or privileged families required the services of men who possessed intellectual ability or diplomatic skill. Authoritarian

theory and Confucian concept, which were being fostered and defined in these centuries, both favoured the growth of a privileged class whose distinction lay in their professional talents.

Such a class was able to consolidate its position and powers during the early and middle empires. By skilfully serving different imperial families or aspirants to empire, groups of officials were able to acquire sufficient landed property to sustain their privileged status. But by the T'ang, and particularly the Sung, periods, economic changes brought a new emphasis to the importance of wealth. New factors resulted from the growth of easier monetary arrangements. The men who commanded wealth could now affect the lives of individuals in equal or even greater degree than the trained official who served the government, and affluence was becoming of as great a value as occupation. Moreover, the high standards originally set for admitting men of distinction to the ranks of the professional class were being abandoned, in favour of ties of kinship, or favouritism due to birth. At the same time, the importance of money in determining social distinctions may perhaps be seen in the rise of a class of hired labourers, whose origins may date from the Sung period.

The tendency for wealth to overshadow service or professional ability continued during the later empires, despite attempts to reassert imperial authority and to enhance the power of imperial servants. Radical change came in the middle of the nineteenth century, with a greatly increased population, with the failure of the privileged minority to provide for the safety and the well-being of the majority, and the compelling need to set labour to work at new tasks, which involved new conditions of employment. The political decline of the Ch'ing dynasty provoked a reassessment of the traditional valuation put on human beings.

Early distinctions of name and kinship

The earliest social distinction to appear with clarity in Chinese literature and tradition is concerned with the possession of a name denoting the clan or the family; and this distinction was perhaps operative in periods which are now described as the neolithic, bronze or early iron ages. The distinction was a clear mark of privilege. Only a small proportion of tribesmen had been designated as identifiable members of a smaller group, and these were associated together by virtue of a more intimate degree of kinship which was denied to many of their fellow tribesmen. The right to use a surname as a symbol of identification, however acquired, was strictly limited to the chosen few, and the distinction between the named and unnamed members is apparent in the religious observances, military functions and economic circumstances of pre-imperial China.

The privileges of a surname

Members of these early communities who were fortunate enough to possess a surname were thereby able to trace their descent from a known series of ancestors, and were therefore both entitled and obliged to perform the necessary religious reverence to their powers; and in turn they could themselves expect to receive the benefits of similar services, duly rendered by their descendants. The principle of privileged worship appears almost in hierarchical form. The Son of Heaven was the only individual entitled to worship at the shrine of Heaven, i.e. of his own ancestor; lesser mortals, who yet possessed surnames, were similarly entitled to worship at their own shrines, which were arrayed in different degrees of honour; but those men who did not possess surnames had no means of performing these rites, and could not expect the blessings that followed such observances.

A further distinction of a religious, ritual or social nature is to be observed in connection with the early arrangements for marriages. When couples who possessed surnames were married, the correct ceremonies were conducted with due pomp; records were maintained and steps taken to preserve the continuity of the name, i.e. of the clan or its constituent families. But for the unnamed majority, unions were formed without formality, record or the same degree of control, and without question of hereditary succession; and on occasion groups of men and women may have been paired off, irrespective of their individual identity.

Similarly, those privileged by the possession of a name could play a safer role in warfare, in a manner which was denied to lesser mortals; for they could enjoy the protection of armed horse-drawn chariots, while the remainder fought as single warriors in the service and defence of their mounted superiors.

Landownership and the peasantry

In addition, there was a sharp difference in the economic circumstances of the two 'classes'. Families which could be identified by the name that had been conferred on their progenitors could usually claim *de facto* and hereditary possession of lands, whose benefit they could enjoy without the burden of personal labour. But the toil of the fields was undertaken by the great unnamed majority, whose efforts supplied the needs of both sections of the community.

This distinction carried with it a further implication. Whereas the few named families, or aristocratic groups as they are sometimes termed, could afford to lead lives of luxury in permanent dwellings, the working community was subject to the needs of the season. According to Chinese tradition and early evidence, in the winter seasons the peasantry lived in hovels that were grouped together as villages; and in the summer they moved to the fields where they worked, there to adopt an open-air existence. The tradition that the privileged families were entitled to expect services from the lower orders forms a cardinal principle of the social structure of imperial times, and its origins can be traced back to the dim depths of unrecorded history.

Landownership and the 'states' of the Spring and Autumn period

A more advanced stage in the process whereby the privilege of a name acquired the distinction of property and wealth is assumed in early Chinese writings with reference to the eighth to fifth centuries. The political developments that were taking shape in those years are closely related to an accentuated distinction between the landowners and the working peasantry. For some generations, landowners had worked their estates with the help of hereditary stewards or servants who supervised the labours of the unnamed tillers of the soil. In the course of time the landowners had been able to consolidate their advantages, and were now forming small units that are conceived as having a political nature. Hereditary and *de jure* occupation of these estates, or states, rested, or was shown to rest on grants that had been made in the first instance by one of the Kings of Chou, i.e. the Son of Heaven himself, whose territorial authority could not be questioned. The more fortunate families could point to written and permanent authority, in the form of bronze vessels and their inscriptions, by which the title to their estates and their claims to noble, privileged status could be solemnly verified.

A feudal age?

Essentially the social distinctions remained as they had been before these estates were being formed into the small political units of the Spring and Autumn period, but it is partly thanks to the compelling need to authenticate these claims to landownership, and to advertise an association between the small states and the King of Chou, that these centuries have been classified as a feudal age, i.e. as an age in which authority and titles to land were derived by direct grant from a superior authority, which possessed the right to assign lands in return for services, and the means to prevent the unrestricted enlargement of territories. However, neither the social nor the political implications of such an arrangement can be easily proved to have existed at this time; and there is little direct evidence to show that the structure of Chou society and polity rested on a deliberate, contractual and systematic grant of lands made by a sovereign to vassal landowners.

In addition the great families of the Spring and Autumn period have been portrayed as being members of an hierarchic nobility wherein each member demanded obedience from his inferiors and enjoyed privileges of rank and status. A correspondence between a society that is described in these terms and some of the mediaeval societies of Europe seems to be even more striking, as the Chinese writers of a later period envisaged a nobility of five degrees, and a system of agronomy in which serf families were bound directly to the service of their lord's manor. However these correspondences may be more apparent than real. Without the benefit of fuller information, properly authenticated and corroborated, the society of the Chou and the Spring and Autumn periods can only be imagined more simply, as including two sections; a privileged aristocracy, dependent on qualifications of birth and the possession of hereditary wealth, and the agricultural workers who constituted the great majority. Between these two extremes, other types intervened, such as the servants of the great houses; but the conclusions regarding the detailed social distinctions of this period can be no more than tentative, as the evidence is scanty, biased and anachronistic.

The new demands of economy and government
The third criterion of class distinction, that of occupation or professional skill, came into prominence during the Warring States' period (480–422 B.C.) and remained dominant throughout much of the imperial age. Its emergence had been prompted by the evolution of new economic standards and new political arrangements. By now, the use of iron had replaced that of bronze; the farmer, road-maker and canal builder could each use sharper tools for his task and produce results more effectively and speedily. Large-scale tasks which were of long-term benefit rather than immediate use were being undertaken corporatively by larger gangs of men, whose activities needed an effective

degree of control and co-ordination. More leaders were needed to organize the diversion of labour to non-productive tasks, and to supervise projects such as commercial exchanges and the transport of agricultural goods.

At the same time a new degree of political organization was becoming necessary; more highly developed forms of government were being adopted by members of the hereditary aristocracy as their domains expanded and their responsibilities grew. In addition, Chinese thought was flowering in such a way that the basic philosophical theories that were to mould the imperial age were being formed, and the intellectual doctrines of the later ages were being defined.

The sale and purchase of land

A further change is to be seen in the conditions of land-tenure. Despite the development of several systems of coinage in these centuries, landed estates still retained their attraction and real value. For coin was minted in small, heavy units, and was both difficult and dangerous to transport; land however could always be utilized, and periodic warfare served to perpetuate its value. As armies in the field required ready supplies of food rather than stretches of arable land, conquering generals chose, or could be persuaded, to leave the land in the hands of the producers; and in a fluid military situation, it could be expected that the conquerors of today would have vanished by tomorrow. For these reasons land remained a safe investment; merchants, iron mine owners and others were willing to turn their monetary fortunes into real property, at a time when the acquisition of land was fast becoming independent of birth or hereditary tenure. In place of the sanction of religious or documentary authority or the investiture from a royal house, possession of land depended now on the disposal of strings of cash.

The need for specialist advisers

By the Warring States period, the prominent families were requiring a different type of service. In place of the hereditary aristocrats of an earlier age with their small domains, China was coming under the control of those few leading houses who governed the Warring States as Kings, or the new type of investor-landowners who had sprung from mercantile origins. The conception of the hereditary servant or steward was now outdated, as there was less need or opportunity for men to run the small estates in the old fashioned way, and the new landowners were strictly practical men, who wished to work their land with a keen eye to business.

A new concept of professional service was being created. The governments of China's Warring States required men of intellectual capacity who could proffer shrewd advice regarding inter-state politics, or who could ably sum up considerations of strategy or tactics. Such men needed a professional training of a new type, and the offices with which they were charged needed a staff of clerks and messengers to suit the new aims of government. The professional bureaucratic class which has long been regarded as the hallmark of Chinese society was brought into being in this way, before the age of empire had dawned; and there was evolved a new criterion of class, based on professional occupation, intellectual capacity and type of service. From early unrecognizable beginnings in the Warring States' period there was to emerge the class of scholar-civil-servant-statesman who dominated Chinese society from the early days of the empires, and whose contribution formed a vital part of the political, cultural and economic growth of the Chinese people.

II. THE DISTINCTIONS OF THE EARLY EMPIRES

Confucian and authoritarian opinion

The distinctions of class that were demanded by pre-imperial politics accorded well with the opinion of contemporary thinkers. Confucius and his disciples were for ever insisting that men of ability must put their skills at the disposal of their ruler, and that the value of the individual's occupation was greater than that of his genealogy; and authoritarian theorists were emphasizing the need and right of the ruler to recruit the most able men that he could find to serve the state. In addition, both Confucian and authoritarian thinkers had reached conclusions regarding the uses, tenure and distribution of land, which cut across the class distinctions of an earlier age.

The distinction between governor and governed is an essential notion in the authoritarian scheme of government. With this must be associated the legalist view that a successful state includes a small class of a cultured intelligentsia and a large class of peasant labour, willing to obey its orders to serve in the fields or in the line of battle. These ideas rest on the desirability of enriching and strengthening the state by means of the services rendered by all members of the community in accordance with their capacity. Although there is a deep and irreconcilable difference with the underlying theory of Confucian government, the two systems can lead to very similar results in practice. As yet, in the time of either Confucius or Shang Yang, no empire existed; but the political needs, administrative requirements, social divisions and ideological doctrines of empire had been partly brought into being by the fourth and third centuries.

The principle of conscripted labour
While rulers were encouraging the emergence of a professional class, their instruments of government (e.g. the control of manpower, measures to maintain security) were leading to the formation of distinguishable sections at the other end of the social scale. By the early empires, these distinctions had become crystallized and were being applied widely. Authoritarian writers had propounded the principle that the state was entitled to require statutory labour from able-bodied members of the community for specified periods each year. Usually the duty was performed locally, for short periods of a month, so as to avoid undue interference with the agricultural production that was the men's first concern. The principle of corvée was fully embodied in the government of the kingdom, and then the empire, of Ch'in, and was duly accepted by succeeding imperial governments. The demand to render this duty was presented universally, exceptions being granted only to members of the privileged classes of imperial times (i.e. the officials and their families; or those who had received some mark of aristocratic status; see p. 134). One important change, which was partly due to the corvée system, was the elimination of the distinction between the named and unnamed members of society. For corvée depended on conscription, which in turn depended on registers or census-returns in which the surnames and members of conscriptable members of society were recorded. It was now necessary for the lower orders to be identifiable by surname.

The treatment of criminals
A marked feature of the government of Ch'in, for which that regime has been execrated by Chinese writers, consisted of the severe code of punishments for criminals. The system probably originated in the fourth century, and provided for sentences of death, mutilation, or hard labour. Penal terms were of fixed duration, often not exceeding five years, and convicts were set to work on long-term building projects under official supervision. It is thanks partly to the labours of the

convict class, which was created artificially by the ordinances of the state, that the palaces and mausolea of the Ch'in emperors were constructed; that imperial highways were laid out and the transport of goods organized; and that the mineral resources of the empire were exploited. In some cases convicts were conscripted to serve as soldiers in campaigns of conquest or to perform the duties of garrison troops on the frontier. The existence of a convict class persisted long after the Ch'in empire.

Official slavery
In addition the penal code of Ch'in was probably one of the main factors behind the emergence of slavery. There is no substantial evidence to show that the purchase and sale of slaves was practised in China before the Warring States' period, although prisoners of war may well have been treated as serfs who possessed no rights. However, there are numerous references to slaves during the Ch'in and Han empires and later, when the class mainly consisted of the male and female relatives of condemned criminals.

For certain crimes, offenders were punished not only personally, but also by the forfeiture of the persons of their relatives; these were confiscated by the state, and put to work for its benefit. In this way, men and women came into the possession of the government; and if the supply was greater than the government's needs, they became available for public acquisition. In such circumstances, slaves could be presented to privileged servants of the state, in return for services rendered; alternatively they could be sold as chattels. The development of a slave market owes its origin to the schemes of government. In theory it was forbidden for families to raise cash by disposing of their own members in the market, but the pressure of economic distress was often more powerful than the official ban; and the non-Chinese inhabitants of southern, unassimilated regions were sometimes forced into slavery by their captors.

The status of slaves and their place in the economy
Early Chinese writers are uninformative and vague regarding the status of slaves. In some references they are treated in the same way as other forms of property (e.g. see Table Eight); elsewhere they are regarded as human beings of an inferior order, being subject to certain restrictions and not expected to attain the highest standards of human conduct. In principle slaves were a self-perpetuating class, in so far as

I

they were entitled to marry only within their own ranks, and their progeny was likewise subject to slavery. By contrast, convicts serving for limited periods of hard labour became normal members of the community, once their sentences were completed.

The importance of a slave-class in the Chinese economy has sometimes been over-emphasized. Clearly, their role as a working force should not be underestimated, but it is highly questionable whether this was ever sufficiently significant to justify the use of the term 'slaveage' with reference to any stage of China's social development. Individual projects may have been undertaken partly, or even exclusively, by slave labour; and some of the large landed estates of the Han period may have been worked by slaves who were bought in large numbers in the open market. But the overall picture of Chinese production is that of projects which were undertaken at the behest of government or of a privileged class of aristocratic, mercantile or bureaucratic origin, and which were actually worked by peasants, convicts, or members of corvée gangs serving for limited periods. In all probability slaves never constituted a significantly large proportion of the population. During the Han period, when conditions of slavery were comparatively highly developed, slaves probably accounted for something less than 1 per cent.

The need of officials
The most notable feature of the social changes of the early empires lies in the formation of the class of officials, that élite group from whom Chinese culture was to draw continual refreshment and perpetuation. During the first century of imperial government (c. 220–120 B.C.) the administration may have been somewhat hampered by the scarcity of trained men who were capable of implementing decisions taken at the centre. At the beginning of the Ch'in and Han regimes it was not possible to repair this deficiency easily; for despite the emphasis placed by leading statesmen on the needs of education, and despite the arrangements made by the authoritarian government of Ch'in to bring a simpler, standard script into general use, there were few facilities for the speedy production of disciplined, literate clerks or responsible officials.

Recommendations and tests for officials
Part of the permanent achievement of the Han empire was the foundation of the tradition whereby the civil servant's profession was treated

with trust and responsibility, and earned its incumbents privilege, prestige and power. From small beginnings there grew up the complex system of competitive examination, whereby men were judged to be suitable for employment and assigned to appropriate posts in the service. In the first instance the most senior advisers to the throne, who had themselves been appointed by reason of their personal loyalties or services, or on account of favouritism, were enjoined to bring forward the names of suitable candidates for employment; and as it was realized that a large staff was required to keep the offices of empire functioning efficiently, governors of provinces were likewise ordered to recommend men of ability for service to the throne.

From the consequent need to verify the value of such recommendations, tests were instituted, at first in the form of requests proffered to candidates to give oral advice on specified topics. The written examinations which were to follow were devised to test ability at composition, power of judgment and familiarity with approved texts. The earliest decrees which can be associated with certainty with the idea of testing candidates' ability date from c. 140 B.C.; already some degree of discrimination was exercised against the influence of the texts of authoritarian writers, and the beginnings had been made of nurturing a tradition of orthodox classical learning. As yet the system and theory of examinations was very rudimentary, as compared with the developments of the middle empires (see p. 140); but already, in the later part of the Han period, successful candidates were being graded into classes according to their performance at the tests.

The career of civil servant and statesman
The men who embarked on careers as civil servants in this way were to become some of the most highly privileged men of China. They were not only regarded as being respectable members of a profession; they were acknowledged to be masters of the only profession. As young men they may have started their careers as humdrum secretaries in the capital city or as humble incumbents of posts in the provinces; as they grew in seniority, so their responsibilities increased, until they found themselves wielding the highest administrative responsibilities in the land and providing the throne with final advice before crucial decisions were taken. For from the outset the career of the civil servant and the statesman was one and the same. The service was organized with a full hierarchy of grades corresponding with a fixed scale of salaries. As a man's authority and seniority increased so also did his emoluments and

131

privileges; in addition, a position in the hierarchy acted as a mark of social status, thereby assuring the holder of the appropriate degree of respect from other members of the community.

In considering the political and social importance of the civil servant in China, due account must be taken of the very great divisions which separated different members of the service. Senior statesmen and provincial scribes were both members of the bureaucracy; but their status and class was no more comparable than is that of a British cabinet minister and a clerk serving in one of the branch offices of local government.

Landowners, tenants and retainers

Simultaneously with the formation of an élite class to satisfy the needs of government, economic changes were stimulating the creation of a class of great landowning families as an integral part of imperial society. This class came into being for two complementary reasons, the desire of the wealthy to invest their riches securely, and the need of a distressed peasantry to procure a stable livelihood. Some of the wealthy families were founded by statesmen whose fortunes rested on their official salaries, or on the discreet, but effective, use of their authority for personal motives. Others had grown rich thanks to mercantile activities. The manufacture and sale of goods had been followed by the investment of the profits in land; this was in turn leased to tenants, and the high rents which were charged had aroused the protests of traditional moralists from the first century B.C. It was clear that landlords could use their economic strength to coerce their tenants, and that in times of bad harvest severe oppression might be practised.

By the second half of the second century A.D., or perhaps earlier, a new class was arising. This was formed by disaffected small-holders or peasantry, who had been forced to flee from their homes as a result of natural disaster, civil warfare or the stringent demands of the tax collector. These were the refugee families who were to be known in the Chinese countryside for centuries; they had been forced to sell the small plots whence they had drawn a livelihood, and were ready to be drawn into rebel bands by competent or inspiring leaders. From about the second century these families were finding advantages in linking their destinies with those of the great landowners, and were willing to become the retainers of the great houses, which provided them with security, livelihood and a settled existence. In the prevailing absence of strong central government, the great families could protect both themselves and their retainers from the interferences of officialdom; in return, the retainers were ready to be used as a labour force, and if necessary to act as armed bands in defence of the great families' estates.

The class of retainers is sometimes regarded as being intermediate between that of slaves and free men. Thanks to economic circumstance they were bound to render loyal service to their masters; and although they were not subject to purchase and sale, as were slaves, they could be transferred from one great family to another, irrespective of their own wishes. The degree of freedom of the retainers was limited not by ties to the soil but by personal ties to individual families.

In this way there came into existence a class of wealthy families able to employ sufficient manpower to exploit their lands. The interests of these families obviously lay in the preservation of their property and the maintenance of law and order so that the full profits could be made. They were thus anxious to provide suitable working conditions for their retainers and to preserve them from danger at a time of banditry or foreign invasion. The great families played an active if unofficial part in the preservation of local communities and their organization for efficient work. Some could trace their origin to the first or second centuries, but the main period of growth and consolidation was that of the following centuries of political disunion.

Reaction against the great estates
It has already been indicated that some degree of overlap existed between the class of senior officials and the great families. Of all situations, the most fortunate was that of those families whose members combined high office with landed wealth, but it is questionable how far such ideal conditions of prosperity could be achieved. Although the same economic interests may sometimes have been shared by both classes, there was ample reason for ideological clash. Officials were nurtured on Confucian precept, according to which the age of golden government was reached when land was allocated on a basis of equality throughout the community. Already in about 100 B.C. protests had been raised against the large estates which were being formed, and about a century later a government tried unsuccessfully to limit the extent of the land-holdings and slaves which individuals were allowed to possess. The growth of both the great families and of the displaced population at the end of the Han period sharpened the contrast between rich and poor; but it was not until the fifth century that a government was strong enough and willing to take measures that were designed to break the

power of the great families by reducing the size of their estates. A difference of interest between the great families and the officials can be seen to persist in subsequent developments (for attempts to restrict land-holdings, and schemes of allocation, see pp. 198 f).

Privileges of rank

The structure of society in the early imperial age must not be over-simplified. Although the main distinctions of class were closely related to those of the bureaucracy, there persisted some privileges which were based on the recognition and use of aristocratic rank, and which were acquired either by virtue of meritorious service or circumstances of birth. In the Ch'in empire a series of eighteen different degrees of rank were bestowed in direct return for services (usually military) rendered to the state. At this time a deliberate break had been made with any traditional system of nobility which was associated with the grant of lands to accompany a title. The eighteen orders of rank carried certain privileges (e.g. reduction of punishment in the case of crime, exemption from corvée duty) and a degree of social status which conferred precedence; and in principle these orders were not held on an hereditary basis.

The orders were retained during the Han period, when the series was actually increased to twenty. They carried similar privileges as in Ch'in, and were bestowed in direct proportion to the value of the services rendered to the State (e.g. the transport of grain to outlying areas). In addition the ranks were sometimes conferred as an act of imperial bounty, designed to advertise the munificence of the Han emperors.

The kings and marquises of the Han empire

The Han governments also granted two orders of nobility in which the principle of hereditary succession was incorporated. The higher of these orders was reserved in principle for the sons, or very close kinsmen, of the emperor, who alone could be officially created 'kings', and whose rank was duly inherited by their eldest sons. The kings not only possessed precedence over all other members of society, including the most senior officials; they also bore direct responsibility to the emperor for the government of provincial territories, which were sometimes of very wide extent. The second order of nobility was formed by those who held the highest of the series of twenty ranks, and this distinction, like that of the kings, was duly transmitted by a man to his son. The holders of these ranks each bore a title, which is usually rendered in English as 'marquis'. The titles were coupled with the right and duty to perform certain administrative tasks, e.g. the collection of taxes, to a carefully specified extent.

In the case of both the kings and the marquises, steps were taken to prevent the undue exploitation of the resulting opportunities. Conferment of the two ranks was probably used as a political device to retain the loyalties of elements who might be dissident, and to provide for a division of administrative responsibilities in the early days of the empire. At a later stage, when officials were being trained and found in sufficient numbers, and when the authority of the central Government had been better consolidated, it was no longer necessary or desirable to use the grant of noble ranks for this purpose.

Nepotism?

Moreover, the principle of hereditary privilege was still maintained in respect of certain forms of appointment. Senior officials were permitted, and even encouraged, to nominate their sons to serve at the palace in the position of 'gentlemen of the court'. In such a capacity, young men could serve either as courtiers around the throne or as men who were available to fill official posts as these were created or became vacant. There was thus likely to be a distinction between officials who had risen to their position after due tests of their ability, and those who had been promoted thanks to their family connections. The practice of nepotism was of greater currency during the middle than the early empires.

Empresses, concubines and eunuchs

The privileged position of the officials was by no means unchallenged by other prominent elements in the capital city of Han China. Members of the imperial family were clearly in a more exalted position than emperor's servants, and were at times able to exploit their precedence satisfactorily. Frequently an empress attempted to obtain similar privileges for her own relatives; and if such men, who were of commoner status, happened also to be men of political ambition and official training, conflicts would break out between different groups of the same type. The simultaneous existence of a number of imperial consorts, of different generations or grades, served only to accentuate these rivalries.

In addition, officials frequently found that their position was threatened by the members of a group which had gained employment at Chinese courts before the imperial age—the eunuchs. Originally these had been used as guardians of the court women, and had come to acquire the status of supervisors or managers of the household. By the time of the Ch'in empire eunuchs had on occasion attained greater responsibility by winning the confidence of their imperial masters, and by being trusted with their intimate plans. From such a position eunuchs were able to procure a hold over weak emperors and to exploit to their own advantage such situations of delicacy as would arise in a court which contained one empress and a large number of concubines. Eunuchs came to possess a mode of access to the emperors which was denied to the officials; and as they had achieved their successes without the rigours of the educational discipline that was required of officials, the latter were naturally envious, mistrustful and antagonistic to the eunuchs and their activities.

With their favourable situation and their large numbers, the two groups of imperial consorts and their families and the eunuchs have at times been able to exercise a dominating influence over China's dynastic and political history. Precise, formal regulation allowed the Han emperors to maintain no less than fourteen different grades of concubines, in addition to their legal consort. The figures that are available for later periods may reflect some rhetorical exaggeration, and probably include the numbers of women who were engaged as servants or assistants in the palace, as well as the emperor's bed-fellows. It is recorded that the T'ang emperor T'ai tsung (627–649) ordered the expulsion of no less than 3,000 women from the palace, and that there were 40,000 women in attendance during the time of Hsüan tsung (713–755). Theoretically the number of concubines serving the Ch'ing emperors was limited to seventy, but there were in addition some 2,000 Manchu girls and women present in the palaces in various capacities.

Figures of the number of eunuchs attending at court cannot be provided for the earlier periods. At the outset of the T'ang dynasty their number was restricted to about 100, but the official register for the year 820 gives the figure of 2,618. In the particularly favourable circumstances of the end of the Ming period, their number may have exceeded 70,000; and at the beginning of the twentieth century the Ch'ing house still contrived to maintain an establishment of 1,500 in the imperial palace.

Religious influences and classes
The characteristic social distinctions of the early imperial age were thus

136

those of the governor and the governed, the scholar and the unlettered, the élite and the majority. These distinctions grew up both during periods of political disunion and those of effective centralized government. The many courts of the pre-imperial age created the demand for a large number of officials; and under the centralized government of the Han empire there emerged a means of selecting the scholar-official and educating him for service. But it is to be noted that no priestly class had arisen to dominate the social or political scene. Under imperial government, responsibility for native religious practices was vested in one of several departments of state, which conducted those ceremonies that were deemed necessary for the general welfare; and the emperor himself took part in some of these observances. Of perhaps greater importance to the history of religion was the persistence of local rites in the countryside and the continuation of practices which can be described as folkloristic, superstitious or religious. Such practices exercised very great influence in preserving different local cultures intact in different parts of China, but they did not produce a distinguishable class of priests, which was of sufficient reputation or strength to monopolize particular social functions.

The place of the Buddhist establishments and their incumbents was perhaps more significant; for here were men and women who were relieved of the obligations owed by other members of society to the state, and who were in theory freed both from the competitive motives which led to a scholar-official's career, and the material ambitions where by the houses of the great landed families had been founded. Buddhist elements played a mixed role in Chinese society; as men and women of religion they earned the respect of other members of the community; as beings who had renounced the cares of this world they may have excited envy, or incomprehension; as beggars who depended on the productive work of others they may have been scorned or even hated; and as the providers of medical attention to the sick and comfort to the needy, they attracted respect and devotion from many ranks of society.

The absence of a military class
Partly thanks to the influence of Confucian and other humanist thought, China has never been dominated by a native class of military officers. The educational aims of the state have throughout been directed to the arts of peace and the cultured life of the learned. Along with the examinations for civil posts there has indeed existed a system

of tests of military ability for those anxious to embark on such careers. But such examinations have always been esteemed more lightly than those of the normal cursus of the civil servant, and success has been regarded as a lesser achievement. Although many dynasties have been founded directly after the successful generalship of leading personalities, either Chinese or alien, it has always been the aim of a newly established regime to demonstrate that its interest lies with civil authority, backed by the traditional service of officials, rather than in the imposition of power through the agency of military officers. There has thus been little incentive to popularize a military career, and the absence of a native class of military leaders has sometimes led to the employment of foreigners in this capacity (see p. 265).

Similarly social structure has not been affected by the need to fill the ranks of the armies, although large forces have often been put in the field, for defensive purposes, or in the interests of expansion or to meet the threats of rebels. In normal times governments have found their soldiers by means of conscription; able-bodied men have been obliged to serve for limited periods of one or two years, either to undergo training or to serve in the defensive garrisons; and in times of emergency such men have been subject to recall to the colours until the particular need has passed. During the early and middle empires attempts were sometimes made to raise professional forces on a basis of more permanent service, but these rarely coincided with a time when a government could offer attractive conditions, or try out such schemes fully. Chinese writers have always been ready to discount the importance of the armed forces as elements of the community, partly because a rude and licentious soldiery cannot be expected to contribute to the nation's cultural well-being.

III. THE SOPHISTICATED SOCIETY OF THE MIDDLE AND LATER EMPIRES

Favourable terms of military service
The principle of privilege persisted during the social distinctions of the middle empires and can be illustrated mainly in connection with the civil service. It is also seen in some of the forms of recruitment to the armed forces of the T'ang empire.

Service on favourable terms, including exemption from the much hated garrison duty of the distant frontiers, was sometimes granted to those whose families were distinguished by merit. These were usually the sons or descendants of those who had fought in the initial campaigns whereby the dynasty had been founded, or refounded after an interval of usurpation. In theory, service in these special privileged units was reserved for those who could be trusted to provide a loyal bodyguard for the defence of the emperor against treasonable elements; and for this reason the units were stationed close to the emperor's person. In practice, admission to these favoured ranks became open to purchase or other irregular means of entry; and the extension of the privilege outlasted a reliable guarantee that the chosen men would render loyal and effective service.

Restricted entry to the civil service
Throughout the T'ang and Sung periods the political and cultural life of China was dominated by the activities of the scholar-officials, as the increasing needs of administration enabled the bureaucracy to consolidate its favoured position. The system of recruitment remained that of competitive examination, whose organization was the responsibility of one of the major offices of state. In theory this method of entry was open to all candidates who presented themselves, from whatever station in society, provided that they possessed the necessary ability. In practice entry was controlled by various devices and factors. Some degree of patronage or recommendation by an existing official was necessary before admission could be sought. Sons of merchants were at times debarred or discouraged from entering, owing to the deep-rooted desire to prevent such a class from infiltrating the ranks of the scholar-officials.

Of equal importance were the economic difficulties which restricted entry to the examinations. Candidates required long hours of leisure in which they could master their texts, perfect their literary styles and immerse themselves in all aspects of China's cultural heritage. Only after such a training could they hope for success, and it was mainly in the houses of the wealthy that candidates could be reared with the necessary facilities for study. Furthermore the sons of officials were themselves in a favourable position for entering the service as they could attend special schools which were reserved for their own numbers. In theory, and according to traditional Chinese boast, a peasant or a swineherd could enter for the examinations and rise to be the most senior minister of state in due course; in practice he could probably not be spared sufficiently from his labour in the fields to enable him to complete his studies. But a remarkable feature of the Chinese scene is the persistence whereby men would make repeated attempts to pass the examinations, undaunted by increasing age, in the hope of bringing honour to themselves and their families.

Manipulation of the system of examinations

For these reasons the bureaucracy tended to become a 'closed shop' during the middle empires, drawing its recruits from its own resources. At the same time, as the system of examinations was controlled by the government, it could be manipulated so as to redress any political imbalance that rested on the dominance of particular families or factions. A classic example of such manipulation occurred in the middle of the seventh century, when the preponderance of the well-seated families of the north-west was forced to give way to new blood, recruited from eastern and southern China. On a lower plane the institution could be used corruptly to satisfy personal ambitions or debts, or to create the political following that a statesman required.

A check to undue abuse was provided by the esteem in which the system was held. A public outcry would ensue, if it could be proved that the examinations had been conducted unjustly or unfairly. Often the most senior officials of the state were associated with the procedure, so as to ensure that the tests were carried out scrupulously; but in such cases there lurked the danger that a senior statesman's name could be utilized as a cover with which to protect irregular practices. In some examinations the questions were allegedly set and marked by the emperor himself; in those cases, an examiner who attempted to abuse his opportunities for personal gain, and whose tricks were exposed, might find himself charged with *lèse majesté*; but an unfounded accusation that an examiner had been guilty of misdemeanour might be tantamount to treason.

Types of examination

The proliferation of the bureaucracy was a marked feature of the T'ang and Sung periods. By now the system of examinations had become highly complex, and took the form of a series of tests, spaced successively over a number of years. In general the first stage took place in the provinces, where local officials were obliged to select suitable men who could be sent to the capital city for further competitive trial. There they faced a series of examinations devised to test their intellectual standard; and successful candidates, who had thereby received their 'degree', were rewarded by gaining permission to enter for a third series, which determined the type of post and salary which a man was qualified to receive. A yet higher series of examinations was used to pick out a very few men for service in one of the highly distinguished and prized academic institutions of the government.

Weaknesses of the system

In all these trials and tribulations, candidates were requested to face tests in much the same subjects, i.e. a knowledge of 'classical' texts and their orthodox interpretation, an ability to compose in varied styles of prose and poetry, and a facility for solving hypothetical problems of procedure or policy. An education which was tailored to procure success at these examinations was often followed by a marked relaxation of intellectual effort, once success had been achieved; and for this reason officials were sometimes prone to intellectual laziness, undue conservatism or lack of initiative. In addition, most officials had been trained with a general education in the classics or arts only, and there was no certainty that they had acquired the necessary knowledge or skill to perform the executive tasks which would face them once they were posted. Thus, successful candidates who were immediately appointed in the provinces lacked both administrative experience and technical knowledge, over matters such as the conduct of judicial cases, the collection of taxation or the maintenance of law and order, which had suddenly become their responsibility.

Metropolitan and provincial posts

After a comparatively short tenure of office (i.e. some three years or less) civil servants could usually expect to be transferred to a different post, and it was the ambition of all officials to serve in one of the departments of the central government. These were situated in the capital city, where there could be found the most distinguished company and finest luxuries of the whole empire. A form of punishment to which unsuccessful officials could be subjected was the disgrace of being transferred to a post in the remote south or west of China; for there, the delights of civilization would not have penetrated, and it could be expected that the company would be rustic, boorish or unlettered.

Irregular entry to the civil service

While the examinations constituted the correct and regular mode of entry to the service, other means could be found. The privilege of nomination which had been practised in the Han empire was followed in the Sung period by various forms of patronage, sponsorship or nepotism. In addition, a hard pressed treasury had long since learnt that there was no shortage of men who would be willing to purchase the titles of offices for ready cash; for it was by this means that the *nouveaux riches* could aspire to join the ranks of the most respected class of Chinese society.

The force of the examinations' system in bringing men of merit to the fore of society whatever their origins varied greatly from the seventh to the nineteenth centuries. During the Sung dynasty the system was used in combination with carefully regulated methods of personal recommendation, which at their worst tended to heighten factional disputes. In the Yüan period the system of examinations was abolished by the alien house, which could not compete with Chinese talent; and even after its reintroduction (1315), the conditions for embarking on an official career were for long abnormal and unattractive. When the foundation of the Ming dynasty (1368) ended the prevailing civil disorders of some decades, there began a particularly favourable period in which a high percentage of successful examination candidates were drawn from humble families who were new to official life. But from about 1450 the prestige of academic qualifications reached in the examination cells was giving ground, as social status became more closely associated with wealth. By the seventeenth or at least the eighteenth century, the opportunities for men of humble origin to rise to the front ranks of the state had been diminished very severely.

The scholar-gentry

It was from the Sung period that the so-called scholar-gentry class rose to a position of extremely great importance in the provincial life of China. The class was composed of men who had attained qualifications for official posts, either by examination or by the less regular means, but who had not taken employment in an official capacity. These men had originated from various types of family, which shared the common feature of possessing sufficient wealth to provide their scions with the leisure, tuition or other necessities for obtaining degrees. On achieving their degrees these men returned to their homesteads in provincial China, if they had been unable, or possibly unwilling, to secure appointment in an official post. Thanks to their family connections, the strength of their families' estates and their newly-won prestige as men of letters they now formed the respected élite of the countryside, while those of their numbers who did achieve appointments in the service formed the respected élite of the capital city.

Members of the scholar-gentry class carried a burden of local duties and responsibilities that was clearly acknowledged if not defined. From their large villas, which were sometimes situated in the small provincial towns, the scholar-gentry commanded powers of leadership with which they were often expected to settle disputes between landowner, tenant and peasant. They acted as intermediaries who ensured that the official tax-collector received his just dues, and that the peasantry was saved from excessive oppression. It was due to the initiative, efforts and resources of the scholar-gentry that measures were taken to alleviate distress, repair the ravages of natural disaster, establish local schools or found charitable trusts. As the gentry families enjoyed the respect and loyal support of the local population, it was often owing to their encouragement that local officials obtained the necessary degree of co-operation for the completion of their administrative work.

The families which produced the scholar-gentry were obviously the best source of recruitment for the bureaucracy, and there was thus some degree of overlap between the two classes of the élite of the country and the town. In times of dynastic unrest or change, it was often the scholar-gentry class which provided social stability and cultural and administrative continuity.

The prominence of the merchant
Other social developments of the Sung period resulted from the newly found power of money. The application of the new art of printing to commercial purposes coincided with economic developments whereby south China was to gain a predominant place over the north. New ways of making fortunes were being rapidly evolved with the growth of crafts and the call for luxury goods that was ever emanating from the sophisticated inhabitants of Hangchow and other cities. In these circumstances the wealthy merchant came to the fore, either by procuring and purveying rare goods or by arranging for their transport and delivery. It was a simple step to invest the profits of such undertakings in further commercial enterprise or as loans advanced to the government, particularly at a time when new means of supplying credit were being evolved.

However, despite their growing powers and fortunes, merchants could not aspire to the most highly esteemed place in society without question. Ever since the Warring States' period, the merchant's avowed object of collecting wealth from other members of the community had been the target of criticism and, occasionally, of governmental interference. Both Confucian and authoritarian thinkers had protested that commerce should be treated as an ancillary occupation only, being relegated to a position of dishonour behind that of agriculture; for while the farmer's products could be used either in the service of the rest of humanity or to enrich the state, the merchant existed to draw profit from his fellow men, or to increase his own fortune at the expense of the government's resources.

The power of wealth
For these reasons historians of the Han and later periods had criticized the merchant and his occupation; but by the twelfth and thirteenth centuries, the merchant's importance and reputation had altered, as the life of the court and the economy of the country was coming to depend on his working arrangements. Although the scholar-official remained the most highly respected member of society, the merchant's obvious wealth was earning him envy. More and more was he able to buy the use of privileges which were properly reserved for the civil service, and more and more was he coming to enjoy a comparable status in practice, if not in theory.

The rise of the merchants to a position of prominence in Chinese society is closely associated with the developments that transformed China's economy from the Sung period. By the fifteenth and sixteenth centuries, the conspicuous places in the society of the towns were no longer reserved exclusively for the established official, or the family whose resources were drawn from landed estates only. The power of those men whose wealth rested on commercial enterprises was now rivalling that of the scholar-official or the landowner; and merchants were sending their own sons to compete in the state's examinations or purchasing offices or titles and their status. An important means whereby rich businessmen could add to their prestige and acquire recognition as benefactors of society lay in their lavish patronage of scholarship and the arts. A number of poets and writers owed their position or comforts to financial subsidies of such origins. Some of the connoisseurs' collections that arose in south China during the Ch'ing period were stocked with books, paintings and other treasures that had been acquired in this way; and the need to satisfy the tastes of this new type of patron no less than the court exercised a marked influence on artistic styles (e.g. in painting and ceramics).

Hired labour

The significance of a monetary economy was also to be seen at the other end of the social scale. In the eleventh century certain statesmen had come to realize that a force of labour could be placed at the disposal of the government more efficiently through the medium of money than under the old traditional system. In place of conscripting gangs of corvée labour to serve for short periods of a month each year, it would be better for the state to raise a monetary tax and to use the proceeds to maintain a permanent force of labour at its disposal. The principle of hiring labour was by no means new to China at this time and had been practised in a number of private enterprises since the early empires; but a new scale was perhaps being envisaged for its application. The logical result of such a scheme would be the creation of a new class of wage-earners. Although the proposals were not yet adopted fully, they may be regarded as a significant, and early, forerunner of the later development of a wage-earning class of modern times. In the fifteenth century, the state-owned iron works employed large forces of wage-earners in the mines and foundries.

The occupations of the townsmen

Visitors to Chinese cities during the nineteenth and twentieth centuries have rarely failed to notice the extreme diversity of the types of townsmen regularly seen in the streets. The Chinese themselves have sought to preserve external distinctions of occupation as a means of maintaining a just pride in the individual's chosen way of life; and the mode of employment has acted as an important symbol of social status. The cities have included men who live by means of semi-professional skills and those who depend on manual toil; and a flourishing underworld has been populated by absconders, beggars and criminals. With the growing prosperity of cities from the Sung period there have appeared a number of external conventional signs whereby a man's occupation can be recognized. Conspicuous robes, badges of rank and means of transport have distinguished the official and his family from lesser fry. The approach of different types of peddler has been heralded by different types of street call, ring of bells or blast of trumpet, whose shrill notes have echoed in the muddy lanes and wide markets; and in the streets there have congregated cheek by jowl, each with his own

7. COAL-MINING

From the *T'ien-kung k'ai-wu*, an illustrated guide to the skilled occupations of farmers, artisans and craftsmen. This book (original edition 1637; the wood-cut shown here is taken from the print of 1771. Original size 20 cm. by 13 cm.) describes the basic resources and technological processes of occupations such as cereal cultivation, irrigation, salt-making, the ceramic industry, iron-working, mining, ship-building, etc. Coal, which is mentioned in Chinese literature in connection with an event of possibly 120 B.C., was used for iron-smelting from the fourth century A.D. The wood-cut shows a ventilation-tube of bamboo, representing measures designed to remove fire-damp, and the installation of pit-props.

prized symbol, the letter-writer, story-teller or fortune-teller; the actor, juggler, undertaker or cook; the coolie, porter, sedan chairman or rickshaw puller.

The status of the alien conquerors
The occupation of large areas of North China by alien dynasties from the twelfth century eventually resulted in the enrichment of the Chinese population by the admixture of new racial elements. Both at this time, and at earlier and later periods, foreign governments were sometimes faced with the problems of administering two distinct sections of their peoples; for their original tribesmen and supporters often led a completely different type of economic life from that of the Chinese, and their social distinctions were far less sophisticated. Sometimes a conquering regime was forced to provide two entirely separate systems of government with which to handle these two elements, but with the passage of years and the influence of Chinese civilization the distinctions tended to become less acute.

On occasion these situations gave rise to new forms of privilege. Under the Ch'ing dynasty, the conquering people was organized as 'banners', units which were of both a tribal and a military significance. This organization was partly applied to the Mongol and Chinese subjects of the Manchus, but the new dynasty soon came to depend on the support of the Chinese civil service and the maintenance of the traditional divisions of Chinese society. Nevertheless the Manchu bannerman long remained in possession of many privileges. His status was superior to that of the leading elements of Chinese society, and until the eve of its collapse the Ch'ing house proudly differentiated between its own native members and its Chinese subjects.

On several occasions alien conquerors have tried to perpetuate a racial or cultural distinction artificially (e.g. by the imposition of a ban on intermarriage between members of the Chinese and non-Chinese races); but it is only exceptionally that such measures have remained in force until the end of the foreign dynasty's political dominion. At other times we hear of deliberate attempts which were made by alien masters to renounce their peoples' native habits (e.g. of dress or language) in favour of those of the Chinese with whom their peoples were fast becoming integrated.

IV. THE FAMILY SYSTEM

Social distinctions have thus arisen in China thanks to differences of birth, wealth and occupation. The social groupings which have been formed will largely be ignored here, with the exception of the guilds to whom reference will be made below (see pp. 179f and 213). In addition the natural units of the family, kin and clan have played so great a part in the continuation of Chinese culture, the success of political administration and economic progress that they deserve brief mention. For the concept and importance of these groups has affected all reaches of society, from the imperial palace to the humblest hovels of the peasantry.

Family, kin and clan
The family was the smallest of these groups and was basically constituted by a man with his wife and children. The size and type of the family varied, according to the inclusion of one or more of the parents' sons after marriage or the members of succeeding generations. Members of the family were associated together by worship of their immediate forbears; and on marriage, a woman left her father's family and was admitted as a member of her husband's. Larger groups, of kin, included the relatives of the parents or the wife; and the different degrees of mourning that were incumbent on the members of the family and the kin were prescribed by Confucian classic or governmental precept. In theory, the clan, or lineage, consisted of all those who could trace descent from a common ancestor, i.e. those who bore the same surname and who were not allowed to intermarry.

The head of the family
The Chinese family has varied very greatly in its extent. It has often been tantamount to a small community, which includes members of up to four generations and which embraces far wider degrees of relationship than those acknowledged in western communities. The head of the family possesses an authority which is accepted without question; it is he who bears responsibility for the upkeep of those religious observances whereby the family's unity has been constituted; it is he who will in turn receive reverence as a departed ancestor; and the head of the family takes the final decisions regarding the disposal of the family's resources. These are owned in common, and their use is in theory available to all members of the family community.

These resources include not only monetary wealth, land and equipment with which to work it; they also include the persons of the family. Thus it is also the head of the family who has the final word in matters such as the preparation of a promising boy for the examinations, or the application of a widow to join a Buddhist nunnery.

The rule and authority of the head of the family was subject to ethical as well as material considerations. For the ideal relationships which should obtain between different members of a family had been of considerable concern to Confucius and his followers, as a means of regulating and improving a general standard of behaviour amongst humanity. The Confucian code defined detailed rules of conduct between father and son, husband and wife or brother and brother. Partly as a result of the meticulous attention to these relationships and those of the kin and clan, the Chinese language includes a rich variety of terms whereby they are expressed. Records of family membership are kept in the family, either by oral tradition or in written form; they are necessary for religious and ethical reasons, as they prevent the infringement of the age old taboo rules that forbade the contraction of marriages by those who bore the same surname.

The power of the family, kin and clan

Rural communities have sometimes consisted solely of single family units, and is it the solidarity of those units that has ensured the success of agricultural production. Family solidarity has shown itself in combatting the encroachments of neighbouring communities (i.e. other families) on land, or of members of the unassimilated non-Chinese tribes of the marshes, woods or mountains. Similarly the clan has been large enough and its interests sufficiently well united to provide an effective defence against armed bandits or beggars, displaced from their homes by stress of natural calamity or war. If a particular section or branch of a clan has been struck by misfortune such as illness, crop-failure or untimely death, common resources can be used to provide relief. In richer cases, charitable trusts may have been founded by a clan, so as to provide food and shelter for surviving widows or for the education of orphans. In such ways is the welfare of the family kin and clan maintained, its claim to respect protected and its ancestors satisfied. Finally, the solidarity of these groups can be strong enough to prevent official oppression or injustice, as it is often easier for a clan or kin to thwart the evil designs of an official, than for an official to bring the forces of administration to bear in all parts of the remoter rural communities.

149

CHAPTER SIX

THE EXERCISE OF IMPERIAL GOVERNMENT

The sources and scope of information

The institutions of government have for long been a source of pride to the Chinese. They have grown up in close correspondence with the social distinctions of Chinese empire and have served to emphasize the force of those distinctions in a practical and visible way. The cultured élite has thrived by means of the institutions which it has itself created; which have derived from both Confucian ideals and authoritarian theory; and which have been strong enough to survive the repeated modifications brought by dynastic change or alien conquest.

It has been the pride, joy and duty of the scholar-officials not only to serve these institutions to the best of their ability, but also to describe their ramifications for the benefit of posterity; for this reason, Chinese literature probably provides proportionately more information regarding the theory and practice of government than do the writings of other civilizations. The dynastic, or standard, histories,[1] which were largely compiled by civil servants, often include chapters which describe the formal aspects of the institutions of government and their divisions of responsibility; in other chapters events or actions are often reported with strict reference to their effect on the fabric of state government; and some chapters consist exclusively of lists of the names of the incumbents of the senior positions of state. Above all, Chinese historians have normally treated individuals as the agents, patients or victims, of institutions; and in biographical accounts, attention has usually been paid to a man's actions *qua* official rather than to his personal character or motives. But it is difficult to handle or evaluate the large volume of material whereby the history of institutions can be studied, as its arrangement is inconvenient and its compilers had no fully critical approach.

---

[1] This term is explained on pp. 280 f.

I. FORM AND THEORY (A) THE CENTRAL GOVERNMENT

From its inauguration, imperial government has comprised two parts: the offices whose work concerned the whole of the Chinese empire, and which were situated in the capital city, and the organs of regional administration whose responsibility was limited to particular areas. These two parts can be described as the central government and the provincial authorities.

The officers of the palace and the administrators of the empire
The central government of imperial China has been formed of elements of entirely different sources which became inextricably associated together shortly after the formation of empire. Many of the principal offices of state had originated from the needs of the palace, i.e. the domestic services required to provide the kings of Ch'in, before the empire had been formed, with security and revenue, and to maintain their establishments in suitable states of dignity. When the palace developed to become the supreme seat of imperial authority, it carried with it some of the same offices; and these were destined to become major elements in central government. Other elements derived from offices which had also been evolved in pre-imperial times, but whose purpose lay in supervising the tasks of state administration. In imperial times these offices came to take a dominant position and to carry the highest responsibilities of state.

The functions and concept of the emperor permitted the co-existence of both these types of senior official, i.e. those designed for the emperor's personal service and those required to govern his subjects. Both Confucian and authoritarian theory envisaged an emperor whose role was inactive rather than positive; ideally his single, comprehensive command to his advisers was to maintain an ordered and fully harmonized control of the world, and from such an order there was to emerge the series of executive functionaries, each invested with authority of a defined scope, and empowered to exact obedience as necessary. But the emperor was also entitled to expect suitable care and attention for his person, and his advisers were obliged to provide him with appropriate comforts and adornments. The central government had therefore to include not only those executive offices which were founded to control the emperor's lands and subjects, but also the organs that were necessary to protect the emperor from danger, to regulate his relations with other mortals and to supervise the arrangements of his household.

Sinecures and shared responsibilities
There are obvious aspects of government in which a certain degree of overlap or duplication could be expected between these two elements. For example, revenue was required both for the administrative needs of government and for the upkeep of the imperial palaces; and a feature of the early forms of imperial government was the existence of two financial organs; each one was concerned with the disposal of monies, but these were collected from different sources and spent for different purposes. A measure of political sophistication can be seen in the processes whereby one of these organs was transformed so as to take part in the government of the state rather than in the domestic service of the palace. Alternately, in some instances it was realized that a single agency was preferable, for administrative purposes, and duplication of similar offices was eliminated. At the same time, such duplication was sometimes retained, in the interests of efficiency, when the existence of two organs possessing similar functions could be used so as to prevent corruption or indolence.

Although the requirements of the administration soon took prior place over the private needs of the emperor, the dignitaries of the palace for long retained a high place in public esteem. As has happened elsewhere, there survived in China obsolete titles or posts whose importance had long been overshadowed by others, but which still carried considerable status and prestige. These were often the officers who had been concerned with the limited cares of running the palace; they had perhaps been responsible for certain matters of prescribed ceremonial or for the conduct of the court in accordance with Confucian precept. It was therefore advisable, and possibly necessary, to maintain such titles with an uninterrupted succession of incumbents, for by that means the majesty of the empire could be demonstrated both to Chinese subject and foreign visitor. In addition the retention of sinecures in the offices of the palace came to possess distinct administrative advantages, for they could be used to provide public employment and salaries for supernumerary advisers for whom there were no vacancies in the hierarchy of executive functionaries.

In the early empires responsibility for the main tasks of administration rested with men whose titles were those of palace officials rather than administrative functionaries. By the seventh century specialist boards, conceived as organs of administration with defined executive responsibilities, had emerged to take a dominant place over the offices of the dignitaries of the palace. However, such officials still survived even into the Ch'ing period; but by then the process of separating the two tasks of imperial government and the regulation of the palace had been far advanced towards a state of completion.

The two layer structure of the early empires
Initially the central government of the Ch'in and Han empires was conceived as a structure of two layers. The emperors relied immediately on three senior consultants, the Chancellor, the Imperial Secretary and the Grand Commandant, who received the highest salaries in the civil service, and who were charged with the general duties of advising the throne. Historically, these three posts had not been associated with the management of the palace. In theory, authority was divided among them in such a way that no single one would be in a position to initiate successful subversive action against the throne; while the Chancellor controlled decisions of policy and was recognizably senior to his two colleagues, the command of imperial forces was vested independently in the Grand Commandant; and the Imperial Secretary was responsible for promulgating orders and recruiting and supervising the subordinate members of the civil service. The post of Grand Commandant soon fell into abeyance and individual general officers were appointed to military commands as the need arose. During most of the early imperial age an attempt was made, with varying degrees of success, to separate supreme military power from the highest civil authority.

The nine senior ministers
The next senior officials of the Ch'in and Han governments bore titles that mostly denote particular services rendered in the regulation of the palace. These nine senior officials or ministers are further to be distinguished from the three consultants just described, in so far as their duties were of an executive rather than an advisory nature. Their titles are given in Table Five, in the order in which they appear in one of the earliest descriptions of imperial institutions.

The growing maturity of these offices and their part in the administrative government can be seen in the tasks allotted to them and the type of their subordinate officials. Thus, the *T'ai-p'u* ('Grand Servant' or 'Grand Coachman') possibly came to be responsible not merely for the transport of the emperor and his entourage, but also for the provision of an adequate supply of horses; and as these could best be acquired or reared in the provinces of the northern borders, the office of the *T'ai-p'u* included some officials who were actually posted to serve there. Similarly the 'Grand Herald' had other duties than those of supervising court protocol during the audiences granted to foreign visitors, and was supported by a staff of interpreters who could parley with alien tribesmen. And as the *Ta-ssu-nung* came to be a minister of agriculture and taxation, his assistants included men who had received the charge of specified granaries.

A private secretariat

In addition to these principal dignitaries or ministers and their growing number of subordinates, there existed some offices of a slightly lower order which also possessed well-defined administrative responsibilities (e.g. there was an office corresponding with a Ministry of Works). Also, there were a number of small executive offices, often staffed by eunuchs, and directed by a separate official who came to possess immediate access to the throne. By reposing greater confidence in these 'Masters of Writing' or 'Palace Writers', and using their services to draft and handle confidential documents, it became possible for an emperor to circumvent the authority of the three consultants or the nine ministers, and to take a personal, and effective, part in the direction of government. Reference will be made below (see p. 165) to the recurrence of unofficial organs and their use as a private secretariat by the emperor or his immediate entourage.

The middle empires: the three departments and six boards

By the seventh century, a new structure of government had emerged and a new emphasis is discernible in the administrative responsibilities of the senior officials. Although the nine senior posts of the Han empire survived in name, they now occupied a completely different place in the stages of government, relieved of their former responsibilities and shorn of their supreme dignities. Government was now delegated in the first instance to three senior departments, the Department of State (*Shang-shu-sheng*), the Imperial Chancellery (*Men-hsia-sheng*) and the Imperial Secretariat (*Chung-shu-sheng*), and the statesmen who presided over these organs occupied the most influential positions of government. As formerly, specialist executive tasks remained in the hands of offices that were conceived at a lower level;

these were the six boards (see Table Five) who were subordinated directly to the Department of State.

Originally the Chancellery and Secretariat were ranked on a par with the Department of State. They existed to provide the emperor with the consultative advice that he needed, to keep him in touch with the major events of the empire and to arrange for the promulgation of his orders. The Chancellery and Secretariat were in a position to concern themselves with any matters of policy, administration or justice; and whereas the Chancellery was the channel whereby representations or information could be conveyed to the throne, the Secretariat was the agency whereby the throne initiated action or published its decrees. The functions of these two departments were complementary, and cooperation between the two was essential if government was to be practised effectively.

The Department of State was responsible for implementing imperial decisions by means of the six boards. Owing possibly to an accident of history, early in the T'ang period the position of head of the Department of State was allowed to fall into abeyance, and its affairs were controlled by two deputy heads of the department. These men were ranked in a lower grade than the heads of the other two departments; and for this reason the Department of State came to occupy a less exalted status than its two fellows.

This more highly sophisticated form of government had resulted from modifications made to an earlier system and from experiments made locally in the long centuries between the Han and T'ang empires. In addition, by the seventh and eighth centuries the means existed whereby a more complex form of government could be operated. The scheme of state examinations that is associated with the Sui and T'ang empires was a far finer instrument than its predecessors, and was attracting more men of ability to the public service. Moreover the hierarchy of the civil service was more exact, and the different grades were defined more clearly than hitherto. As well as the large number of officials proper, government was conducted by clerks or scribes of a lesser calibre, who were employed to perform the less responsible work of administration, and who were graded in their own hierarchies, comparable with those of the 'career' civil servants.

The highest organs of the later empires
The significance of the six boards as the executive organs of government persisted from the T'ang to the Ch'ing period, despite some

degree of reorganization and considerable changes which occurred in the direction of policy at a more senior level. Early in the Ming dynasty (1380) an endeavour was made to reassert the power of the throne. The Secretariat, which had lately been exercising control of the six boards, was now abolished, and the boards became responsible to the emperor directly, and independently of each other. Similarly, the emperor assumed immediate control of twenty-four *ya-men*; these were offices which were set up to perform specially assigned tasks of administration; they were staffed by eunuchs.

But the Ming and Ch'ing periods witnessed various changes in the degree of mastery achieved alternately by emperor and statesmen through the foundation or manipulation of official institutions. The Grand Secretariat (*Nei-ko*) had come into being somewhat informally from about 1400 to provide the emperor with the secretarial assistance that he needed; later it was to become an agency whereby statesmen-scholars were able to regain some measure of powers as against those of the throne. The Grand Secretariat acted as a consultative council, and was duly taken over with other institutions of government by the Ch'ing emperors. But perhaps the nearest approach to a cabinet ever evolved in imperial China was the Grand Council, or Council of State (*Chün-chi-ch'u*) that was founded in 1729. This body was formed at a time of military emergency, allegedly so as to provide a stricter control of the armed forces and a higher degree of military security. In fact it constituted an organ whereby once more an emperor could exercise a personal influence over the conduct of central and provincial government. While routine business remained in the hands of the six boards and the Grand Secretariat, matters of special importance were brought before the emperor himself and his immediately available advisers of the Grand Council. By the middle of the nineteenth century members of the imperial family were serving in this body, sometimes for lengthy periods and in dominant positions.

TABLE FIVE

THE PRINCIPAL CIVIL OFFICES OF STATE

The following are the principal offices of state that are listed in the accounts of Chinese institutions. As those accounts were based on formal concepts rather than practical conditions of government, it should not be assumed that the theoretical establishment that is envisaged corresponded exactly with the organs of government that actually existed throughout the dynastic periods that are concerned.

TABLE FIVE (continued)

1. THE HAN EMPIRE

(a) The Three Consultants (*San-kung*)

The chancellor (*Ch'eng-hsiang*)
The imperial secretary (*Yü-shih-ta-fu*)
The Grand Commandant (*T'ai-wei*)

} *For the division of responsibilities see p. 153.*

(b) The nine ministers (*Chiu-ch'ing*)

	Responsibilities
The grand ceremonialist (*T'ai-ch'ang*)	The observance of religious ceremonial; some educational services; record keeping; observation of stars; medical care for the emperor.
The supervisor of attendants (*Kuang-lu-ch:ang*)	Superintendence of the court and imperial household; control of certain advisers to the throne and troops used for ceremonial purposes.
The commandant of the guards (*Wei-wei*)	Physical security of the palace; control of the imperial guards.
The Grand Coachman (*T'ai-p'u*)	Care of the imperial stables and carriages, and of governmental pasture grounds.
The commandant of justice (*T'ing-wei*)	The infliction of punishments.
The Grand Herald (*Ta-hung-lu*)	The receipt of homage from foreign tribes owing allegiance to the emperor.
The director of the ancestral clan (*Tsung-cheng*)	Maintenance of records of the imperial family and regulation of their degrees of precedence and other matters of protocol.
The grand controller of agriculture (*Ta-ssu-nung*)	Collection of state revenues and direction of working projects (e.g. state monopolies).
The lesser treasury (*shao-fu*)	Charge of the privy purse of the emperor.

2. THE T'ANG EMPIRE

(a) The three departments (*san-sheng*)

The imperial chancellery (*Men-hsia-sheng*)	Received imperial commands and reports submitted from members of the central and provincial government for deliberation; brought the necessary information and advice to the attention of the emperor; kept custody of the imperial seals.
The imperial secretariat (*Chung-shu-sheng*)	Drafted and promulgated imperial edicts; kept custody of official documents.
The department of state (*Shang-shu-sheng*)	Implemented policy decisions through the agency of the six boards, which it controlled.

(b) The six boards (*liu-pu*)

The board of civil appointments (*li-pu*)	Staffing the civil service; duties included the conferment of grades, assignment of officials to posts and (until 736) conduct of the examinations.

157

TABLE FIVE (continued)

The board of finance (*hu-pu*)	Collection of taxation and supervision of the empire's resources of land, grain and other products.
The board of rites (*li-pu*)	Religious matters, the receipt of foreign dignitaries; from 736, the conduct of the examinations.
The board of war (*ping-pu*)	Supervision and appointment of military officers and defensive equipment and services; control of foreign subject peoples.
The board of punishments (*hsing-pu*)	The administration of justice and initiation of procedure against state criminals.
The board of works (*kung-pu*)	Care of state buildings and projects (including schemes of irrigation and transport).

(c) The Censorate

The Censorate (*Yü-shih-t'ai*) was controlled by a presiding official and his two assistants, and consisted of three divisions:

(1) An office concerned with general affairs; six censors, who attended imperial audiences, were responsible for impeaching officials in cases of injustice or irregularity.

(2) An office concerned with the affairs of the palace. Nine censors were charged with the duty of inspecting aspects of imperial protocol and procedures in which the palace was concerned.

(3) An inspectorate. Fifteen censors were responsible for inspecting the work of officials, and making the necessary enquiries in the provinces regarding their efficiency, quality and integrity.

3. THE SUNG EMPIRE (for the period 960–1080)

(a) The Council of State

This council was formed of five to nine members, who held senior posts in the Secretariat-Chancellery and the Bureau of Military Affairs (see below). The council was concerned with administration and the conduct of justice, and drafted decisions for the emperor's approval. The council's work was subject to modification either by the emperor's personal action, or by the advice offered to him directly by officials of two types: (i) the scholars of the Han-lin Academy, who provided technical assistance; (ii) officials charged with the duty of criticising the administration, including members of the Censorate (see below).

(b) The administration

Authority was divided between three main organs, which worked under the aegis of the Council of State.

	Responsibilities
The Secretariat-Chancellery (*Chung-shu Men-hsia*)	Control of a large number of offices and agencies which had been inherited from earlier regimes, and which had specialist duties (including judicial administration; recruitment and supervision of the civil service; foreign relations; state protocol; educational and scholastic institutions).

TABLE FIVE (continued)

The Finance Commission (*San-ssu*)	Economic administration. Three offices were responsible respectively for Salt and Iron, Revenue, and the census of the population. The duties corresponded roughly with those of the T'ang Board of Finance, and included those of the Board of Works.
The Bureau of Military Affairs (*Shu-mi-yüan*)	Planning the defence of the empire.

(c) The Censorate

The Censorate was similar to that of the T'ang system, with the addition (1045) of members who were responsible for criticising the policy of the most senior officials of state.

4. THE MING EMPIRE

(a) The Grand Secretariat

The Grand Secretariat (*Nei-ko*) consisted of between three and six Grand Secretaries, who assisted the emperor in supervising and co-ordinating the work of the six boards or ministries.

(b) The six boards or ministries

These bore the same titles as the six boards of the T'ang system. The Senior official of each ministry, who was termed the *Shang-shu*, controlled a number of subordinate offices, each of which was headed by its own senior officials. The responsibilities of administration were divided between the six ministries in much the same way as they had been during the T'ang period.

The board of civil appointment (sometimes termed the Ministry of Personnel)	There were four offices, responsible for appointments, honours, records of service and evaluation of performance.
The board of finance (Ministry of Revenue)	This comprised thirteen offices, each one of which was assigned responsibility for one of the thirteen provinces and comprised four specialist sections (population and census, general accounts, special accounts, and granaries).
The board of rites (Ministry of Rites)	This was divided into four offices, responsible for ceremonies, sacrifices, the reception of visitors, and provisions. In addition, the board was responsible for regulating some affairs of the Buddhist and Taoist priesthood.
The board of war (Ministry of War)	There were four offices, which were responsible for (1) the appointment, etc. of officers; (2) the supervision of operations; (3) equipment; (4) military supplies.
The board of punishments (Ministry of Justice)	Organized with thirteen offices on a territorial (provincial) basis.

TABLE FIVE (continued)

The board of works (Ministry of Works)	Responsibilities were probably more complex than under T'ang, embracing schemes of construction, the conscription of manpower for state service, the manufacture of equipment for the government, land and water communications, standardization of weights and measures, control of certain forms of produce (i.e. from hills and lakes). The board was divided into four offices, and controlled a number of warehouses, factories, etc.

(c) The Censorate

The Censorate (re-named the *Tu-ch'a-yüan* from 1380) comprised two censors-in-chief, a number of deputies and four subordinate offices which were concerned in handling the censorate's correspondence and administrative business. The main power of the censorate lay in the persons of 110 investigating officials, who were employed to observe the conditions of government in all parts of the empire, so as to bring to light cases of inefficiency, malpractice or corruption. The censorate was also in a position to criticise the actions of senior state servants and even the emperor himself.

The official's powers

The organs of central government were thus evolved without giving rise to a distinction between the legislative, administrative and judicial aspects of government. No specialist independent departments of state were formed so as to separate these functions, and officials of the civil service found themselves entrusted with the duties of law-maker, executive functionary, judge or jury. There was no recognition that an individual subject of the emperor possessed the right to question the legality of decisions or actions taken by properly constituted authority. If it was claimed that the demands of an official were unjust or extortionate, protest could be made to the highest authorities on the grounds of corruption or oppression, but it was often difficult or impossible to lodge such claims effectively. In theory the throne was ready to listen to any suggestion, from whatever quarter, whereby the welfare of its subjects could be improved; but opinion could not always be voiced in such a way that it would be favourably received, particularly if it was radical or protestant.

The emperor and his advisers

The ideal whereby the emperor's part in government was conceived as negative and quiescent was very rarely achieved, and was often not intended seriously. Many of the major decisions of policy were taken after the receipt of memorials, i.e. written suggestions humbly submitted for the emperor's scrutiny, and followed in due course by the publication of decrees to order the necessary action. The conduct of government through the agency of the emperor in council derived in the first instance from the acknowledgement of the emperor's supreme authority. It was also stressed by Confucian writers from the Han period onwards that one of the major virtues of sovereignty lay in the willingness of the emperor to listen to protest or admonition, and imperial governments have usually included a complement of official critics.

On occasion the Han emperors showed themselves ready to invite senior advisers to report on individual problems with their suggestions for a solution; sometimes several statesmen were ordered to confer together to discuss a particular designated topic. In the T'ang period the government's policies were discussed at daily meetings which were attended by the senior officials of the three departments of state and other elder statesmen who still remained in favour. The results of these deliberations were conveyed to the emperor for discussion and the necessary administrative arrangements followed.

The emperor's personal influence
The degree to which the emperor was able to exercise a personal influence over decisions of state depended partly on his own character and the uses to which his office could be put. Occasionally it is possible to trace the impress of a strong emperor on his environment or matters of policy; and means could be devised to by-pass the restraints of the bureaucracy (see p. 165). Alternately weak emperors would become little more than tools in the hands of their advisers, or could seek refuge from the cares of state in the practice of lengthy religious ceremonies or in a life of seclusion.

But the single effective way in which an emperor could dominate the political scene lay in the choice which he made of his senior ministers. By this power, his authority could be expressed forcefully and decisively, and for this reason the question of the imperial succession was always present in the minds of statesmen or men of ambition. In practice this supreme authority could be flouted by bringing irresistible pressure to bear on the emperor's person, and intriguing factions sometimes found reason and means to depose an emperor, and to replace him with an infant who could be effectively controlled. Such incidents must be set against examples in which emperor and statesmen have lent each other loyal support and co-operation, in the interests of conducting a just and efficient administration.

The checks to excessive power monopolies

Imperial government comprised a number of built-in devices whereby a check could be imposed on the acquisition of excessive power and the resultant threats to the survival of a dynasty. Reference has been made above to the formal distribution of authority among the three senior consultants of the Han system, and the same principle operated during the T'ang dynasty. Here the direction of administrative arrangements was placed independently of the other two main departments of government; and it is noteworthy that these two, which were responsible for advising the throne, were each controlled by a pair of presiding officials, whose rank was theoretically equal. In addition the two departments were dependent on each other's goodwill for the operation of government. For although the Chancellery was the channel for bringing information and suggestions to the attention of the emperor, the files of state papers and records to which that body might wish to refer were housed in the Secretariat; and whereas the Secretariat was the correct organ for the promulgation of imperial decrees, the seals needed to authenticate such documents were kept in safe charge by the Chancellery. In theory, each of the two departments could act as a check against the other, and each depended on a third department to take suitable action to implement its decisions.

In the somewhat different circumstances of Ch'ing government, which was conducted under the auspices of a conquering alien house, the practice arose of appointing two incumbents simultaneously to the more responsible posts of government, one being Chinese and one Manchu; and the same principle was adopted at some of the lower levels (e.g. the thirty-two secretaries who served the Grand Council comprised sixteen Chinese and sixteen Manchu). Here the intention was perhaps not only to scotch any hint of anti-Manchu opposition, but also to provide the untutored Manchu officials with the benefit of the bureaucratic skills of the Chinese.

The Censorate

A characteristic feature of Chinese government was formed by the censorate. This independent institution whose importance grew principally from the T'ang period was charged with the duty of investigating all cases of official injustice, oppression or corruption, and by this means a further control could be imposed on the growth of subversion at all levels of central and provincial government. The censorate can be traced originally to the appointment of special officials (106 B.C.) who were ordered to inspect the administrative work and achievements of senior provincial officials; and the inspectors worked directly to the central government. By the middle and late empires the scope of the censorate's activities had become very wide, and few political leaders or men of intrigue could afford to ignore the potential strength of the institution. At the same time the efforts of the censorate were directed equally against the corrupt practices of established authority. Classic cases of bravery in which censors were willing to risk their lives in order to lay bare the abuse of power or to denounce the extravagances of the court can be quoted for the Ming and Ch'ing periods.

The division of the armed forces

Just as an attempt was made to divide the control of civil authority, so was the command of the armed forces divided among different units or general officers. At the capital city a standing garrison was frequently formed into duplicated units (e.g. those of the northern and the southern barracks); or some units were placed in a separate and privileged category, such as might excite envy or rivalry rather than encourage co-operation in subversive activities.

The place of written law

Imperial government in China has never relied solely on a systematic compilation or constitution in which the rights, duties and functions of officials were legally defined and the requirements of popular obedience categorically asserted. Ideally the statutes or regulations of a dynasty were regarded as expedients of secondary importance only; for the qualities of the emperor were supposedly sufficient to attract the voluntary co-operation of his peoples, and laws were needed only as a means of compelling the obedience of recalcitrant elements of the community. In practice, however, individual laws have been framed as devices to ensure the effective exercise of authority, and have of necessity been backed by a rigorous and cruel code of punishments. It is with such aspects of authoritarian compulsion that the Chinese have associated the concept of law. The Chinese distrust of legal codifications is usually traced to the revulsion felt in the Han period against the harsh severities of the Ch'in regime.

It will have been clear from Chapters Three and Five that a European concept of citizenship is quite alien to Chinese political thinking. There is thus no question of the place of law as a protective guardian against the excessive or unauthorized demands of officialdom; and as a means of deciding civil disputes, codified law has often been of minor importance as compared with the force of custom.

From the second century B.C., central governments have compiled lists of the statutes or ordinances that have been decreed by the centre and have promulgated them for the guidance of local officials. Major innovations of the T'ang and Ming dynasties resulted in the production of documents that can possibly be classified as legal codifications. The T'ang code, which is China's earliest code to survive in entirety, largely influenced contemporary practice in Japan. The Ming code was in turn adopted and modified during the Ch'ing dynasty, and it is in respect of Ch'ing practice that we possess most information regarding legal theory and procedure.

The Chinese compilations consist, very generally, of two parts; a statement of injuction or prohibition, followed by the penalties that can be exacted in case of non-compliance; and, secondly, cumulative lists of exceptional circumstances in which the relaxation of penalties has been justified; the second part can almost be regarded as a commentary on the initial statements. The Ch'ing documents suffer from poor arrangement and a lack of systematization, and it is not surprising that they contain inconsistencies and ambiguities.

Criminal cases

Criminal cases were handled at different levels of government, depending on their degree of seriousness. Minor offences came before local authorities in the country districts; other cases were sometimes passed from one authority to another, in an ascending order of seniority, for reconsideration in each office; and if the most severe punishments might be involved, cases were transmitted, at least formally, to the throne, before a final decision could be taken, and sentence duly executed. Authority to support this complex procedure was found in the stress laid by Confucius on the need for just treatment and the exercise of mercy. There were also reasons of expediency; the re-consideration of important cases would tend to discourage official malpractices or the miscarriage of justice; and the more numerous and more senior the officials who were involved in, e.g. cases of high treason, the smaller was the chance of complicity in high places.

At the lowest level, a local official was forced to institute a trial if an accusation of an offence was brought to his attention. The procedure required that if the accused man was not convicted, his accuser was thereupon indicted for bringing a false accusation. Local magistrates themselves performed the duties of detective, jury and judge; and, if necessary, torture could be used during the course of a trial, to exact the confession which the law required in order to establish guilt.

The less regular means of government
In the foregoing pages an attempt has been made to consider certain aspects of the operation of imperial government by its duly recognized organs. A further aspect, which reveals the Chinese stress on form at the expense of substance, is seen in the devices whereby actual authority was exercised by organs of a different type, or by individuals whose powers were defined less regularly. During the Han and T'ang periods, for example, there were times when the all important responsibility for the issue of decrees was removed out of the hands of the most senior officials of state, and came under the control of the members of a select privy committee. These men often drew salaries from sinecures; they were engaged as the personal assistants of the emperor; attended him personally and provided him with the machinery of government for immediate use, wherever he happened to be residing.

These committees had sometimes won their initial powers by means of the loyal and necessary services that they had rendered in times of emergency or imperial exile; later they enabled an emperor to entrust favourites with the highest powers of government. Such methods appealed directly to emperors who were anxious to evade the moralist strictures of Confucian statesmen; to initiate action which accorded ill with the traditional tenets of Chinese statecraft; or to exploit their exalted position for personal gain.

The powers that the private advisers could grasp were obviously enhanced if they had once performed an action of an illegal or unauthorized nature on behalf of their master (e.g. the confiscation of property in the personal name of the emperor). It is not surprising that the *Shang-shu* (Masters of writing) of the Han dynasty (see p. 154 above), the *Han-lin-yüan* of T'ang or the *ya-men* of the Ming period (see p. 156 above) provided an irregular mode of entree to high responsibility for eunuchs or for men who had not embarked successfully on an official career. The simultaneous retention of the duly constituted offices, bereft of effective authority, and the highly powerful private organs of control is but a single example of the Chinese genius for preserving form, however different the practice may be.

II. FORM AND THEORY (B) THE PROVINCIAL AUTHORITIES

The feudal and provincial systems

The two principal methods of governing the Chinese sub-continent are often described as a feudal and a provincial system. Ideally the 'feudal' system has consisted of the investiture of certain rights and responsibilities over defined territorial areas; such investiture has usually been made to members of the imperial family, whose loyalties are owed directly to the emperor rather than to organs of central government. They pay homage at set times, forward counts of the population of their areas to the emperor, together with certain monies that they have collected therefrom; and at their deaths the benefits, cares and responsibilities of their lands pass into the hands of their eldest sons.

Under the provincial system, governors of defined areas are appointed as salaried officials who are subordinated to senior officers of the central government. They must regulate the affairs of their areas to the satisfaction of the centre, forwarding reports when necessary, and carrying out the tasks of government (e.g. the collection of tax and the dispensation of justice) in accordance with procedures laid down for general compliance; on death, promotion, dismissal or retirement they are replaced by other nominees of the central government.

The growth of the provincial system

In many dynastic periods a compromise has been reached whereby both of these methods are practised. At the foundation of the Ch'in empire (221 B.C.) a discussion took place regarding the advantages of both systems, and a provincial system was introduced exclusively, in the interests of establishing firm authoritarian government, with a precise hierarchy of control, throughout the realm. Although this particular dynasty ended soon, many of the provincial boundaries which it adopted (and which were partly based on the divisions of the pre-imperial age) have persisted as significant territorial divisions ever since. In the succeeding Han dynasty, however, it was found that imperial government could not be based exclusively on a provincial system, and 'feudal' modifications were introduced. For there was no sufficiency of trained men who could be appointed to fill the vacant posts of provincial governor and to satisfy the full needs of a provincial system.

Furthermore, by conferring territorial rights directly on individuals, a victorious emperor could reward the successful soldiers who had brought him to power, settle them in remote areas and divert their energies to the organization of a more prosperous and efficient way of life for the population. By the same means, an emperor could share the cares of government with his sons or near kinsmen, and by giving them a share in the disposal of empire bind their loyalties to his own person.

The first of the Han emperors, then, arranged for the central part of China to be governed by means of a provincial system; at the same time he conferred comparatively small estates on his immediate supporters (i.e. the marquises), while reserving larger investitures for his own sons, and one other supporter, who were given the rank and title of 'King' (see p. 134 above). The history of the Han empire is marked by the growing preponderance of the provincial system at the expense of feudal arrangements. The kings were brought under a closer measure of control by the centre when they lost the right to appoint their own advisers, and were forced to accept the men deputed for their service from the central government. The territories of the kings were divided into smaller kingdoms, or taken over by the centre and placed under provincial governors; and by A.D. 1 only a very small proportion of the Han empire still remained under the sadly diminished authority of the kings. Elsewhere territory was organized on a provincial basis, and this has remained the principal means of government ever since. A reaction, in which a further trial of feudal arrangements was made c. 300 A.D., seriously weakened and ended in the break-up of that particular empire (Western Tsin); and although there were numerous occasions in later dynasties (e.g. T'ang, Ch'ing) when estates were conferred on members of the imperial family, they had no decisive influence on the development of provincial administration.

The advantages of the provincial system
The adoption of the provincial system has thus proved dominant, and its success may be partly related to the variations of the extent of successive empires. For the provincial system is cellular in nature; the size of provinces can be altered without affecting the structure of government; further provinces can be founded as a result of successful campaigns, or large provinces can be divided into two or more units to suit administrative needs; and several provinces can be grouped together, to form larger regional units, should the need arise. Above all,

in times of political disunion, a dynasty which controlled only a part of China could do so by means of a provincial system and maintain the fiction that it was ruling an integral empire in traditional and legitimate style.

The province as the basic administrative division

The term province is used somewhat loosely to translate a variety of Chinese expressions which are alike in so far as they have been used at different times to denote the largest administrative units of the empire. With political and dynastic change, the size and concept of such units has altered considerably, with the result that the Han empire of some 100 provinces (*chün:* sometimes rendered 'commandery') was followed in due course by the T'ang empire of some 400 provinces; but by the Ming and Ch'ing periods, the largest administrative units numbered no more than twenty. But despite frequent changes of Chinese nomenclature, and the territorial extent, the significance of the provinces in the administration of empire has remained largely unaltered. Although the provinces have themselves been constituted by numerous minor units, known usually as prefectures, or counties, and have sometimes been grouped together in major units, the province can best be taken as the basic organ whereby the government of empire was supervised.

The seat and extension of provincial authority

The officials who were responsible for the provinces were appointed by the central government. Sumptuous residences, manifold offices and staff were established in the centre of the region over which they operated. Usually this was situated in the most important walled town which lay within their indicated sphere of activity, i.e. the city which boasted the greatest economic prosperity or the largest number of inhabitants; or the one which could be defended most securely, or which was best placed as a centre of communications. These cities were situated in one of the constituent prefectures of the province, and may have housed the organs of prefectural as well as provincial government.

The authority of provincial officials was exercised outwards from their 'capital' city. Originally the scope of this authority was bounded by natural barriers rather than artificial boundaries, e.g. the larger rivers or more impenetrable mountain barriers could effectively block the exercise of provincial authority. In some areas the limit of authority was reached at points where the territory of adjacent provinces met, and the officials of the two units confronted each other. In such cases a line of demarcation may have been agreed locally or determined by the central government.

The closer that provinces lay to the centre the more effective was the jurisdiction of their governors. Despite the impression given by most historical maps of Chinese empires, it should not be assumed that full authority was exercised throughout the provincial areas. Many of these (particularly in the south, south-west and north-west) comprised large wastes of mountain, jungle swamp or desert, which could perhaps support a sparse and non-assimilated population, but which would not admit the attention of the official representatives of Chinese government.

The tasks of provincial officials

Provincial authority was originally split among three officials, with separate responsibility for administering the civil population, for the inspection of officials' activities, and for military matters. These senior officials worked directly to the centre whose orders they implemented; they forwarded part of the revenue they collected, either in coin or kind, to the central government; they called up civilians to serve as conscript soldiers, trained them in their duties or despatched them where they were needed; they received care of some judicial cases from the prefectures, and in turn forwarded serious cases which lay beyond their jurisdiction for the judgment of senior offices in the capital city; they conducted provincial tests to prevent unsuitable candidates from attending the metropolitan examinations, and they sent up reports on the conduct and efficiency of their subordinate officials. But in many respects the provincial officials were removed by at least one stage from the actual exercise of power, as the greater part of their work lay in handling papers or passing instructions to their juniors in the prefectures. For most matters of everyday administration, the personal contact between a subject of the emperor and his immediate governing authority was maintained only on the lower, prefectural level.

The number and size of the provinces

The very considerable variation in the number and size of provincial units (see Table Six) illustrates the growing intensity of Chinese imperial government. In A.D. 1–2 the Han empire was organized in a total of 103 such units; however, the T'ang empire of the early eighth century boasted some 350 provinces, excluding those of the border areas inhabited by a semi-assimilated population. As the actual area of the Han and T'ang empires corresponded very roughly to the same territorial extent, the increased number of provinces indicates a new degree of intensity with which Chinese officialdom had been established and to which it was able to penetrate. It will be shown (p. 171) that the large number of provinces of the middle empires became too unwieldy for effective control, and during the later empires there were established giant provincial units (Chinese term, in use today: *sheng*) which numbered less than twenty.

Prefectures and magistrates
Prefectures can be partly considered as smaller versions of provinces, and corresponded in size to English counties. The officials of the prefecture bore authority to govern the town where their offices were situated and the surrounding countryside. Their jurisdiction was extended outwards, in the same way as was that of the provincial officials. The senior official, or magistrate as he is often called, worked directly to his superiors of the province, who were entitled to present him with demands and to inspect his activities. Usually the magistrate had no means of direct contact with the central government, but this was provided by special arrangement for areas or towns of an exceptional character. It was by the magistrates and their staff that most Chinese were brought face to face with the inescapable requirements of authority; they paid their taxes to his officers; they endured conscription as members of his labour gangs; if they were involved in judicial processes or litigation, they awaited their magistrate's decision, received his sentence of punishment or suffered his reference of the case to superior quarters.

Reliance on the elders
Magistrates of prefectures have possessed no subordinate organ at a lower level to whom administrative work could be delegated. Local leaders of the country districts, e.g. members of the gentry families, have acted in the capacity of advisory elders capable of bringing considerable influence to bear on the community. Natural leaders of the villages have acquired positions of honour and respect, without recognition as men who held salaried posts; and they have assisted the magistrates by compelling their flock to obey his orders and by reinforcing the rule of custom on which Chinese government relied so greatly. In the interests of security and integrity, governments have usually prescribed that officials cannot serve on the prefectural staff in their own home areas; and magistrates have therefore been handi-

capped by an ignorance of the local conditions of the areas in which they served. The arrangements made to supplement this deficiency will be considered below (see p. 178).

No accurate or representative figures can be provided with which to estimate the size of prefectures during the imperial age, and allowance must be made for very considerable variation. In the Han period there were in theory two grades of prefect; those of senior rank governed prefectures with a population of over 10,000 families (i.e. *c*. 50,000 individuals), while the governors of less populous areas were of a lower grade. The few figures available for the population of some of the more prominent prefectures of Han China (in A.D. 1–2) vary between 40,000 and 80,000 families (from 100,000 to 250,000 individuals); these refer to the inhabitants both of the prominent cities of the prefecture and the surrounding country.

The needs and dangers of larger units
At its greatest extent, a Chinese empire consisted of several hundred provinces, some of which lay at a distance of six or seven weeks' journey from the capital city. It was thus not always easy for the central government to keep in direct contact with its provincial officials, who could therefore acquire an independent control of large resources of money or grain, arms or manpower. These dangers were most marked at the perimeter, where disloyal officials might espouse the the cause of hostile leaders rather than protect the interests of the central government.

As early as 106 B.C. a system of inspection was initiated so as to reduce these dangers. Some dozen independent officials were appointed by the central government to positions whence they could test the efficiency, integrity and loyalty of provincial governors. Each of these inspectors operated by travelling in a small number of adjacent provinces and reporting back to the centre directly. By this means the provinces were grouped together in thirteen geographical groups. By virtue of the powers that he exercised over the provincial officials within such a group, an unscrupulous or ambitious adventurer who had been appointed to be one of the inspectors possessed easy means of establishing a separatist regime in defiance of the central government. Some of the dynastic developments that took place between the Han and T'ang empires arose as the result of such situations, whose potential dangers became gravely accentuated during the eighth century. To preserve security on the borders, or to co-ordinate defences

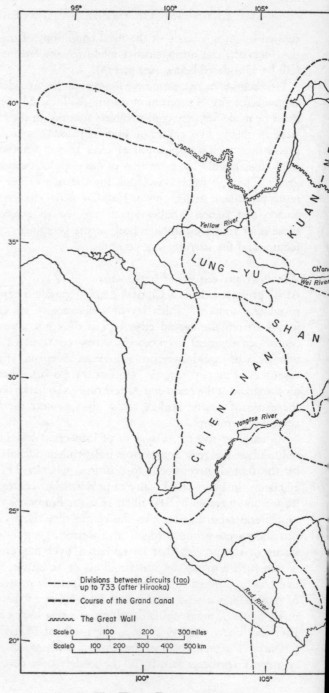

MAP 6. The T'ang Empire (about 630)

40°

HO-TUNG   HO-PEI

HO-NAN

35°

Yellow River

Lo-yang   Pien-chou
(K'ai-feng)

HO-NAN

Huai River

Yang-chou

NAN   HUAI-NAN

30°

Yangtse River

HIANG — NAN

25°

LING — NAN

West River

Kuang-chou
(Canton)

20°

against particular enemies, special commissioners were at times given wide authority over a number of provinces, comprising both military and civil powers. At times, non-Chinese obtained such positions; and although the delegation of authority over wide areas of strategic importance had been introduced to safeguard the interests of the central government, it could actually lead to an empire's dismemberment. The political history of China from 755 to 960 is largely concerned with the rise and fall of small impermanent regimes established in this way and their effect on the central government.

The tao (circuits) of the T'ang empire

The division of China into a few large units of provincial administration was evolved from what was at first the somewhat unsystematic practice of the T'ang period. In the seventh century a few imperial commissioners were ordered to inspect the needs and efficiency of provincial officials in certain designated areas. The idea was not applied as universally or as extensively as it perhaps was during the Han period; but from these arrangements, there soon arose the concept of the empire as consisting of ten (later fifteen) tao (i.e. circuits; the term is sometimes rendered as province). But the circuit did not comprise an independent organ of government of a provincial type; it was the approved area of operations for commissioners, who had been appointed as itinerant representatives of the central government itself.

The Ming and Ch'ing provinces

It was not until the Yüan and Ming dynasties that effective arrangements were made to govern China by means of a few large provincial units. These empires were divided into thirteen sheng or provinces; these were composed of a number of the older and much smaller provinces, which were themselves still subdivided according to the territorial divisions of the original prefectures; and with the addition of a further authority, at an intermediate level, there came into being a provincial and local structure of no less than four levels. The same basic arrangement was adopted during the Ch'ing empire, which is often described as consisting of the eighteen provinces (sheng) of China proper, in addition to those of the other territories (Manchuria, Tibet and Turkestan).

The strength of provincial authority

It will be clear from the foregoing pages that considerable differences existed between the *chün* of the Han and the *sheng* of the Ch'ing empires. Intermediate stages probably came into being in two very different forms. There were times when large regional units, corresponding with the later *sheng*, had acquired an existence *de facto*, despite the disapproval of a powerless central government. Alternately, in later times, despite its constitutional existence, the *sheng* sometimes lacked sufficient authority to exercise a co-ordinated control over the large areas that were involved, and the conduct of administration devolved in effect on its constituent units. Ideally, provincial government is depicted as a pyramid of authorities; a possible criterion for the cohesive nature of imperial government may be seen in the degree to which the theoretical hierarchies were actually maintained or flouted.

TABLE SIX

UNITS OF PROVINCIAL GOVERNMENT

Han A.D.1–2		103 *chün*, etc.			1587 *hsien*
Han 140		105 *chün*, etc.			1180 *hsien*
T'ang *c.* 742		328 *chou*[1]			1573 *hsien*
Sung 997		322 *chou*, etc.			1262 *hsien*
Ming (end of period)	13 *sheng*	159 *fu*	240 *chou*		1144 *hsien*
Ch'ing	18 *sheng*[2]	*c.* 400 *fu* and *chou*[3]			16–1700 *hsien*

[1] Not including units at the borders inhabited by semi-assimilated peoples. For the period 742–58, the term *chün* was used in place of *chou*.

[2] I.e. the eighteen shown in Table One, excluding those of Manchuria, Tibet and Turkestan.

[3] In the Ch'ing period the structure was somewhat complex, comprising sometimes three and sometimes four levels of authority.

Different English equivalents have been variously adopted for the technical terms that designate the units of provincial government:

Han period	*chün*	commandery (or prefecture)
	hsien	prefecture (or district)
T'ang, Sung periods	*chou*	prefecture
	hsien	county
Ming, Ch'ing periods	*sheng*	province
	fu	prefecture
	chou	sub-prefecture (or department)
	hsien	county (or district)

III. PRACTICE AND PROBLEMS

The aims and instruments of government

Although imperial government developed as a compromise arrange-

175

ment that rested on Confucian and authoritarian principles, the main duties of its officials have been directed more to the materialist ends of strengthening the state than to the philanthropic purposes of improving the lot of its subjects. The most conspicuous objects of government have been the exploitation of natural resources as fully as possible; the maintenance of imperial prestige and power; the collection of revenue; the preservation of civil discipline; and the provision of effective defences against China's enemies.

The basic instruments whereby these objects have been achieved were evolved very early in the imperial period, and originated in part from earlier experiments of the independent kingdoms; they have included a count of the population, in which the individual's age, liability for service and legal status have been recorded; a register of land, with information of its quality, uses and capacity (i.e. whether best used for the cultivation of crops, for orchard land or for forest); a calendar, calculated on a luni-solar basis and made out to satisfy the requirements of the agricultural year; and a system of post-stations and horses, for the conveyance of officials or their mail. By these means governments have attempted to organize the working activities of the population; to prevent the occurrence of refugee conditions of a displaced, uncontrolled peasanty; and to ensure that agricultural work is initiated at the correct season. To preserve law and order, governments have relied on a series of rewards and punishments whose validity has been manifestly demonstrable and whose application has been theoretically universal.

The formulation of policy
The officials of the central government were largely engaged in the collection of information, in advising the throne of suitable measures, and in ordering the implementation of their decisions; they thus tended to be more concerned with policy and theory than with direct action. The provincial authorities however were faced with problems that arose during the course of administration, with the tasks of making contact with individuals, and with handling the goods and monies of the government. Nevertheless, provincial authorities possessed some means of influencing decisions of policy. Governors were alway free to submit memorials to the throne in which positive suggestions could be made or the solution of problems propounded (e.g. in regard to the establishment of local schools, negotiation with unassimilated tribesmen, or difficulties of irrigation or transport). Similarly, by precipitate

action a provincial commander of troops could commit the central government to new ventures in foreign policy; and in the prevailing difficulties and delays of communication, it sometimes happened that a local commander was forced to take decisions of far-reaching importance, without the opportunity of consulting his masters at the capital city.

The difficulties of implementing decisions
The final stages of policy discussion took place between the senior ministers of state and the emperor. However, there was no guarantee that their decisions would necessarily be effective, as there were numerous opportunities for opposing political factions to gain personal access to the palace and to frustrate the plans of the statesmen who were nominally in control of the government. In addition there was no certainty that those decisions had resulted from consulting the most suitable advisers, as the most appropriate members of the civil service might not be employed in capacities or grades whereby their specialist advice could be sought or tendered. Suggestions emanating from the provinces or from junior officials could easily be deflected from reaching the highest quarters.

The number of men employed in the civil service cannot be determined with accuracy, but it is clear that the complexity of the service, and the sheer weight of its numbers, could only militate against the speedy workings of government and the individual assumption of responsibility by those most qualified. Despite repeated protestation and decree, political ability would not necessarily be rewarded with high office. Posts would not always be available for the immediate employment of all successful candidates at the examinations, with the result that the civil service sometimes included supernumerary members, who carried no portfolio in which their competence could be displayed. Alternately, there was no guarantee that suitable men would be available to fill the vacancies in the service that were caused by death, retirement or dismissal; and in such events there might be a missing link in the hierarchy and the smooth transmission of authority would be precluded.

Weaknesses in the prefectural system
At the lowest level of government, the offices of the prefectures, there could be no question of delegating responsibility for the prime tasks of government, i.e. the administration of justice, the collection of revenue, the maintenance of security, the upkeep of communications, the care

M

of state stores and granaries and the registration of the land and population. Magistrates were responsible for these duties over areas which were in some cases larger than English counties, and were rarely supplied with a sufficient staff to perform them efficiently. In addition some degree of administrative continuity was essential, and the technical nature of many of the tasks demanded the attention of men who possessed a detailed local knowledge.

Unfortunately the system of civil appointments was not designed to meet these requirements. Prefectural magistrates were usually appointed for short terms of office, sometimes of only three years or less; and in some cases they were officials who had been drafted to the prefectures as a form of punishment, or who had been placed in remote regions so as to silence their criticism of the government. Their few subordinates could not possibly bring authority to bear in all parts of the prefecture in an even, unbiased way, and there were regions where the voice of other elements, such as the gentry families, Buddhist foundations or bandit leaders, could be heard more forcefully than that of the government's accredited representative. Moreover, magistrates did not always command sufficient public funds to enable their work to be done without corruption, extortion or malpractice. The means of overcoming these difficulties are best seen in some of the arrangements practised during the Ch'ing period.

The magistrate's staff

Employees of two types were available to assist a magistrate in the execution of his duties, those provided by the government and those whom he engaged personally. The clerks, who were paid by the government, were taken on for longer periods of service than the magistrates, and were therefore often waiting in office to receive a new magistrate on his arrival in his district. The clerks were thus in a position to control the magistrates' files and records, and could supply, or withhold, that essential local information on which government relied. Similarly the magistrates' staff of runners, who acted as messengers or policemen, or conveyed the magistrates' orders to members of the public, were also employed by the government. By contrast, the magistrates themselves were obliged to engage and pay their secretaries and personal servants. These acted as specialist consultants who could advise a magistrate on matters such as judicial procedure or the formulation of documents, and who could sometimes be used to counterbalance the strong position of the clerks and runners.

Customary fees

At all stages of government, local officials were accustomed to supplement their salaries by the collection of 'customary fees'. When members of the public had business with the magistrates' representatives, they were obliged to pay fees to ensure the satisfactory completion of the transaction and the discharge of their obligations. If they refused, the necessary certificates would perhaps be withheld. In addition the practice of collecting fees prevailed between different levels of government, e.g. in the dealings that took place between prefecture and province. Obviously, any official faced with the need to make these payments would take steps to reimburse himself by a similar procedure with his subordinates; and eventually it was from the civilian population that the source of these sums was found. The collection of customary fees was a regular practice acknowledged by the central government, and is to be distinguished from the illegal collection of money by means of unbridled extortion or corruption.

The force of the family system

The operation of government depended largely on the force of custom and the pressures that were exerted by unofficial or semi-official organizations. Custom operated as a cogent force at most levels of society; it was seen in the accepted authority of the village elders or the heads of families, and it was felt at its strongest in the power exercized by a father over his son. This type of natural authority was recognized alike by government and its subjects as a useful and workable means of maintaining public order and discipline. The head of a family could force a member to fulfil his obligations to the state, punish him for misdemeanour and prevent his criminal adventures. Since the days of the Ch'in empire the state had supported the principle that small groups of families or individuals bore collective responsibility for the misdeeds of any one of their members; and as the failure of a family's head to restrain a man from criminal action could lead to his own indictment, magistrates could rely on the family and its structure to check violence or misdemeanour. Moreover the formal processes of the law that were conducted by magistrates or their superiors were fraught with considerable dangers and severities. In case of dispute, individuals were in practice discouraged from initiating litigation, if a fair decision could be reached by referring to the arbitration of the head of the family.

The guilds

The essential co-operation between the inhabitants of the towns and their governors depended partly on the force of the guilds. These semi-official associations had been formed by members of a particular craft or occupation, whose interests lay in presenting a bold, united front to officialdom. Some of the guilds were formed by men whose homes had orignally been in the same district of rural China, and who wished to retain some measure of cohesion and corporate action. In each case the guild provided its members with material benefits and represented their interests in negotiations with authority. For its part, the government was prepared to accept the leadership of the guilds and to recognize the powers that they exerted over their members. In return, the guild did its best to prevent crime or sharp practice, and forced its members to perform their duties to the state and to conform with the accepted standards of commercial or other practice.

Local disaffection and banditry
According to Confucian theory it was the duty of government, and particularly of its local officials, to take active steps to ascertain the cause of popular grievance or disaffection. In practice, it was left to the initiative of such officials to decide how far they would interest themselves in their subjects' welfare. Magistrates who took their duties seriously and respected Confucian precept would indeed attempt to find out what their flock was suffering or feeling; others would ignore the existence of grievances, and it would be left to an illiterate population to voice its protests by action. In this way complaints against government, whether based on true or false assumptions, could easily lead to outbreaks of banditry, or, at least, to a refusal to meet the magistrate's demands. As disorders of this type reflected on his efficiency, he would do his best to scotch such activities at the earliest possible stage. If the situation became uncontrollable he would still be loath to report outbreaks of violence to his superiors or to ask for their assistance; for such reports could easily end in his own disgrace or dismissal. The temptation to conceal the true state of the country from senior officials could sometimes mean that the central government, or even the emperor, was suddenly confronted with an ugly situation of which he had received no prior warning.

From the magistrate's point of view the rural population could be divided into two categories; the law-abiding members of society, who lived in settled estates or farms, whose names were duly entered on the registers and who met their obligations of tax and service without difficulty; and those who had evaded such controls, and led an unsettled existence, fleeing before the magistrate's officials and seeking a livelihood as they best could. These latter families or displaced elements were regarded by officials as outlaws or bandits; and they were easily recruited into those rebel groups whose rise against the properly constituted authorities of the state often heralded the disruption of an empire.

Judicial procedure

It was open to any member of the public to bring the magistrate's attention to cases in which the laws had been broken, or to appeal to his jurisdiction in civil dispute with a neighbour. Once an accusation had been laid before a magistrate he was in duty bound to try the case, and a man who was accused of legal infringement was treated as guilty and required to prove his innocence. If he succeeded in doing so, his accuser promptly became subject to trial for perjury or misrepresentation, with the result that judicial cases were certain to end in the conviction of at least one party.

The magistrate and his staff acted as investigator, jury and judge; he was able to disregard evidence in the course of trial and was empowered to use torture as a means of extracting confessions. Once a charge was proved, the punishment was determined by reference to the laws of the empire. As the magistrates were entitled to sentence criminals to minor punishments only, the more serious cases were referred for retrial to the senior officials of the province; and from that level cases were sometimes transmitted to the central government or even to the emperor himself. The punishments of the state were extremely harsh, involving criminals in mutilation, flogging or other forms of suffering; in some periods, punishments were extended to a convict's kinsmen. Privileged members of society, such as those who held aristocratic rank (Han period), or officials, were punished less severely than others; at times the criminal members of a non-Chinese conquering people, such as the Mongols or Manchus, were treated less harshly than the Chinese.

IV. THE WEAKNESSES OF IMPERIAL GOVERNMENT

The exercise of imperial government has suffered from three major weaknesses. These comprise faults inherent in the system of recruitment; the difficulties of delegating authority; and the excessive attention which has been paid to form rather than substance.

The shortage of skilled executives and the employment of foreigners
The constant references in documents to the need to find men of high
integrity and intellect to serve the state may sometimes sound forced
or unreal. But in fact, despite the prestige of the profession, the acute
competition to join, and the large numbers of men who were at times
accepted for employment, the civil service often suffered from a deficiency of men of suitable calibre or specialized training (e.g. in judicial
or financial matters). Governments were therefore forced to call on the
services of those who had received no formal training, with the result
that undesirable elements could at times gain control of civil or military
powers.

Similarly foreigners were recruited for the service of the state in
time of shortage, and included expert soldiers from central Asia who
were used to campaigning in conditions to which the Chinese were
themselves ill-suited. Other types of foreigner could help an emperor
with talents that were less familiar to Chinese skills, such as Marco
Polo (during the period 1276–92) or the Jesuit fathers who served the
Ming and Ch'ing courts, and whose engagement can only have been
galling to traditional Chinese officials. The need to employ foreigners
as army commanders arose partly on account of the contempt in which
the profession of arms was held, and the difficulty of maintaining adequate imperial defences in Chinese hands involved the government in
obvious dangers.

The shortage of civil servants of adequate integrity sometimes prevented a fair trial of proposed schemes of administration. If men of
questionable morality or poor intelligence were appointed to executive
positions, it could become impossible to introduce new plans without
encountering deliberate obstructions or even sabotage. Alternatively,
career officials who lacked integrity, and who wished to repay themselves for the expenses incurred in attaining their positions of eminence,
could exploit their newly found authority to practise extortion, to
misappropriate public funds or to demand bribes from their subordinates.

Excessive conservatism
The academic training of the civil servant usually tended to encourage
undue conservatism and to leave little scope for innovation. A radical
approach to the problems of government was highly exceptional, and
the official debates that took place at the capital were more usually
concerned with method or degree than with principle or policy. Very

few successful civil servants had opportunity to suggest administrative change that fully accorded with contemporary social or economic development; and although some problems may have required exceptional treatment (e.g. as demanded by abnormal conditions in the far-flung quarters of the empire), compromise between the formal precepts of central government and the practical needs of reality was rarely acknowledged officially. The continual recourse to the precedents of an ideal past is seen in the compilation of encyclopaedic works designed to guide the civil servant in times of perplexity, and in the arguments propounded by statesmen in their advice to the throne. A basically conservative outlook, coupled with the lack of a specialist training in government, forced officials to rely excessively on their inferiors, and laid them open to deception or manipulation.

Factionalism
Civil servants who reached the culminating points of their careers as the presiding statesmen of the government could hardly do so without involvement in factionalism. Probably they had been forced to express preferences or loyalties at earlier stages of their careers, and had benefited from the patronage of senior colleagues. Such support was rarely given without its price; loyalties were demanded in time of crisis, and rewarded if the outcome was successful; and in this way a man's political affiliations would be clearly committed. In the course of professional promotion the process became accentuated, and senior statesmen often became *de facto* leaders of particular groups or factions. But the interests of rival factions were more material than ideological and the objectives of political groups was usually concerned with the acquisition and use of salaried position than the implementation of defined measures of government. Personal or family interests were of greater consequence than party programmes.

The control of the frontier commanders
The problems of controlling delegated power was highly marked in provincial government and military dispositions. The needs of defence entailed the establishment of static garrisons at places which were widely separated from the centre by long distances and slow communications. The commanders of these forces bore final responsibility for the security of their areas; failure to prevent invasion could result in impeachment, but any action which they initiated, and which ended in military catastrophe, could be followed by their degradation or

183

punishment. Army commanders were sometimes tempted to act independently of the central government and to withhold news of their activities or losses; and instead of applying for reinforcements to the centre, they would supplement their strength by the local recruitment of unassimilated natives. By this means armies were formed whose primary loyalties lay with their regional commanders; and these were soon excellently placed to launch separatist campaigns against the centre. As the army commanders often controlled military forces, local products and occupations and the lines of communication, they could deny the central government its accustomed sources of revenue, and establish their own independent regimes.

Less conspicuous, but equally dangerous, examples of separatism could be seen at the lower level of prefectural government. There were few means whereby the central government could check the accuracy of magistrates' reports. In remote areas it was perfectly possible for a magistrate, with the connivance or at the instigation of his subordinates, to retain a large proportion of the tax that he had collected for his own private uses. Whatever regulations were introduced to prevent such malpractices, magistrates possessed the final means of supporting their action, in the census returns, land surveys and tax returns which they themselves compiled.

The façade of government

The preservation of form, whatever the actual practice, is seen in the structure and working of both the central government and the provincial authorities. While the sacred edifice of imperial institutions, with its formal provision for the smooth delegation of responsibility, was maintained in fiction, practical arrangements for administration may have been based on the realistic conditions of a slowly evolving society or economy. But the deliberate retention of obsolete forms could easily lead to the abuse of power or the failure of government to meet its responsibilities. For rational criticism levelled against existing practices could be answered with the plea that well-established traditions were being maintained and should not be lightly cast aside.

The results of this lip-service to formal procedure are sometimes misleading. Chinese historians have maintained the fiction that all under the heavens is subject to the emperor's decrees; so that, when changes of practice have occasionally been noted, they are represented as following directly on imperial orders or as permission graciously given to introduce new schemes. In fact, however, many edicts should be interpreted not as the authority needed to take action but as the formal and grudging acknowledgement of practical changes that have already occurred.

The close of the imperial era
The failure of the traditional system of government to withstand the changes in the nineteenth century requires little explanation. The introduction of new concepts of government in China coincided with a time when the current dynasty was fast losing its authority. In traditional terms, such processes would doubtless be described as the forfeiture of the mandate of Heaven, and the situation would be regarded as little different from those many earlier occasions when a ruling house had shown itself unworthy of rule and incapable of government. In the nineteenth century such incapacity was being demonstrated, as formerly, in the selfish use of resources by the imperial house, and the growth of corrupt practices between officials and the public. But new factors were present in the demands of new industries, the adoption of modern methods of communication and the manifest impossibility of disregarding the strength of foreign powers. Without authoritative leadership or visionary inspiration it could not be hoped that the procedures of the old China could be reconciled with contemporary demands, and the eventual emergence of a new order can hardly be regarded as surprising.

CHAPTER SEVEN

THE OPERATION OF THE ECONOMY

Few Chinese statesmen or philosophers have failed to stress the importance of China's natural resources and to imply that responsibility for organizing their exploitation is one of the primary tasks of imperial government. From the fourth century B.C. or earlier, Confucian and authoritarian theorists enjoined the sovereigns of the small kingdoms, and then of the empires, to pay due attention to this task, either as a means of improving their subjects' standard of living or in the interests of strengthening the state's resources. But although government has been largely and consciously directed to the organization of this work, the sources of information regarding economic practice are by no means satisfactory.

The lack of hard evidence
Proposals made to improve the volume of production, to lighten the burden of taxation, or to speed the processes of transport figure frequently in memorials submitted to the throne; but although they are sometimes supported by theoretical calculations, or by reference to a notional figure, there is little means of relating such assumptions to actual working conditions. Thus, a figure may be quoted as an average assessment of grain production, but it may be impossible to apply it to a particular part of China or to a specified type of crop. Similarly those chapters of the Standard Histories which attempt to describe economic practice more often consist of an explanation of theoretical systems than detailed accounts of the basic tasks of production, manufacture and distribution.

Unfortunately there exists very little archive material or statistical evidence whereby the general, and often rhetorical, statements of historian or politician can be tested against hard fact. Although the work of provincial government depended largely on the upkeep of local registers of land and population, and the central government required the regular submission of these *data*, the basic documents have perished almost entirely. For the Han period, the theoretical statements of the Standard Histories can be corroborated by the fragments of a few records, but these may not represent normal and regular administrative procedure, and they are not primarily concerned with economic practice. For the T'ang period there exist rather more numerous and more complete pieces of registers used in imperial administration, and it is possible to draw some general inferences; but it is only from c. 1000 or later that statistical and descriptive accounts exist in sufficient quantity to be of wide and authoritative significance.

The duty of working the land

From the earliest times the Chinese have expressed a high regard for agriculture. This is illustrated in one of the legendary accounts of the beginnings of Chinese civilization, and the debt that is acknowledged to those heroes who evolved agricultural techniques or implements. From the beginnings of the imperial age, decrees have habitually stressed the importance of this work, partly by way of contrast with the occupations of those less fortunate mortals who lived beyond the influence of imperial government. Such tribes have been regarded as leading a less sophisticated form of nomad existence, without the benefits of the settled livelihood that farms and land-holdings permit. The exploitation of the land has been regarded, perhaps unconsciously, as one of the means whereby the Chinese peoples can fulfil their purpose of spreading a more civilized form of life amongst the uncultured savage; and most statesmen have appreciated that the survival of the Chinese has depended, first and foremost, on the production of adequate food supplies from that small portion of the sub-continent that is arable.

Land was held in trust by the emperor who was empowered to dispose his officials so that its benefits could be obtained efficiently and enjoyed universally. He was also empowered to organize the labour of his subjects so that products would be made available as necessary. Theoretically, land could be bestowed only as an act of trust, and such conferments could be regarded in the first instance as the delegation of responsibility for agricultural work in specified areas.

The scope of agricultural production

By the imperial age it was generally accepted that agriculture was the normal occupation of the majority of the population. Other occupations, which were concerned with manufacture or distribution, were of

187

a secondary nature, and engagement therein might need to be explained, excused or controlled. It was recognized that imperial authority was justified in organizing the utilization of the land, and that it was entitled to devise institutions and to establish offices for this purpose. It was also acknowledged that the rural population could be expected to provide not only for its own needs, but also a sufficiency for that part of the community whose labours were not immediately or visibly productive. This fraction included the cultured élite of the court, urban dwellers engaged in non-agricultural work, corvée labourers and members of the imperial forces who were engaged in training or active service.

The main uses of the land have been to provide grains and materials for textiles (i.e. hemp, silk and, more recently, cotton). Other crops have included tea, whose culture was of profound significance in the development of a modern monetary economy, and timber, whose importance has been greater than that of grains in some areas, and whose resources could sometimes be exploited more profitably (e.g. at times of a building boom). The products of lakes and forests have always been recognized as contributing to the communal prosperity, and have formed an important secondary means of earning a livelihood.

Some of the principal ordinances of government have been directed to the control of arable land and its tenure and the distribution of its products. These subjects must figure predominantly in any account of the Chinese economy. But before considering these problems, attention must be paid to two basic factors, the population and the means of exchange.

I. POPULATION

The success with which governments have been able to administer the land has been intimately associated with the vital factor of population, and imperial authority has from earliest times recognized the need to estimate the number of mouths to be fed and the extent of the manpower whose efforts it could conscript. But although census counts of the Chinese population have been made from the Han period onwards (the first extant example relates to the year A.D. 1–2), the surviving figures are difficult to interpret and must be regarded with considerable reserve. Some of the reasons for these difficulties apply to other evidences and problems and therefore merit consideration in some detail.

The surviving estimates

From the Han period, a census was theoretically made at frequent and regular intervals (i.e. roughly every three years) for the sake of efficient administration, but in view of the obvious difficulties of the work it is very likely that the counts were not taken as often as was prescribed. Unfortunately only a very few examples survive, and we are dependent almost wholly on the figures which happen to have been included in the Standard Histories. These are spaced at irregular intervals, and we have little means of estimating the regularity with which the counts were actually made or how easily a government could refer to records of the past. It is only from the Ch'ing period that regular annual estimates become available.

There is usually no means of checking whether the figures preserved in the histories can be accepted as accurate copies of the original documents on which they were based. In some cases the validity of the figures is obviously questionable, in view of arithmetical errors or inconsistencies. The fullest counts give the figures of both the households and the individuals for specified areas such as provinces, together with total sums for the whole of China. Doubts are raised if the addition is incorrect; or if the proportionate size of the household varies inexplicably from the norm for one particular area. Omissions (e.g. a zero) can sometimes be detected, or the figures may be suspiciously round. Above all, the census counts of the Chinese empires were made neither for the benefit of the statistician of the twentieth century nor exclusively to fill the immediate needs of government. Allowance must be made for the formal aspects of Chinese administration, and the surviving figures may at times represent little more than an official's endeavour to satisfy the theoretical prescriptions of his task.

The different conditions of the census

In comparing the population counts for different periods, it must be remembered that the basis of the census may have varied from one dynasty to another (e.g. slaves, convicts, or soldiers who were absent on active service, may or may not have been required in the family's return), and allowance must be made for contemporary political or military upheaval. Thus the census for 140 gives a smaller population for many of the northern and north-western provinces than does the corresponding count for A.D. 1–2; the differences may well be due to the invasions launched into China *c.* 140, and the subsequent withdrawal of administrative offices from the northern areas. No significant comparison can be made between the total figures of, say the Han and the Sung periods, in view of the differences in the areas which were held under effective official control. Similarly the very different counts that are given for 742 (8,525,763 households) and 760 (1,931,145 households) can be ascribed to the occurrence of major rebellions between those years, and the loss of administrative efficiency by the central government.

Uneven density
A high proportion of the population has been concentrated in comparatively narrow expanses of the sub-continent. Even when the figures are available for separate provinces they may still be misleading in this respect, as they give a false impression of an even spread of population over comparatively wide areas of territory. However, rural settlements have followed the presence of natural advantages or topographical features, and have been situated far more irregularly than is indicated by the bare figures; and the colonial inhabitants of the provinces of the perimeter have been grouped in small pockets rather than in even density throughout the area.

Deliberate falsification
The census figures that are retained in the histories can hardly be accepted as realistic estimates of the total population of China. Obvious consequences of a somewhat unpleasant nature followed the inclusion of a family in the count, such as liability for poll-tax or for conscripted service. There was thus every temptation to a man to conceal himself from the eyes of the census-official, or to seek temporary refuge in the large areas of hill, forest, or marsh where such authority could not penetrate. The registers could not include members of such refugee families or the unassimilated alien tribesmen of those areas. Similarly, in the interior provinces the families of the great estates might well prefer to conceal the actual number of retainers who were tilling their fields.

In addition, the counts may have been subject to deliberate falsification by the officials themselves in a contradictory, and perhaps counterbalancing, manner. The success of provincial government was sometimes measured by the prosperity of the local population and its numerical increase; local magistrates might therefore be tempted to exaggerate the size of their communities, so as to enhance their reputation with their superior officers at the centre. By contrast, unscrupulous officials who retained for their own pocket a part of the taxation that they had collected would be tempted to show a return for a less populous community than was actually in existence.

Details included in the census (see Table Seven)
The census comprised the number of households and the number of individuals. The household (*hu*) was for long the taxable unit, and must be distinguished from the basic social unit of the family and the small communal units formed so as to bear collective responsibility for crime (see p. 179 above). Fragments of original census returns or similar documents that have been found in central Asia refer to the Han and T'ang periods. They include the essential information whereby an individual's liabilities could be assessed, i.e. sex, age (whether subject to service or not), or distinction of privilege (e.g. marks of social status which carried exemption from obligations, or reduction of punishments; see p. 134 above). Taxable units have usually been shown as consisting of four or five members. There is hardly any evidence whereby the proportion of urban to rural inhabitants can be calculated.

Natural and human calamities
The expectation of life of the Chinese has always been low, and frequent disastrous reductions have been brought about by flood, drought, famine or plague. In addition to natural calamities, political upheavals and constant warfare has taken further toll of the population. No accurate statistics can possibly be available to measure the effect of these events, although the Standard Histories frequently provide rhetorical figures designed to impress the reader. But the grim references to cannibalism in those documents are not necessarily hyperbolical and serve to emphasize the precarious nature of the existence to which most Chinese have been born.

The migration to the south and its growing importance
Between the Han and the Ch'ing dynasties the balance of the Chinese economy changed completely, as the southern part of the sub-continent and its population gradually came to acquire a greater importance than the north. From at least the twelfth century the Yangtse valley and the provinces on its south bank have exercised a more dominant influence on China's production, commerce, transport and expenditure; but the shift of emphasis had started at an earlier stage, when Chinese families began to migrate southward. From the fourth century, the pressure of

the northern invader has from time to time resulted in the flight of the court, the leading families and China's working peasantry from the occupied and dangerous zones of the north towards the safer and less populous areas of the south. These movements have sometimes been prompted by famine, which has resulted from warfare and the impossibility of cultivating the fields. Alternately, the actions of a strong and settled government have sometimes impelled families to move; for there persists the ever optimistic hope of the peasant that he can settle in a remote region that lies beyond the reach of the official and his demands for tax and service.

The flight to the south is well evidenced during the early part of the T'ang period. In the succeeding centuries (i.e. from 755 to c. 960) the north was subject to a far more severe state of disruption than the south, where the comparatively recent settlers were able to develop their sources of production more securely and effectively. The occupation of K'ai-feng in 1127, which prompted a new wave of migration, was comparable with the fall of Loy-ang in 311. The continued migration and search for lands that could be cultivated easily, peacefully and without official interference were among the causes that led to the economic preponderance achieved by the lower Yangtse valley over the traditional grounds of Chinese agriculture in the north.

The changes of the Ch'ing period

Examples of some of the official estimates for China's population are given in Table Seven. When due allowance is made for the difficulties of interpreting these figures, it can still be observed that the most conspicuous and explosive increase of the population occurred during the last dynasty. It has been estimated that there was a threefold increase between c. 1650 and 1850, when the figure perhaps mounted to 430,000,000. The more gradual increases of earlier centuries had been accompanied by the discovery of new resources or the evolution of new and better methods of production. But the dramatic growth that started in the seventeenth century was not matched by industrial, commercial or productive improvements of a correspondingly radical nature, and since the middle of the nineteenth century a new type of economic balance has necessarily been imposed on the Chinese way of life.

TABLE SEVEN

ESTIMATES OF THE CHINESE POPULATION

1. The figures that are given below are taken directly from Chinese sources. Although they can sometimes be proved to be inaccurate (e.g. for A.D. 2 the sum of the counts given for the 103 provincial units actually amounts to 12,366,470 households and 57,671,400 individuals), for the sake of uniformity they are given as they appear in the original sources.

date of census (A.D.)	number of households	number of individuals
2	12,233,062	59,594,978
140	9,698,630	49,150,220
(unspecified year between 742–55)	8,958,334	51,035,543
1292	11,633,281	53,654,337
1393	10,652,789	60,545,812
1662	19,137,652 ⎱	not
1711	24,621,324 ⎰	given

2. The figures that are given above refer to periods when Chinese empire was effective over most of the sub-continent. However, they cannot be taken as referring to precisely comparable areas, and the basis of census was almost certainly different for each case.

The following figures, or estimates (as given in Chinese sources) apply to periods of incomplete or newly founded empires, or to periods of disunity, and illustrate the lesser degree of intensity to which the census was taken at such times.

280 (Tsin)	2,459,840	16,163,863
464 (Liu Sung)	906,870	4,685,510
577 (North Ch'i)	3,032,528	20,006,880
580 (North Chou)	3,590,000	9,009,640
589 (Ch'en)	500,000	2,000,000
760 (T'ang)	1,931,145 ⎱	not
841–6 (T'ang)	4,955,151 ⎰	given

3. The relationship between the foregoing, official, figures, and those of real population may be extremely questionable. Estimates that have been made recently for the Ming to Ch'ing period can be summarized as follows:

(a) During the early part of the Ming period, the actual population was probably over 65,000,000 (cf. the total of 60,000,000 given above).

(b) Official data for two selected years are:

1741	143,411,599 (individuals)
1775	264,561,355

There are grounds for assuming that the actual population during this period was at least 20 per cent in excess of the officially registered population.

(c) Assuming an even rate of increase between 1779 and 1850, it is likely that the actual population of the entire country increased to 430,000,000 by 1850.

N

II. THE MEANS OF EXCHANGE

Shells, tools and early coins

The first medium of exchange to be used in China was probably the cowry. These shells have been found in the treasure pits of the Shang kings at An-yang; and the Chinese pictogram for cowry is included in a number of compound characters which were evolved at an early period to convey the meaning of treasure or commercial transactions. Cowries were almost certainly strung together to form units of an accepted value, but nothing certain is known regarding the system of exchange or the methods of valuation that were then in vogue. With the bronze age a further medium of exchange soon emerged into use. For while bronze implements were still rare, agricultural tools such as knives or shovels were exchanged by barter; and from direct barter there arose the use of these objects as a constant and reliable means of valuing other goods. The use of real shovels and knives for this purpose can be inferred from the later development, in which small imitation tools were made in bronze, deliberately for monetary purposes. The first examples of these early 'coins' were comparatively large, being made as replicas of the actual implements. In time they were replaced by smaller, stylized copies, which sometimes carried a short inscription indicating the place of minting or the coin's value (in terms of weight). Replica knives and spades were widely used in different parts of China during the Spring and Autumn and Warring States periods, and by the ?sixth century B.C., some of the states were minting smaller coins, cast in a new fashion as circular discs.

Imperial minting

With the replacement of the many states by the single empire of Ch'in and Han, effective measures were taken to standardize monetary usage, and to restrict the manufacture of coin to mints that were owned or controlled by the government. With a few exceptional periods, discs have been used as the standard and regular form of coin throughout the imperial age. Usually they have been cast with a central hole, either circular or square, through which a string or leather thong could be threaded. In general copper coins of a single denomination (the so called 'cash') were used, as experiments at multiple units proved to be unpopular and unsuccessful. At times, ingots of gold, or more recently silver, were used in major transactions, with a standard rate of valuation fixed in terms of copper coins. Governments have been free to specify the weight and shape of the copper coin, and have been able to manipulate the economy by means of debasement.

The circulation of coin from Han to T'ang

The use of coins became generally widespread under the settled conditions of the Han empire. The salaries of officials, though graded theoretically in terms of measures of grain, were actually paid partly in cash and partly in kind (grain or cloth). The Han poll-tax was raised on a monetary basis, and was payable, at least in principle, in coin; and records from central Asia illustrate the use of coin by soldiers or colonists to make personal or official purchases. With the breakdown of stable government from the third century or earlier, barter arrangements on a basis of cloth or grain tended to become popular; for there was no effective central authority to control the minting of coin and thereby uphold its value in the face of counterfeiting. When the state's monopoly of minting was reaffirmed under the T'ang government, a new coin of high quality, and bearing new features, was circulated; and under the new dispensation of government the use of a single denomination was retained. Multi-denominational systems were tried occasionally by a hard-pressed treasury, and could be used to introduce a measure of debasement. It is not surprising that such schemes failed to be popular or successful. For large transactions, the T'ang governments sometimes encouraged the use of bolts of silk or precious metals.

Cash strings

From the Han period it had been necessary for businessmen to string coins together by the hundred so as to form larger units than the single cash, and owing to the low value of the basic unit the custom necessarily persisted. By the thirteenth century the value of currency had been considerably depreciated; in official transactions, calculations were made on the basis of the string of 1,000 cash; and in private commerce a nominal unit of 100 cash was used, with a real value that varied from the fifty-six to seventy-seven coins that were actually strung together.

Paper money and inflation

However, a far more radical development had been taking place from the ninth or tenth centuries, in the emergence of the banknote. Commercial enterprises, whose interests lay in widely separated parts of

China, were demanding a new medium of exchange which could be handled more safely and with less labour than the heavy and unwieldy string of copper cash. At the same time the government itself was beginning to experience difficulty in transferring large sums of money from one part of the empire to another, and was recognizing the folly of such undertakings. The bills of exchange or letters of credit that were issued by business houses soon developed into banknotes of a recognizably modern type, and by the eleventh century the issue of this type of currency had been finally taken over by the government with a view to a more general circulation.

The introduction of paper money owed much to the contemporary development of printing and the shortage of copper. For some time the dangers of issuing unlimited quantities of notes were rashly ignored, as the Sung governments felt free to print money, without securing adequate reserves to back the issues. Inflation was partly curbed during the Yüan (Mongol) dynasty, when efficient arrangements were made to issue a whole series of notes, ranging in value from 10 to 2,000 cash. The extensive use of these notes was partly due to the imposition of strong government over a wide area, and their successful circulation is testified by Marco Polo's[1] frequent references to the peoples of Asia and China who were 'idolaters and subjects of the Great Khan, and used paper money'. But once again a breakdown of stable government led to a change of monetary practice. Units of silver were brought into use during the Ming dynasty; and as both the Ming and Ch'ing governments generally preferred to work with hard cash than to face the dangers or difficulties of inflation, the issue of notes was strictly controlled, and related to the reserves actually held in the treasury. Copper currency was supplemented not only by the new source of silver that was being mined in Burma and south-west China but also by the adoption of coins that had been minted abroad (e.g. Spain, Mexico and the United States of America).

The purchasing power of cash
Owing to variations of time and place, and not infrequent occasions of inflation, no general statement of significance can be made regarding the purchasing power of these coins or notes. The Standard Histories frequently refer to fluctuations of price (usually of grain), but the examples that are quoted are usually abnormally high, so as to demonstrate the dire effects of a food shortage, or exceptionally low, so as to

[1] For Marco Polo, see p. 238.

illustrate the material benefits of a particular emperor's reign, or the result of a glut. Only very rarely is it possible to relate the values of different commodities to each other, or to make a realistic appraisal of current prices. Examples of a few figures are given in Table Eight.

TABLE EIGHT
THE VALUE OF MONEY
(1)

The following information is derived from fragments of documents that have been found in north-west China and which can be dated between 100 B.C. and A.D. 100.

(a) Part of an assessment of property belonging to military officers, made out for purposes of taxation.

2 slaves, non-adult, male	value	30,000 cash
1 slave, adult, female		20,000
2 light vehicles, horse-drawn		10,000
5 horses (for farm work)		20,000
2 ox-drawn carts		4,000
2 yoke-oxen		6,000
1 dwelling		10,000
5 ch'ing [i.e. land measures] of arable land		50,000

(b) The foregoing values can be compared with the monthly salaries paid to officers serving in north-west China at this time; these varied from 300 to 3,000 cash, according to rank. Junior officers who were in command of defensive posts, manned by four men, received 900 cash monthly, and the same sum was paid to the civil officials who were attached to the platoons (i.e. the command posts which controlled some six of the defensive posts mentioned). These salaries were paid in coin, and on occasion in the textile equivalent (two rolls of silk to 900 cash).

(2)

The following prices have been selected from a long list of entries in an account book that was kept by a Buddhist temple. The fragments of the book, which is to be dated in the seventh or eighth century, were found near Khotan.

Man's wages for sewing a fur-robe	150 coins
1 chin [·6 kilograms] glue	150
1 tou [5·9 litres] wine	40
1 tou hemp, for use of oil extract	90
1 tou millet	15
1 roll of paper	45
1 writing brush	15
2 sieves for kitchen use	30
1 jar of preserves [i.e. syrup or pickles]	1,000
1 mirror	300

(3)

The list of comparative prices given below includes a few items that have been selected from a long list of values made out to assess the official worth of goods in 1368. They apply to a time when the Yüan dynasty was on the point of collapse, after the outbreak of a series of rebellions, and following a decade or more of inflation. Prices are quoted in strings, i.e. notes with a nominal value of 1,000 coins.

1 *liang* [37·3 gr.] gold	400
1 *liang* silver	80
1 horse	800
1 camel	1,000
1 sheep	40
1 dog	10
10 melons	4
100 peaches or pears	2
1 pair of shoes (calf)	10
1 door	5
1 wooden plank [15 × 30 × 150 cm.]	4
2 umbrellas	1
1 iron ploughshare	2
1 vehicle, large	300
1 vehicle, small	24
1 *tan* [71·6 kg.] coal	8
1 *chin* [·59 kg.] tea	1
10 *chin* [5·9 kg.] salt	2½
100 sheets paper	from 7 to 40
1 *chin* [·59 kg.] ink	8
10 writing brushes	2

III. THE LAND AND SYSTEMS OF TAXATION

The conditions whereby arable land has been owned, leased and worked are basic to the economy of China and bear an intimate connection with the main systems of taxation. Broadly speaking two views regarding the principles of land-ownership have been propounded; the Confucian theory whereby the land has been regarded as subject to state ownership, so that corporate working can be organized satisfactorily; and the realist or legalist theory whereby individual enterprise has been encouraged in the interests of increasing production. In practice a compromise has often been reached between the two views.

The possession and distribution of land by the state
Confucian theorists of the imperial age have sought authority for their views in the precedents envisaged for a golden age of the dim past,

when saintly rulers were assisted by outstanding counsellors in the government of a thoroughly loyal population. In such an era, it was held, all arable land had been the property of the monarch; it had been worked by means of a corporate system in which eight families were grouped together as a farming unit, and further reference to this idealized system, which is termed the 'well-field' system, will be made below. The principle implies that land cannot be acquired by purchase, as ownership and the right of disposal is vested solely in the sovereign. In imperial times the principle was invoked to support schemes whereby land tenure was to be brought under the direct control of the government. Theoretically, such an authority should be responsible for the fair distribution of allotments on a basis of equality, and in this way a means of livelihood would be provided for all members of the community.

The political use of land control
Sponsors of schemes to control possession of the land could draw support from the Confucian faith in moral values and the government's duty to provide for its subjects' needs. In addition, controls of this sort would commend themselves to the established authority of a dynasty, as they could be used to justify measures that were actually designed to break up the influence of potential rivals. By insisting on the universal distribution of land on a basis of equality, a government could foster the growth of small landowners and prevent the emergence of powerful subversive elements. A few instances can be quoted in which a newly founded dynasty, or an usurping authority, has tried to woo the loyalties of small farming communities by initiating a programme of equable distribution.

The failure of ideal schemes of equality
In theory such schemes should prevent the exploitation of the poor by the rich, for all families would be provided with a sufficient means of livelihood on a secure basis. Practice has not unnaturally failed to live up to such expectations. The Confucian view of society has comprised the existence of privileged classes who have been entitled to receive land in larger allotments than those distributed to the general public; and from such beginnings the growth of larger estates has speedily followed. In addition the successful operation of a scheme of distribution by the state depends on conditions that are rarely fulfilled. The forces of nature must first be ready to co-operate with the

government; for in an era of poor communications, the incidence of crop failure, drought or flood can play havoc with the artificial values placed on land or the arrangements devised for systematic distribution or economic working. Moreover, the distribution must be conducted regularly and by an impartial authority whose integrity is beyond question. In practice the executive has rarely possessed the means of implementing these schemes justly or without corruption.

Free enterprise and the growth of large estates
The realists or authoritarians have recognized that individuals are ready and willing to exploit the land in their own personal interests, and have been ready to make full use of these natural ambitions. They have seen no reason to prevent the free sale and purchase of land, and have rather encouraged such transactions in the hope of achieving a more prosperous agriculture. It is no accident that early measures to facilitate these ventures, such as the provision of a standard and trustworthy currency, were taken by the governments of Ch'in. The value to the government lay in the reclamation or exploitation of land that had hitherto been unused, and in the eventual possibility that excess population from crowded areas could be induced, or forced, to settle in farmlands newly established in virgin ground.

The practice of free enterprise resulted in the appearance of a very rich and a very poor class. The rich class consisted of families which were able to thrive on their large estates and to extend them as opportunity offered. Such families possessed sufficient resources to survive natural calamities without suffering economic ruin; for their lands were probably scattered over different areas, and were thus not all subject to the impact of local disasters. By contrast the small landowners suffered severely on such occasions. The localized floods of a single valley could destroy the basis of a smallholder's livelihood; he would then be forced to sell his land to his grand neighbour, and to seek terms whereby he and his family could remain *in situ*, working as the tenants of a rich man's estate.

The high capacity of the greater estates
Despite the accentuated disparities in wealth which resulted from the free sale of land, the amalgamation of smallholdings into large estates permitted considerable advances in economic production. Large landowners, such as the gentry families or the Buddhist establishments of the third to ninth centuries, could utilize their accumulated resources

to initiate large-scale enterprises designed to improve irrigation or transport. Local losses or poor harvests could be offset; the necessary funds existed to buy seed, animals or implements in bulk, and these could be used economically in the general interests of a comparatively large farming unit. Similarly money could be invested in buildings or mills, in the hope of long-term gains, and labour could be found to dig channels and keep the sluices open. By contrast, under the ideal theories of the Confucian school, private enterprise would not be strong enough to initiate such schemes; these would depend on the government's willingness to devote corvée labour to the work, and the impersonal supervision of officials who might easily be disinterested in the success of the ventures.

Varied conditions of tenure
Periods in which schemes were adopted to control land ownership have alternated with those in which free rein has been given to private enterprise. There have emerged many types of family whose livelihood has depended on the land, ranging from the large estate owners living on rents, to the peasantry eking out a bare existence in field or hovel. Between these extremes there have existed many different types of leasehold farmer or working tenant, whose obligations and dues have depended on the institutions of government or the goodwill of the landlord. Changes in the conditions of tenure have often been brought about by variations in the concept or systems of taxation.

The idealized 'well-field' system
Literature dating from the fourth century B.C. or earlier refers to the practices of the Chou dynasty in somewhat idealized terms. There are references to the levies in kind that were required by the model kings of the past and which amounted to a ninth, tenth or eleventh part of the produce. There may also be references to different methods of assessments, i.e. on a strictly realistic rate, calculated according to the amount of each year's crop, or on an average rate taken over a number of years and irrespective of temporary variations. Above all, there are references to the 'well-field' system[1] as being the most just and efficient means of agricultural exploitation.

According to this system, a number of plots of land were owned by

---

[1] The name 'well-field' derives from the Chinese character 井 . The basic meaning of this character, which happens to give a pictorial representation of the land system in question, is a water-well.

an acknowledged nobleman (one of the possessors of a surname), and the work of the fields was undertaken by members of the peasantry. Eight families were together responsible for working each plot, which was divided into nine equal portions. In this way they provided both for their own needs (eight portions of land) and for those of their superiors (the ninth portion); the social order was maintained and an élite class was permitted to live a life of leisure; and the authority of noblemen, landowners and kings was provided with revenue in kind.

Intensive cultivation

The references to this system are somewhat enigmatic and have aroused considerable controversy. They can perhaps be taken to represent a definite stage of intensive agricultural development, which was being reached during the Chou period (i.e. from c. 1000 B.C.) after a long period of evolution. The stage formed a marked improvement over the primitive practices of the neolithic ages, when small clearings were made by farmers who worked independently and moved from one settlement to another so as to work successive plots. By the Chou period, agriculture was being practised in a more permanent fashion, in settlements which could not be extended indefinitely and which were best worked by means of a corporate effort. By now the habits which have moulded much of China's agricultural practice were already being formed. The farmer concentrated his main attention on that small proportion of the countryside that was arable, and mobilized all available labour, male and female, old and young, for its cultivation. Intensive agriculture utilized all available resources and contrivances to raise the yield to its highest possible amount.

The extent to which the idealized well-field system was ever put into practice is a matter of dispute; some scholars regard the scheme as being wholly theoretical, and impossible to operate. Perhaps the main importance of the well-field system lies in its concept, as it has been consistently quoted by later protagonists of state schemes of land ownership as an early example of communal co-operation and equable distribution.

The sale of land

While Mencius (c. 390–305) was praising the virtues of the well-field system, other developments had been taking place. Iron had been coming into general use, and the land was being worked more effectively; coins were being circulated more generally, and a few merchants were beginning to accumulate large fortunes. In the unsettled conditions of these centuries, land provided the safest form of wealth, and merchants were ready to turn their heavy purses of copper spades and knives into real property. Legal sanction to the exchange of land for ready money was specifically given in Ch'in, and owed much to the theories of politics and economics that were being voiced by Shang Yang (c. 390–338).

Land-holdings and taxation (Han period)
Purchase remained the regular means of acquiring land during the early empires, and the system of taxation was arranged accordingly. The imperial revenue of Han was largely based on the collection of a land-tax calculated according to a man's actual holding, and a poll-tax levied in respect of his own person and his family. Land-tax was paid in kind, at a rate that was fixed first at one fifteenth and later one-thirtieth part of the produce. The poll-tax was usually paid in coin, but at times local products could be used as a substitute. The rate of poll-tax varied in respect of an individual's age, as did the demands that were made on him for military service (normally two years of duty) and corvée (one month annually). For this reason, the classification of the population as children (aged 14 and below) adults (15 to 56) or veterans was an essential part of the census compiler's task. The rate of the poll-tax could also be changed in accordance with the needs of the exchequer; during the Western Han period it varied between 40 and 190 cash for each adult male.

Early attempts to restrict the growth of estates
By about 100 B.C. protests were being raised against excessively high rates of taxation, and the imposition of disproportionately heavy burdens on the poorer members of society. To find the money for their own dues and to acquire sufficient income for their own purposes, landlords were probably collecting as much as 50 per cent of their tenants' produce. The resulting state of economic disparity offended all statesmen who claimed to be governing in accordance with Confucian ideals.

The first attempt to reform the economy of the empire by imposing legal restrictions on the extent of land-holdings and the slaves used for the work was made by Wang Mang, who succeeded in establishing himself as emperor for a short time (9–23). But the attempt failed to attract sufficient support and was soon abandoned. In the succeeding centuries of the Eastern Han empire and the age of political disunity, unstable conditions favoured the large landowners. In the absence of a central authority, social and economic stability was being provided by those prominent families who were able to build up large estates and work them by means of tenantry or dependent clients (see pp. 132f). Similarly it was during this period that Buddhist establishments were increasing their properties, largely thanks to the gifts of land that were being consigned to them by pious benefactors.

But there were reactions against the growing preponderance of private wealth. Even in the third century a military leader (Ts'ao Ts'ao), who founded a short-lived regime in north China (Wei 220–264), had tried to improve agricultural production and distribution by establishing a series of official colonies under the control of the state; in the succeeding Tsin dynasty advantage was taken of these arrangements to introduce measures to restrict the permitted size of land holdings. Under the comparatively stable conditions of the northern Wei dynasty (386–534), it was realized that the wealth and power of the great families was sufficient to threaten the well-being of the government, and measures were proposed to protect the state's interests. These measures provided for a scheme of land distribution that was closely linked with new systems of taxation; and at the outset of the T'ang empire (618) the same principles were incorporated in a state scheme which it was hoped to operate on an empire-wide scale.

The T'ang system of land allocation and taxation
The scheme was based on the undertaking of the government to make equal allotments of land available to all registered families of the population. The greater part of the allotment was to consist of arable land, which was due for return to the state when the holder died or reached the age limit; a smaller part, which was intended for long term use as orchard land or for mulberry groves, remained permanently with the holder and his family on an hereditary basis. In return for these allotments the holders paid regular dues of grain and cloth, and were liable to render a basic twenty days' service annually.

If it had been operated effectively, the scheme could have been used to eliminate the growth of the large estates, and the newly founded T'ang governments were doubtless anxious to achieve this result. In addition, the scheme could be used as a means of stimulating agricultural effort, by encouraging the peasantry to migrate from crowded areas to regions ready for exploitation. However, government was not yet sufficiently rational, disinterested or effective to operate the scheme to full advantage. Exceptions, whereby officials could own or buy land in excess of the normal allotment, vitiated the principle of equality from the start. Variation of topography led to the distribution of allotments of uneven size, and there was no guarantee that allowance would be made for qualitative differences of the soil. Moreover, in some areas it was possible and profitable for the peasantry to remove to a further distance from the seat of authority, and to draw a living from lands that were not subject to official restriction or demand.

Nonetheless there is evidence to show that the scheme was put into practice in some measure, if not universally, during the seventh century, and records of allotments that were made in the extreme north-western parts of the T'ang empire happily survive. But by the eighth century, the system was failing to provide the government with sufficient revenue from direct taxation, or to act as an effective means of controlling the growth of large estates.

The principle of the quota of taxation
The breakdown of the initial T'ang system of land distribution and taxation can be dated some time before 755, the year which saw the outbreak of a series of large-scale rebellions which nearly destroyed the dynasty. As early as 736 the failure of local officials to make adequate arrangements to collect tax had resulted in the imposition of a quota system, whereby they were notified by the central government of the amounts of revenue which they had to procure; and they were free to collect these as they saw fit. Thereafter the quota system formed a regular feature of Chinese financial administration for some seven centuries or more. It was embodied in arrangements that were introduced from 780, when a weakened government was forced to yield actual, if not nominal or formal, control of large areas of China to semi-independent regional governors. By now, land was falling more and more into the possession of a comparatively small number of large landowners. It was admitted that the system of allocation had led to a multiplicity of taxation without ensuring fair means of collection or providing financial stability. It was therefore recognized that the state would forego its claim to distribute land holdings, and that purchase should be accepted as the general and legitimate means of acquisition.

Measures to rationalize the T'ang finances (780)
Under the new scheme of 780, taxation was still levied in respect of

land, its produce and its occupiers; but the earlier division into three types of payment (grain, cloth and service) was abolished, together with many supplementary, indirect taxes that had become necessary. The new simpler system was based on payments which were to be made twice annually. Of greater significance, in place of the levies raised on the theoretical holdings of land to which families were formally entitled but which they had not necessarily occupied, the tax was in future to be assessed realistically on the basis of land actually in possession. An important element of rationalization was introduced by the provision that a budget should be drawn up to show what expenditure was necessary, and provincial governors should be charged with the task of raising the quota specified by the central government. By this means, a weak government that lacked effective authority could retain some measure of income from the remoter areas if it was ready to forfeit its control over the methods of collection.

While receiving more responsibility for the collection of taxes, provincial authorities were also empowered to distribute the taxes in a more practical way. As early as the Han period (*c.* 100 B.C.), a writer had employed vivid and rhetorical terms to describe the wastage consequent on the despatch of tax grain to the capital city, where unmanageable surpluses would lie rotting. In 780, provincial authorities were formally authorized to retain part of the taxation which they collected for their own local use. And although tax was still paid principally in kind, changes in the basis of assessment marked an advance in the process which was to lead eventually to the collection of China's main taxes in money.

The suggestions of Wang An-shih

The success with which the measures of 780 could be operated was strictly limited by unfavourable political conditions. From the ninth century the economy was marked by the continued growth of the large estates, owned by gentry-families and worked by tenants or hired labourers. Further attempts to rationalize the financial system which were suggested in the eleventh century envisaged a fuller application of the quota-system, and means whereby the state would help the small producers to maintain a state of solvency. Such proposals were associated with the far-sighted statesman Wang An-shih (1021–1086). As they ran counter to the interests of conservative statesmen and wealthy merchants, it could hardly be expected that such radical measures would be accepted and introduced effectively.

The 'single whip system' of the Ming dynasty

From the earliest times, the imperial tax systems had comprised a demand for regular annual service to be rendered by the individual as an integral and regular part of his obligations. By this means imperial government was able to call on manpower for projects of state building or other tasks. However, with the developing economy of China's towns and countryside, the system was becoming less suitable to the government's needs. It was appreciated, at least by Wang An-shih (c. 1069), that, rather than conscript labour on a temporary basis, it would be more efficient to raise a regular and special monetary tax on a universal level, with which to hire a force of labour on more permanent terms. Again, Wang An-shih was voicing reforms before the time was ripe for their acceptance, and it was not until the Ming period (middle of the sixteenth century) that a determined attempt was made to merge the obligations of service with those of the land-tax, in the form of single payments to be made in money rather than kind.

The 'single whip system' of the Ming governments constituted a radical change from earlier procedures; like the reforms of 780, the new system was aimed at simplification. It was hoped that it could be applied universally, and that the greater part of the dues could be collected in ingots of silver, which was now coming into greater use as a medium of exchange. However these hopes were not completely fulfilled in the Ming period. The Ch'ing governments retained the main features of the system. Changes in the methods of assessment and registration which were introduced in the middle of the eighteenth century resulted in a more effective merger of the two types of dues under one heading. However, some reliance was still placed on corvée, and the collection of taxation in kind remained one of the duties of provincial and local officials. And, in addition to the normal land-tax, a special collection of tribute-grain was made in certain areas, specially to supply the particular needs of the official residents of Peking.

Other means of direct taxation

In addition to the imposts raised on the land or as a capital assessment, Chinese governments have sought to increase their revenues by other types of direct taxation. These have included dues payable on the produce of forest and lakeland; on transactions in the tea business (from the eighth century); on plots used in the official markets or business premises; or on vehicles used in transport. Capital levies have occasionally been raised on the declared monetary property of the rich, and in times of emergency a forced loan has been demanded. Further means of supplementing revenue are seen in the sale of titles of honour, offices in the civil service or certificates of ordination as Buddhist dignitaries; and in the Ch'ing period an important source of income lay in the tariffs which were levied on all merchandise that passed through some thirty points of control inside China. In addition, State monopolies were sometimes established to organize the production of minerals or certain manufactures, and these provided governments with a further source of income.

IV. THE GOVERNMENT'S MONOPOLIES

The economy of imperial China has throughout depended on agriculture, and the staple diet of the population has been provided by the cereal crops that the farmers have grown. In these circumstances two mineral products, iron and salt, have come to play an essential role in Chinese life and have sometimes been brought under the state's control.

The traditional attitude to the iron and salt industries
However, Chinese authorities have not always been willing to give full recognition to the importance of these products. Owing to the stress that has been placed on agriculture, the occupations of the mineowner, the manufacturer and the commercial distributor and their workmen have often been regarded as secondary, despite the farmer's use of iron implements and his need of irrigation channels dug by iron tools.

There may be practical reasons which account for the traditional scorn of the industrial worker and the shopkeeper that arose during the Warring States period. Although the use of iron had been introduced for some centuries, technology was still somewhat primitive and manufactures were limited in quantity. Probably iron was first used more to provide the soldier with his weapons than the peasant with his tools; and the scarcity of such objects not unnaturally enhanced their value and their makers' opportunities for gain. Statesmen, whether advocates of Confucian or realist theories, may have been aware of the dangers that would accompany a large-scale flight of labour from the ill-rewarded drudgery of the fields to the more profitable work of the mines or the foundries. To ensure that the production of essential food took priority over that of less important goods or even luxuries, it would be necessary to discredit the occupation of the artisan or the shopkeeper; it would also be necessary to ensure that the small supply of iron and its manufactures was being used to benefit the community at large, and not simply to enrich individual mine-owners.

Monopolies or free enterprise?
Salt was produced not only from coastal sources but also from a few mines that lay scattered in different parts of China. While the process of extracting and drying marine salt was considerably easier than that of mining either salt or iron, the establishment of fair and efficient means of supply posed considerable problems. For to a community which depended on a cereal diet, salt was essential; and as the sources of marine salt were somewhat localized, it would be possible for powerful merchants to exploit the difficulties of distribution so as to establish a commercial monopoly in their own interests, and to the grave disadvantage of the peasantry. Such a result would meet with the disapproval both of those who desired the well-being of the population and those whose prime concern was the enrichment of the state.

As with the case of land-ownership, two principles emerged regarding the production of minerals. The case for free enterprise was doubtless supported by those few families who had succeeded in making their fortunes from the salt or iron mines during the Warring States period, and who were anxious to hold fast to their sources of profit. Their opponents however could find a precedent for the establishment of a state monopoly which would control the industries and the distribution of its products. This was ascribed, perhaps anachronistically, to the court which had governed East China during the seventh century B.C., under the direction of Duke Huan of Ch'i and his adviser Kuan Chung.

The Han monopolies as part of a major economic policy
Shortly after the beginning of the imperial age, a progressive government introduced measures to bring these industries under the direction of the state. The establishment of iron and salt monopolies under official commissioners (*c.* 119 B.C.) marks a new stage of political sophistication. But these measures should not be regarded in isolation as a single act of government, as they formed part of a general policy of economic expansion. Contemporarily with the take-over of the iron and salt industries, arrangements were being made to improve the

o   209 disposal of the state revenues that were being received in kind. A timely adjustment of the coinage resulted in the introduction of a coin which was destined to remain in circulation for some centuries; and it is possible that the progressive statesmen of Han who arranged to take over the mines could appreciate the value of promoting an external trade between China and her neighbours (see p. 255 f).

Conservative elements at court could not permit the adoption of these policies without protest, and the issues were debated by protagonists of both sides. In the account of one such debate (81 B.C.) which has happily been preserved, the conservative elements are shown as worsting their progressive opponents; but it is noteworthy that the official control of iron and salt was none the less retained.

The Han monopolies were controlled by commissioners (about forty for iron and thirty for salt) who were stationed locally to supervise the work of particular mines or centres of marine salt production. The commissioners may have been able to call on convict labour or the corvée to perform the necessary work. Salt and iron products were sold to the public by the same official agencies, and iron goods were sometimes inscribed with the name of the agency and date of manufacture. Money could be raised for the government as an indirect tax levied during the process of sale.

The salt monopoly of the T'ang and later governments
The salt monopoly was reimposed by the T'ang government in the middle of the eighth century as a means of raising much needed revenue. Commissioners were responsible for production, and sold salt to the merchants for general distribution; at the same time there was imposed a very high tax, which sometimes rose to ten times the market value of the salt; and this was duly passed on to the public by the merchants. This source of revenue was soon to form the major stable element of the T'ang government's income, with the result that the Salt Commissioners, whose headquarters were placed at Yang-chou, could assert themselves as the chief financial power of the empire. The highly complex system of control whereby traffic in salt was regulated invited attempts at manipulation or evasion of the law, and the continuation of the monopoly during succeeding dynasties encouraged the growth of salt smuggling and other abuses.

No attempt was made by the T'ang governments to institute a state control of iron products, but during the later empires, the industry was worked partly under the government's control and partly by private enterprise. Other monopolies which were imposed less regularly or successfully have included liquor (in the Han and T'ang periods) and tea (T'ang).

The control of the salt industry that was adopted by the Ming and Ch'ing governments was more advanced than that of their predecessors and provided an important source of revenue. The monopoly allowed scope for private enterprise, as licences (i.e. exclusive rights) were granted by the government to those private businessmen who were anxious to engage in this highly profitable industry. China was divided into some dozen regions wherein the production, distribution and sale of salt was strictly regulated. Smuggling was practised very extensively.

V. COMMERCE

The conflicting interests of state and individual
Traditionally merchants have been subjected to even greater scorn and disapproval than manufacturers and artisans. For not only did merchants engage in occupations that were of secondary importance to the production of crops from the fields; their living depended not, as did the farmers', in the growth of material goods for the benefit of society, but on the extraction of profits from their fellow-men, in return for supplying them with their needs.

In the centuries immediately preceding the formation of the Ch'in empire, there had emereged two types of merchant; the wholesalers, who dealt in large quantities over long distances and employed large numbers of assistants to run their business; and the retail shopkeepers whose business was confined to local markets and particular wares. As conspicuous examples could be quoted of wholesale merchants who had amassed large fortunes from their undertakings, their occupations were regarded with horror and distrust by early Confucian writers, and with anxiety, or alternately envy, by realists. For the conflict between the interests of state and individual could easily become acute. The Han government was anxious to produce and distribute grain and other staple goods as widely, cheaply and fairly as possible; such ambitions were perpetually threatened by the merchant adventurers, whose best chance of profit lay in exploiting a shortage of necessities.

Attempts to limit transactions in grain and cloth
In the early empires steps were taken to restrict the scope of mercantile activity and to deflect its attention from staple commodities to non-

essential manufactures or luxuries. Such an objective depended on the part played by the government in distributing staple goods. The Han system of taxation provided for the collection of grain and cloth by authorities of the government, and for the use of corvée labour for its transport to non-productive regions. By paying its officials and military officers partly in kind, the government could hope to prevent the growth of markets wherein the élite class of town-dwellers bought their supplies. Ideally, it could be hoped that the farming community would be self-sufficient, and would have little reason to rely on merchants. But in practice considerable traffic in grain and cloth took place. High-ranking officials needed or wished to dispose of surplus quantities which they received as part of their salaries; and in years of plenty the peasantry would wish to sell their surplus stocks. The volume of these transactions must have varied greatly; but the existence of commercial opportunity is shown by the steps that Han governments thought of taking to control the growth of excessive profits from a trade in essential goods. It is significant that at the time when the monopolies were being established in iron and salt, measures were also being taken to stabilize the prices of staple commodities, and to provide for their regular transport where they were most needed.

The control of the markets
Merchants were thus discouraged from making large profits on essential commodities and prevented from trafficking in objects of state monopoly. But life in the early empires was enlivened by brisk marketing in manufactures or luxury goods such as pickled foods, fruits or animal hides; rare horns, cinnabar, or livestock such as horses or cattle; carriages to be drawn at speed by horses, or more sedately by oxen; wooden or bamboo wares; copper vessels or lacquered boxes. Attempts to control commercial activity are seen in the imposition of an official supervisor over the market places, which were built in carefully specified areas. And the merchant was subject to some degree of social ostracism. For although wealth could perhaps enable a merchant to enjoy the leisures and material luxuries of the scholar officials, as yet it could not bring him the recognition of superiority that was accorded to the educated class or the means of joining its ranks.

The developing trade of the T'ang, Sung and later periods
Between the Han and the T'ang dynasties the practice arose of holding fairs and markets in the grounds of Buddhist temples, initially on

specified festival days. In addition, it was from beginnings in Buddhist establishments that there grew the earliest pawnshops and agencies on which marketing thrived and from which the intricate system of credit and banking was to develop. A substantial advance in commercial activity took place from the T'ang and Sung periods, partly as a result of the more highly sophisticated habits at home and the extension of contacts deep into Asia and beyond. The products of the Middle East were becoming known and appreciated; faster communications now existed for the conveyance of perishable goods; and increasingly more demands were being made by the wealthy town dwellers for luxuries that were brought from afar.

With the newly found means of monetary exchange of the Sung era—the bank-note—commerce thrived with increasing prosperity, Earlier regulations whereby shops were restricted to a few designated market places were now rescinded, and retailers could purvey their goods where they chose. The old custom of grouping shops together if they dealt in the same commodities still persisted; for in this way retailers could easily form their guilds and determine on corporate action in time of need; and the conduct of business between wholesaler, agent and retailer could be managed more easily. From the Sung period warehouses began to be established, either by the government or under private hands. Trading continued to take a more important part in the economic development of China, and eventually give rise to the flourishing emporia of the Yangtse valley whose prosperity and activity so impressed the European visitors in the nineteenth century.

The place of the guilds
The marked growth of commercial activity that occurred from the Sung period can be illustrated by the rise of the merchants' guilds which can be dated at that time. These were organized on a formal basis; they appointed their own officers and drew up their own rules of membership and professional conduct. The guild could protect its members from unfair external competition or official oppression, and could relieve members' distress in times of material want. The heads of the guilds dealt directly with the tax-collectors, having themselves collected the necessary sums from members or sometimes paying a fixed quota of money on their behalf. At times the guilds could bring effective pressure to bear on all tradesmen of a particular type so as to enforce membership; and in the case of the state monopolies, the

213

guilds were sometimes recognized as operatives to whom the government delegated responsibility for the distribution, transport or sale of selected products; the guilds were willing to pay handsomely for such lucrative privileges.

Restricted capitalist enterprises

From Soochow and other centres the merchants of the fifteenth century had been engaged in the profitable trade of supplying northern customers with the porcelains and silks, cottons and teas that were manufactured or processed south of the Yangtse. By the eighteenth century it had become possible for some groups of merchants to launch into ventures of a larger scale, and to found fortunes of unprecedented wealth. A good example of such success is seen in the case of the salt merchants, whose highly profitable industry comprised a whole hierarchy of greater and smaller operatives, and whose activities took place with the co-operation and even the blessing of the government. However, the fortunes amassed by such means were rarely of long duration, and the failure to use these resources to found capitalist enterprises of a western type has yet to be fully explained.

Some of the reasons may lie in the nature of Chinese society, wherein initiative had long been directed to other paths; or in the deep-seated faith placed by the Chinese in the value of land as against other enterprises. Perhaps the merchants' rise to prominence (see p. 143) occurred at too late a stage of China's social and political development; and by the time that large fortunes were being founded and could have been used to promote truly capitalist enterprises, institutions had long been devised to direct individual energies to supporting the emperor's government and to discourage the diversion of resources to private purposes.

Chinese traders abroad

Whatever the original inhibitions against the merchant and his occupation, active engagement in trading has remained a characteristic of Chinese city life in the succeeding centuries from the T'ang and Sung periods. This feature has perhaps been more marked in the southern than the northern provinces. As most of the Chinese who emigrate overseas have originated from the southern cities, they are often to be found in neighbouring lands pursuing the same occupation to which they and their ancestors have been accustomed, that of the tradesman. Further developments which have affected the south rather than the north have followed the growth of an export trade with foreign countries and will be considered below (see p. 270).

VI. COMMUNICATIONS AND THE CAPITAL CITY

The problem of supply
The effective strength of imperial government has frequently been limited by the lack of adequate natural lines of communication for the easy delivery of products to these areas where they are most needed. Populous cities have sometimes arisen at some distance from the grain producing areas, or in secluded positions chosen for the sake of their natural defences. Chinese governments have been faced with the major problem of conveying supplies from the great plain of north-east China, and later from the Yangtse valley or the southern provinces, to the cities that lay hidden in the stronghold of the north-west or the south, or to the more distant garrisons facing central Asia.

Poor natural communications
While the natural lines of communication that run from east to west are only partially usable, there is an almost complete absence of natural links directly connecting the north and the south. From about the region of K'ai-feng, navigation down the Yellow River is seriously impeded by flooding and frequent changes of the river's course. Further upstream, the large rocks (situated at the San-men gorge) have often prevented or delayed the westerly progress of grain-laden barges; and the Wei River, whose course appears to form a westward continuation of the Yellow River, is subject to considerable silting and is unserviceable for all vessels except those of the shallowest draught.

Mountain ranges (the Ta-pa-shan and Ch'in-ling-shan) lie athwart the path of the traveller wishing to transport his goods from the Upper Yangtse valley to the old metropolitan area (modern Shensi). From the Han period the government had tried to make use of small tributaries of the Han and Wei rivers to form a link between Ch'ang-an and the Ssu-ch'uan basin, but such endeavours were frustrated and no regular means of transport could be found.

Land traffic
Deliberate attempts at road building have been made by governments from time to time, but these have usually been directed to improving the efficiency of government and its controls rather than to easing the

problems of the economy. The Ch'in government built a series of roads to aid the deployment of their armies. In the Han period a fast postal system was developed, so that officials and despatch riders could travel at speed from one end of the empire to the other. At this time it took some six or seven weeks for the delivery of mail from central China to military posts established at the north-western extremity of Chinese penetration. More conspicuous and successful attempts to organize an empire-wide postal service were initiated by the T'ang and particularly the Yüan governments. The system of official postal stations, with remounts and hostels, that was established by the Ming governments was inherited by its successors, and in 1842 the official schedule for the express delivery of mail from Peking allowed thirty-two and forty days for the journey (by horse) to Canton and Yün-nan; K'ai-feng and Mukden were reached in eight days, Nanking in thirteen. But for a number of reasons roads have been of less importance to the development of the economy than waterways. Quite apart from the incidence of mountain ranges and the geographical difficulty of planning a major scheme of road transport, the actual means of travel by road have been limited. Horses have never been available to the Chinese in great supply, as pasture grounds are scarce and the animals are ill-suited to the climatic conditions of the south or the precipitous nature of so much of China's territory. The horse has usually been reserved for the use of the official, travelling on fast business at the expense of the government, or for the merchant who has been wealthy enough to maintain his own stables. For the humdrum local distribution of bulky staple commodities, transport has depended, if not on water, on the mule or the ox-cart.

The growing importance of the south and the north-east
The problems of communication were intimately related to two processes which have affected the economic development of China, the preponderance of the south over the north and the shift of emphasis in the north from the west to the east. Reference has been made above (see p. 191) to the migrations of the population to the south which had started and sustained the growth of productive power in the lower Yangtse valley. This tendency was promoted by the political and dynastic events of the Sung and subsequent periods, and by the successful experiments which markedly increased the yield of the land in these areas.

In the meantime the old metropolitan area of the north-west was forfeiting its strategic significance. The Liao and Kin empires had arisen in the north-east, and had extended their hold on Chinese territory thence in a westerly direction. It was therefore more natural for their capital cities to be situated in the east (e.g. the city later called Peking) than on the western side of the T'ai-hang hills. With the reunification of north and south by the Mongol emperors there was already a long history of administration conducted from centres lying in the north-east; and the reasons that had enhanced the value of the north-west as a well-defended stronghold had disappeared. The Yüan dynasty's seat of government was established at the site of Peking by 1272, and China's imperial capital has remained there, with short interruptions, ever since.[1]

The choice of a capital city and the Grand Canal
The foundation of the capital city at Peking was the last move in a series of changes, which can be partly explained in terms of transport and communications. The difficulties of supplying Ch'ang-an have been discussed above, and partly for this reason, Lo-yang was often chosen as the centre of the administration, from the Eastern Han period onwards; for Lo-yang lies on the south bank of the Yellow River, some fifty miles below the obstruction of the San-men rocks.

In the T'ang period Ch'ang-an and Lo-yang were both used as the seat of government. By now the problem of supply was somewhat different from what it had been in the Han period. With the development of the Yangtse area, a high proportion of grain was being brought from the south rather than from the east, and a series of canals had been dug to facilitate transport. These canals were unified into a single system under the Sui emperors, and served to link the northern and southern part of the empire by a route leading from Hangchow to K'ai-feng. This system of waterways, which is known as the Grand Canal, was supplemented by routes which carried goods to the north-west where they were most needed. When the Sung capital city was set up at K'ai-feng (960–1126) the same overall conditions applied; but with the split of China into two empires during the twelfth and thirteenth centuries, there was no immediate need to maintain the link between north and south, and the system of canals fell into disuse. From the Mongol period a new problem of communications was posed in the need to convey supplies from the south to the north-east instead

[1] Nanking was used as the capital city in the early part of the Ming period (1368–1420) and at times between 1911 and 1949.

of the north-west; the original concept of the Grand Canal was now obsolete and new measures were necessary.

The second Grand Canal

The Yüan governments attempted to solve this difficulty by utilising both sea-routes and inland waterways. Before then a coastal route would have been of little value in solving the problems of transport that faced dynasties seated at Lo-yang or Ch'ang-an; and it was only from the Sung period that the Chinese had been building strong vessels capable of plying the high seas. The value of sea traffic during the Yüan period was somewhat limited owing to the toll taken by pirate and typhoon, but it nonetheless constituted a valuable secondary means of transport.

A more effective and permanent solution lay in the construction of a second Grand Canal. As before, this was designed to bring north traffic that originated from below the Yangtse and passed through the Huai River valleys, and it was possible to repair some of the earlier stretches of canal for re-use. But it was also necessary to construct a new course to meet the new needs. The second Grand Canal was directed to the north rather than the north-west, so that it crossed the Yellow River itself, and came to an end very close to Peking.

This series of waterways, which was completed c. 1295, has acted as a key line in China's system of communication until the advent of railways in the nineteenth and twentieth centuries. However, the efficiency of the system has often been impaired by natural causes. Stretches of the canal are sometimes subject to severe silting, and require constant dredging. Should the Yellow River make a drastic alteration of course (e.g. the shift from the southern to the northern side of the Shantung peninsula, which took place between 1852 and 1855) the value of the waterway may be destroyed, together with the fleets of junks and the installations by which vessels were raised or lowered to suit the different water levels. Reasons such as these had forced the Yüan governments to try the transport of grain by sea; and a further cause, the occupation of south China by the T'ai-p'ing rebels (c.1850–65) forced the Ch'ing emperors to adopt similar measures.

Waterways and government

The Grand Canals form conspicuous, but by no means the only, example of the attention paid by imperial government to the efficiency of transport. Since the Han period it has been appreciated by Chinese

8. IRRIGATION

Form the *T'ien-kung k'ai-wu* (see note to Figure No. 7); original size 20 cm.
by 13 cm. Mechanical devices to raise water for irrigation or other purposes
originated about A.D. 100 or perhaps a little earlier. The wood-cut shows a
square-pallet chain-pump, the most widespread of Chinese water-machines.
The removal of water for these purposes sometimes conflicted with the need
to maintain the requisite depth in the communications' channels for the use
of transport barges.

statesmen that if taxation is to be collected in kind, the strength of empire will depend on efficient distribution; and the government has perforce been concerned with establishing and maintaining the means of transport under its own control.

Attention to these matters has often been combined with a deep interest in other projects to control or utilize water, e.g. for irrigation or conservancy. As with the transport canals, so in these projects large forces of manpower have been needed for the initial construction and subsequent upkeep; and as the use of water for major schemes of transport has sometimes conflicted with parochial needs for irrigation, an overall co-ordination and direction of available labour has been essential. There has always existed an interdependence between economic stability, the exercise of effective government and the use of sufficient manpower by the state. Failure to maintain artificial waterways, or to control flood damage, may be one of the first signs of imperial weakness or the first effects of rebellion.

CHAPTER EIGHT

THE GROWTH OF CITIES

I. EARLY BEGINNINGS

The pre-imperial age

The growth of cities has depended on both economic and strategic considerations. In recent decades archaeologists have succeeded in isolating sites and identifying them as the remains of large settlements of the neolithic and bronze ages, equipped with defensive walls and designed to house the ruling families and to protect their bronze treasures. Comparatively more is known about the communal settlements of the early iron age (from *c.* 600 B.C.), but it seems that the formative stage in the development of early cities coincided with the other economic, social and political changes of the Warring States period.

The reasons why particular sites were suitable for the rise of cities before 221 B.C. have remained largely unaltered, although the localized sites of settlements may have shifted a few miles during the passage of time. The cities of pre-imperial China arose at points which suited the administrators of the new kingdoms or their defending generals; or along the natural lines of communication where communities could best engage in trade or industry. Since 221 B.C., cities have served the same purposes at the same original sites, while fresh economic ventures have necessitated the growth of new urban settlements in the Yangtse valley and beyond, or on the sea coasts; and a very recent development is the rapid growth of industrial cities in Manchuria. But despite the greater economic significance of the south during the last 1,000 years, the cities of the Great Plain and the Yellow River valley have been endowed with permanent advantages. They can boast a continuous history to the Warring States period, and have still retained a large measure of their early significance.

Early centres of government

Before an empire had been formed, cities were built to house the kings or noblemen of the smaller states, together with their courts and administrative assistants. A palace required the services of numerous attendants and an effective defence against intruders; and there grew up the walled city, surrounded by high ramparts and protected by a permanent garrison. The assembly of a non-productive court, the officials of the administration and defensive troops stimulated the growth of trade and required the support of supplies grown in the country to provide for the needs of the townsmen. In time these processes were to lead to political maturity, and, eventually, to the elimination of the small states and their replacement by a single regime. Although in imperial days government was organized from one, or sometimes two, capital cities, owing to the wide extent of the Chinese empires the towns that had acted as the capital cities of the earlier kingdoms still remained important regional centres of trade and administration.

The use of two imperial capitals
Some dynastic houses have been glad to make use of two towns as their capitals, possibly as a means of advertising their strength or displaying their pomp. There have also been realistic reasons for the practice, e.g. the alternate use of two centres in accordance with economic, political or military pressures (e.g. famine or invasion). There may also have been ethnic reasons for a non-Chinese regime to retain an acknowledged seat of authority in an area that lay beyond the Chinese pale, whence their own followers had originated. Thus, the capital city of the T'ang emperors was situated sometimes in Ch'ang-an, sometimes Lo-yang; and the Ch'ing court, which started by maintaining a base in Mukden, also possessed a summer palace in Jehol, where a refuge could be found from political turmoil until the very last days of the dynasty, whose principal palace was in Peking.

The many small towns of the empire
Small towns, possibly of some 5,000 inhabitants, have grown up in most of the 1,500–2,000 prefectures of the Chinese empires. Originally they may have acted as the seat of the local official and his small staff; or they may have emerged in obvious centres where roads and rivers meet, where goods may be safely stored and exchanged, or where minerals were known to lie below the earth's crust. These country towns, whose number can be estimated at between 1,000 and 3,000, have been more characteristic of town life in China than the very few cities which have played a significant role in the cultural or political

development of the country, and which therefore feature more fully in Chinese writings. But owing to the nature of the evidence and the limitations of space, we are necessarily concerned here with those few cities of China that are much larger and that have acted as dynastic capitals, commercial centres or international emporia.

The regional growth of cities

From the Warring States period, major towns have sprung up along those stretches of the Yellow River which are safe from flood (Lo-yang, P'u-yang), or in the deep recesses of the natural fortresss of the north-west (Ch'ang-an, Hsien-yang). They have been built in the Shan-tung peninsula to serve the needs of an active trade and industry (Lin-tzu) and in the rich valley of the Huai River and its tributaries (P'eng-ch'eng, Junan). Other cities have long existed in the south-west (Ch'eng-tu, Chungking) and on the banks of the Yangtse (Chiang-ling, Ho-fei). With the shift of economic emphasis that is perhaps to be dated from the T'ang period, the southern cities began to rival those of the north, and maritime trade stimulated the prosperity of towns such as Canton or, by the thirteenth century, Ch'üan-chou or Fu-chou. Cities of the lower Yangtse valley were sometimes founded as centres of the southern regimes that existed in times of political disunity, but their development as thriving centres of a prosperous trade dates from the latter half of the imperial age. Ports such as Amoy, Shanghai and Tientsin are largely the products of the late nineteenth or twentieth centuries, whose growth was stimulated by Europeans under the Treaty-port system. Twentieth century developments are seen in the industrial cities of Manchuria.

Changes of site and name

In choosing the sites for their cities, the Chinese have sought to exploit natural advantages such as protection from invader or flood, or a ready supply of water. If cities have been destroyed or depopulated, official attempts at resettlement have been made either in the same locality or at a short distance (a mile or two) from the original site. Such removals are perhaps to be ascribed to the stern needs of communications or economy; or they may have been prompted by the need to found a larger city than the predecessor. Sometimes the choice of a new site has been represented as being due to a geomancer's advice, so as to avoid the displeasure of those supernatural beings who control the fortunes of local inhabitants. Alternately, the appeasement of these powers has been achieved by changing a city's name. Such changes were also made so as to provide a new centre with felicitous association, or almost as a slogan with which to advertise the hopes and intentions of a new dynasty.

II. CHARACTERISTIC FEATURES

Planned cities and the spontaneous growth of towns

Some of the best-known Chinese cities were purposely planned so as to confirm with a specific design; but the great majority have come into being naturally as a result of increasingly active human occupations. Sometimes, a plan which was originally imposed to suit the needs of defence or administration has restricted urban development along natural lines; sometimes the original features of a city's design have been obscured by later spontaneous extensions. In general the planned cities were built in answer to dynastic needs or with the deliberate intention of founding new centres of habitation or administration; and the cities that have grown up naturally owe their origins and prosperity to private enterprise.

Planned cities came into being if a new dynasty wished to establish a new seat of government free from the baleful influences or traditional associations of its predecessor; towns arose, or were extended, spontaneously so as to accommodate the larger numbers that came to be engaged in industry, commerce or communications; and in building both types, full advantage was taken of the predominant natural features of hill or water supply. The unplanned towns testify to the growth of material prosperity, and there is no basic distinction to be drawn between the towns of this type that were built in China or elsewhere in East Asia. But the planned city of China perhaps symbolizes some of the formal aspects of Chinese civilization and expresses Confucian ideas in a material form. As the planned cities are characteristic of Chinese civilization, and have been imitated in other countries of the Far East, they deserve greater attention than the more numerous towns that have grown up naturally. In the following pages an attempt will be made to describe some of the general features of the planned city, before considering a few examples.

Defensive walls

Before the formation of empire, cities were built as fortified strongholds, enclosed within two sets of concentric walls. These were usually

9. THE KUANG-AN GATE, PEKING, ABOUT 1939

Photograph from *Peking to kamera* (Kokka shoten, Peking, 1939). The scene shows a street in Peking, looking inwards from one of the gates on the west side of the city. The arrangement of an inner and outer wall, which is partly retained here, can be traced to before the imperial period. In the foreground a female figure wears her hair in a queue; this Manchu custom was imposed on Chinese males after the Manchu dynasty was founded (1644) and compliance became obligatory until 1911. Between the two walls a *fen-fu*, or sewage collector, is seen making his way into the city.

10. THE GREAT WALL

Views of the wall near Pa-ta-ling, north of Peking. Photographs by S. Takaya, Kyoto, 1960. The present structure, which dates from the Ming period (1368–1643) has recently been restored in its original style.

built in square or rectangular fashion, and the wide intermediate spaces between the walls were reserved for cultivation, without buildings. Privileged inhabitants jealously guarded the right of cultivation there, in view of the obvious advantages of working productive land that lay within the safe keeping of the ramparts; but the main importance of these plots lay in their potential use at a time of siege, which could be withstood by a defender just as long as his supplies lasted. The defensive walls were built to form a massive protection, impenetrable by wild beast or enemy forces. By the Warring States period, cities were acting as the safe depositories of treasure (bronze, gold and jade) manufactures (iron-made tools and weapons) or raw materials (grain and cloth) and constituted valuable military objectives. Many of the recorded exploits of arms of these centuries were concerned with the siege and capture of towns rather than with destroying enemy forces on the field of battle.

Access to travellers, and water supplies
Gates were placed at regular intervals along the walls to permit access to travellers, and imposing towers flanked the gateways, so that traffic could be effectively controlled. In addition the walls may have been pierced to allow passage to controlled waterways, which were led naturally or artificially from nearby sources. A favourite stratagem adopted by a besieging army to hasten the fall of a city lay in interfering with these arrangements. Either the main source of water could be diverted, so that the parched defenders were forced to surrender; or the dykes that ran along the major source could be breached in such a way that the city would be flooded.

The grid-plan
Some of these features were retained in the cities of the early empires, but accurate or precise information is not available. By the sixth century A.D. the form of the planned city had been crystallized, elaborated and applied to a far more sophisticated way of life. Further attention will be paid below (see p. 233) to the noble city of Ch'ang-an (modern Sian), built by the Sui and T'ang emperors to house the palace and the administration, but the city must first serve as an example of a type for general consideration. For Ch'ang-an was planned as a rectangular walled city, set square to face the four directions of the compass. Broad, straight streets ran up and down or across the city at set intervals; and the city was thus divided, chequer-board fashion, into small rectangular

P

units. These units usually formed residential sections, or wards, each one being bounded by its own walls, which were considerably lower than those of the city's perimeter. Entrance to the ward was controlled by gateways, placed regularly on each of the four sides, and giving access to the main lanes that traversed the interior of the ward. These lanes were wide enough to accommodate mounted riders, and they ran from north to south or east to west, so that they were directly parallel with the main streets of the city. Minor lanes which divided the ward yet further were probably not so straight or regular. Although houses and gardens reached to the external wall of the ward, only the most highly privileged families were permitted access to their homes from the main streets.

Control and isolation

The grid-plan on which Ch'ang-an was built enabled authority to control the inhabitants, who were forbidden to walk the main streets once the curfew had tolled. It was also possible to isolate special areas for private or non-residential purposes, to accommodate the imperial palaces, the offices of the government, market-places, military barracks or temples. Such sites were usually placed symmetrically; and the market-places, which were subject to official supervision, also comprised meeting places where exhibitions or entertainments could be held. Some of the wards were reserved for special groups of inhabitants, e.g. foreign traders, diplomatic missions, or that glamorous class of females to whom the Chinese were wont to repair for artistic entertainments or other forms of relaxation.

Compromise between design and spontaneity

The T'ang city of Ch'ang-an was the classic example of a city that was built on a grid-plan. Between this type and the contrasting examples of towns that grew up naturally without official planning, there exist intermediate cases in which some of the features of the planned city were incorporated. Areas were sometimes reserved for particular types of residence; or across the irregular pattern of crooked streets and lanes, wide straight avenues were laid out, lined by trees to form a highway fit for imperial progress.

Hangchow or Lin-an, where the southern Sung court fixed its capital (1136) was a compromise between the two types. The town had been built with defensive ramparts, and the extensions outside derived from individual initiative. Although the city was partly adapted to meet imperial needs in the thirteenth century, there could be no question of re-building it entirely in grid fashion; and the demands of a fast develop-ing society and economy gave rise to certain changes naturally. As has been noted above (see p. 213) the establishment of a few select market places was giving way to the dispersal of shops throughout the city; places of entertainment were being built where townsmen could enjoy their leisure; wharves and warehouses were fast being constructed to serve the needs of the trader and his customer.

A compromise of a different type is seen in Peking, where a city has probably existed since the Warring States period. The modern city comprises two parts, of which the northern one (designed in the Yüan period and later) is an excellent example of a city built on a grid-plan, set to face the south and bounded by thick defensive walls; but im-mediately to the south of this city there lies the second section, also walled, and rectangular, but crossed by the irregular streets and narrow lanes that satisfy the needs of a growing population.

Foreign examples of the grid-plan city
The example of Ch'ang-an, specially designed to advertise dynastic prestige and to express the formalism of Chinese culture, was shortly to be copied by foreign imitators. It was used as a model for the capital cities that were built in Japan, where a new degree of national unity was being attained in the seventh century. These cities were laid out at Nara (in 710) and Hei-an (from 793), which is better known under its modern name of Kyoto. At the outset, Kyoto was planned on too grandiose a scale, and the failure to occupy the whole city resulted in the early decay of its western half. By contrast, the modern city, which boasts a population of 1,500,000, has been extended far beyond the original limits as these were conceived; but the rectangular layout of the main streets and lesser lanes still characterizes this stately town. The influence of Chinese design can also be traced in other cities of neighbouring countries.

The lack of municipal arrogance or power
The Chinese city has developed somewhat differently from its counter-part in Europe. Until recently there has been little sense of municipal pride or privilege, and no concept of municipal self-government. If a city has been fortunate enough to be chosen as the capital of the empire, its inhabitants have been happy to pride themselves on their good fortune. The proximity of the palace and the court has been

sufficient to attract local loyalties and to detract from a distinct or rival sense of communal unity. Elsewhere, if commerce has played the dominant role in the growth of a town, individual residents have trusted to specialized professional groups, i.e. the guilds, to watch their interests, rather than to any representations they could make to a power-ful municipal authority. With some notable exceptions, special organs of government were rarely introduced to administer the large communities of the towns, which have remained as constituent members of the prefectural or provincial units. In view of the nature of Chinese society and the prestige of service in the central government, municipal leadership was not an ambition to which men of distinction would aspire. Municipal independence or pride failed to develop until very recently, and the loyalties of Chinese cities of the imperial age hardly constituted a crucial factor in determining the fate of a dynasty.

III. ASPECTS OF A FEW CITIES

It is not possible, nor would it be wholly representative, to trace the history of a particular major city throughout the imperial age, and the very great varieties of time and space preclude any appreciation of a general nature. In the following pages an attempt will be made to note the conspicuous or characteristic features of a few cities that have drawn the attention of Chinese writers or foreign visitors. The cities chosen for consideration are Ch'ang-an (in the Han period), Lo-yang (Han to T'ang), Ch'ang-an (T'ang), Canton (T'ang to Ch'ing), Lin-an (Sung) and Peking (Yüan to Ch'ing).

Ch'ang-an in the Han period
The somewhat questionable facts and figures that are given in Chinese sources for the size of Ch'ang-an are being supplemented by recently found archaeological evidence, but there is still much that is unknown about the city. The decision to establish the Han capital at this site was taken after due consideration of the rival claims of Lo-yang, and it was only from 194 B.C. that the work of building defensive walls was put in hand. Large forces of labour, possibly amounting to over 140,000 men, were engaged on the work during the following years, sometimes for periods of no more than a month at a time. A somewhat dubious source relates that the walls were designed to rise to a height of 35 feet[1] from a width, at base, of 15 feet, and that they were tapered

---

[1] I.e. Han feet. The Han foot measured c. 10½ inches (23 cm)

so as to measure 9 feet wide at the summit; but the remains of walls that have been dated in the early Han period show that these were much wider, measuring some 16 metres (or 60 Han feet) at base. Each of the massive gates which gave entry to the city was built with three passage ways; in one instance, these three were separated from each other by a distance of 4 metres, and each was some 8 metres wide.

While the eastern, and perhaps the western, wall was built in an uninterrupted straight line, the other two sides were somewhat less regular, as they included indentations and excrescences. But the city was basically of square shape; it was set directly to face the four points of the compass, and was divided by some eight or nine principal streets that ran from north to south or east to west. These were laid out with sufficient breadth to accommodate twelve mounted men riding abreast, and were lined with decorative trees to shade the traveller. Restrictions imposed on the use of one of these avenues—the Imperial Highway—forbade the general public to enter; and it is related that even the Crown Prince was once forced to make a detour, to avoid infringing the ban. The main course of the Wei River flowed in an easterly direction outside and parallel with the northern side of Ch'ang-an. Small tributaries, which were similarly situated on the eastern and western sides, were connected by a channel that was led through the walls to traverse the lower part of the city.

Imperial residences

Nine authorized market places were established within or slightly without Ch'ang-an; but the most conspicuous features of the Western Han capital were its palaces, set arbitrarily in and among the residential districts. Each palace comprised a set of buildings made to house the emperor or a leading member of his family such as his mother or his son (the Crown Prince). A double wall enclosed the palace grounds, wherein audience halls, repositories for books or treasures, and domestic quarters were arrayed in symmetrical, or at least formal, fashion. Entrance to the palaces was made by way of imposing and highly decorated vestibules and gateways; these were sometimes named with grandiloquent titles, chosen to evoke the moral precepts of Confucian teaching; or they were known after their function, e.g. 'The gate of the southern guards'; and sometimes their titles followed local features, e.g. the 'Gate of the gilded steeds', so-called after the bronze figures of horses that had been erected nearby. A straight road

229

led due north from the main entrance of the palace grounds, and visitors were conducted through courtyards and up stairways, until they finally reached the audience chamber, where the emperor sat enthroned, facing directly to the south.

The Wei-yang palace

With the exception of the founder, all the emperors of the Western Han dynasty resided in the Wei-yang palace, which was situated in the south-western corner of the city. An early text gives the dimensions and describes the elaborate nature of the very wide audience hall that had been built as part of this palace during the time of the emperor Wu ti (141–87). '. . . magnolia wood had been used to make the ridge-poles and rafters, and decorated apricot wood for the beams and pillars. Golden clasps held securing rings, on doors studded with jade, and rings of jade were suspended from the gay struts of the roof. Chased columns rested on base-plates of jade, and the hall was divided by a set of horizontal rails that were formed of carved poles. The gateway and porch were richly engraved and decorated, the one in blue and the other in scarlet; and the approach-way was divided into two parts, with steps on the left and a ramp on the right. Battens of gold [ran along the walls ?], carrying here and there the finest jades and gems, ready to tinkle in the breeze. . . .'

This somewhat fanciful description cannot be corroborated directly. Remnants of the Han palaces include carved decorative pieces made of white stone rather than jade, and fragments of plaster walls that had been brightly painted. Numerous semi-circular tiles used in roofing have been found both at the site of Han Ch'ang-an and elsewhere. These half-cylinders were closed at the end by a full circular medallion, embossed with decorative designs or with the characters of contemporary slogans praising the achievements of the Han emperor or praying for his eternal felicity.

An emperor's pleasure-grounds

Beyond the western wall of the Han city of Ch'ang-an lay the imperial pleasure-ground, which included artificial lakes and waterways, and hillocks topped by multi-storey towers. In this extensive parkland were kept the specimens of foreign beasts or birds submitted for the imperial delectation from foreign parts, and which were maintained to enhance the splendour of the imperial court.

The site also included a further set of palace buildings, whose construction was started in 104 B.C. Of the settlements that have been built on this site in the twentieth century, one bears the name of the 'Encampment of the Twin Phoenixes'; and two mounds that lie to the east of this village have been identified as parts of the northern gateway of the Han palace. Originally, this rose to a height of 175 feet (Han), and it was surmounted by a pair of phoenixes cast in bronze. The site of one of the Han ornamental lakes can also be identified.

The life of the slums
Literary descriptions of Ch'ang-an fail to mention the seamy side of the life of a great capital city that flourished in the Western Han period. There are no references to the slums, where the great majority of the inhabitants lived in primitive hovels, and which may even have flanked the Imperial Way. We do not know how rigorously public order was maintained, or with what degree of cruelty the laws were imposed. Nor do we know what facilities existed for the conduct of daily life; how living accommodation, or supplies of necessities could be acquired; how the dead were disposed of; or what arrangements existed for sewerage. We can only assume, on the basis of conditions which existed in Chinese cities in later ages, that the population included a high proportion of vagabonds and beggars, and that many of the inhabitants spent their lives in conditions of filth and squalor, disease and misery.

Lo-yang as a capital city and a religious centre
With the restoration of the Han dynasty's authority in A.D. 25, the decision was taken to move the capital city to Lo-yang, which lay some 200 miles to the east, on the south side of the Yellow River. Again, the choice of a capital city had not been undisputed; but the advantages of Lo-yang, with its traditional evocations of the Chou period and the benefit of its easier communications, outweighed the value of the natural defences which enclosed Ch'ang-an. The move involved the transfer of the court, and the bulky records of government, which had been written on wooden strips, were transported to their new home by the cart-load. Lo-yang was used as the capital city by a number of dynastic houses between the first and tenth centuries; and the precise site, together with the style of the city, has been changed on several occasions.

While Ch'ang-an's importance lay in its use as the centre of the first permanent empire of China and as an advertisement of the authorized form of government, part of Lo-yang's significance lay in the welcome that it gave to Buddhism, and the splendid buildings whence the message of the faith was propagated. Lo-yang was not only one of the first towns at which an organized religious community is known to have been founded (from at least the middle of the second century); it remained a centre of Buddhism during the succeeding centuries, supported at times by the patronage of the court. Certainly the large number of Buddhist temples formed as conspicuous features of Lo-yang as had the imperial palaces of Ch'ang-an.

An early Buddhist temple

A sixth century account of the famous Buddhist establishments of Lo-yang, which is open to some statistical exaggeration, opens with a description of the Temple of Eternal Rest, built in 516. There was a timber-built tower, or pagoda, constructed in nine storeys and rising to a height of 900 [sic] feet. A finial added a further 100 feet to the building, which was visible at a distance of 100 li [i.e. some 30 miles] from the city. When the builders began digging to lay the foundations, they came across a large number of golden statues. The empress dowager, who was sponsoring the erection of the temple, took this event as proof of her faith, and proceeded to plan a building that would be more elaborate than any yet seen. Above the finial there was suspended a golden vessel large enough to contain 25 full measures of liquid; and below the vessel there were no less than thirty golden dishes, laid one on top of the other and designed to catch the falling dews. Golden bells hung down on all sides, and the finial was locked to the main tower by four iron hawsers. These were surmounted at the four corners by more golden bells, each the size of a full measure. Further bells were hung to adorn the nine stages of the tower, so that in all the structure boasted no less than 120 bells.

The tower was four-sided; each side was pierced by three doors and six windows, painted with scarlet lacquer. Over these apertures there were arrayed five rows of golden fastenings, so that the twelve doors and twenty-four windows were adorned with a total of 5,400 such pieces. Chased golden rings were held by bosses which were shaped in the form of animals' heads. 'There can be no finer examples of the craftsman's skill or the designer's art, and the extent to which this Buddhist temple was decorated defies the imagination. The rich ornamentation of the pillars and golden bosses was little less than startling; when the winds rose up during the long stillnesses of the night, the bells tinkled and reverberated in harmony, and the sound of their chimes could be heard at a distance of ten *li* or more.'

Ch'ang-an in the T'ang period

In 582 the newly established Sui dynasty readopted Ch'ang-an as the capital city of the empire. A new site was chosen, lying to the south-east of the Han city, so as to provide greater scope for the large number of buildings that were planned. In addition it was hoped that a more plentiful supply of water would be available, and that the new dispensation would avoid undue association with the earlier regimes that had been settled in Ch'ang-an. The new city, which was further developed by the T'ang emperors, was designed in the light of new concepts of grandeur and spaciousness. The area within the four straight walls of the perimeter included stretches of spare unoccupied land that was left free of buildings; an ornamental lake was laid out in the extreme south-east corner, and the supplies of water were so contrived that springs and streams could be used decoratively to enhance the beauty of landscape or garden. The main streets were broader than those of the Han city; palaces and offices were grouped together in the northern quarter, instead of the less regular dispersal of earlier days.

But above all a new degree of symmetry was attained by the city planners. The systematic design of eleven main streets running from north to south and fourteen from east to west resulted in the formation of 108 residential wards,[1] in addition to those areas which were set aside to accommodate palaces, government buildings, and market-places. When the T'ang emperors sat facing the south to receive their servants in audience, the whole city lay stretched out at their feet. The vertical axis which split Ch'ang-an into equally sized eastern and western halves ran for some six kilometres from the palace gates to the Gate of Brilliant Virtue, which stood at the central point of the southern wall. To the left and right of the audience chamber, the courts and halls of the palace were laid out to match one another in symmetrical arrangement, and so to give physical expression to that idea of a balanced cosmos on which Confucian society and polity rested.

[1] See pp. 225 f above.

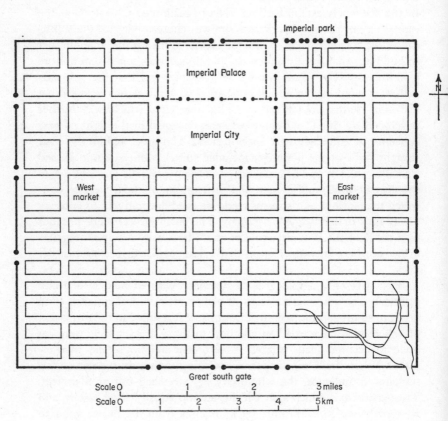

Ch'ang-an under the T'ang Dynasty

Ninth century Canton

While the administrative centre of T'ang government lay at Ch'ang-an or Lo-yang, other cities were fast developing a new state of prosperity. Since the Han period, a settlement had existed on the site of Canton, almost at the southern extremity of the empire, and often acting as the first port of call where sea-borne foreigners encountered Chinese authority. A recent author has described the main features of the T'ang city in vivid terms[1]:

But of all the cities of the south, and of all the towns where foreign merchants congregated, none was more prosperous than the great port of Canton, the Khanfu of the Arabs, the 'China' of the Indians. Canton was then a frontier town, on the edge of a tropical wilderness populated by savages and wild beasts, and plagued with unpleasant diseases, but handsomely set among lichees, oranges, bananas, and banyans. During the reigns of the T'ang emperors it became a truly Chinese city, even though a large part of its population of 200,000 was 'barbarian'. It was a wealthy city, but a flimsy one: its triple wall surrounded a crowded mass of thatch-roofed wooden houses, which were repeatedly swept by disastrous fires, until, in 806, an intelligent governor ordered the people to make themselves roofs of tile. In the estuary before this colourful and insubstantial town were ' . . . the argosies of the Brahmans, the Persians, and the Malays, their number beyond reckoning, all laden with aromatics, drugs, and rare and precious things, their cargoes heaped like hills'. In exchange for their fragrant tropical woods and their almost legendary medicines, these dark outlanders sought bales of silk, boxes of chinaware, and slaves. They enriched the Chinese businessmen who were willing to give up the comforts of the north for the profits of the south, and made possible the high state of the governor of the town and province, ' . . . who carries six yaktails, with an army for each yaktail, and who in his majesty and dignity is not to be distinguished from the Son of Heaven'.

Many of these visitors settled in the foreign quarter of Canton, which by imperial sanction was set aside south of the river for the convenience of the many persons of diverse race and nationality who chose to remain in Canton to do business or to wait for favour-

---

[1] Edward H. Schafer, *The Golden Peaches of Samarkand*, Berkeley and Los Angeles, 1963, pp. 14f. Citations derive from an account of the city which was written by a Buddhist priest in 748.

able winds. . . . Here, in short, foreigners of every complexion, and Chinese of every province, summoned by the noon drum, thronged the great market, plotted in the warehouses, and haggled in the shops, and each day were dispersed by the sunset drum to return to their respective quarters or, on some occasions, to chaffer loudly in their outlandish accents in the night markets.

Canton and foreign trade

But like other cities, Canton has known its hours of sorrow. In the course of a rebellion launched against the T'ang dynasty, the city was besieged and finally captured (878), with catastrophic results for its foreign community. According to a contemporary description by Abū Zaid of Sīrāf, 120,000 Moslems, Christians and Jews were massacred, and the lights of this glamorous city were extinguished at a single blow. But by the thirteenth century Canton had partly regained its position as a prosperous international emporium, and was eventually to attract the commercial instincts of European seamen. By the end of the eighteenth century, a British government was seeking means to persuade the Chinese authorities to relax some of the restrictions against foreign traders and thus to increase the possibilities of further ventures. It was for this reason that a mission was sent to secure an audience with the Ch'ien-lung emperor under the leadership of Lord Macartney, who arrived at Canton in December 1793. His journal includes the following references to the city (entries for January 2–7, 1794)[1]:

As none of the gentlemen of our Factory had ever been within the city of Canton, except the Commissioners, when they went to deliver the Chairman's letter announcing my intended Embassy, I had a strong curiosity to see it. I entered it at the great watergate and traversed it from one end to the other. It covers a great extent of ground and is said to contain a million of inhabitants. This account may possibly exaggerate. . . . The streets are narrow and flat paved, much resembling those of Hangchowfu. No wheel carriages are admitted, not did I see any horses in the town except those which my servants rode upon. It is full of shops and trades, and has in general a gloomy appearance, except in two or three large open squares, where the Viceroy and other great men reside.

All the people seemed very busily employed, chiefly in making

[1] J. L. Cranmer-Byng (ed.), *An Embassy to China*, Longmans, 1962, pp. 209f.

either silk boots or straw bonnets, in the working of metals, and the labours of the forge, and most of them wore spectacles on their noses. The walls are kept in good repair, but no guns are mounted on them. The ordinary troops here, instead of a blue uniform and red lace as elsewhere, are clothed in red with a blue lace. . . .

Macartney refers elsewhere to the duties raised by the Chinese government on foreign merchandise and the corrupt state of the local administration at Canton. He was struck by the skill of the Chinese goldsmiths, metal-workers and glaziers of the city, and the prevalence of veneral disease. He was also impressed with the efficiency and speed of the courier service which conveyed express letters from Peking to the provincial authorities.

The temporary capital of Lin-an (Hangchow)

Lin-an is known more widely under its modern name of Hang-chou, or its earlier courtesy title of Kinsai or Quinsai. Until the twelfth century it had grown up as a small provincial city lying beyond the range of major dynastic events or upheavals. The town possessed good natural defences, as low lying marshes prevented easy access by hostile forces, and it was perhaps for this reason that it was chosen as a refuge for the emperor and court when north China was overrun and the Sung dynasty was driven from its capital of K'ai-feng (1126–7). For long the fiction was maintained that Lin-an was no more than a temporary resting place, favoured by the emperor for a short sojourn, and little attempt was made to adapt the existing provincial buildings for the more splendid purposes of a central government; but by the middle of the thirteenth century, Lin-an had been greatly expanded and was fulfilling its purpose as the capital of an enlightened empire and the centre of a prosperous trade.

The situation and form of Lin-an

Of all the capital cities of the Chinese empires, Lin-an has been admired as the one that is most beautifully situated. The town had been built on the north bank of the river Che, whose main course protected the southern and eastern sides. To the west a large artificial lake had been constructed, mainly to ensure that a plentiful supply of fresh water was available. The lake was divided by a series of dykes, and was studded by a few islands which were crowned by an occasional ornamental building. The hills surrounding the lake feature in many of the paintings which the city has inspired from the Sung period and later. The ramparts which delineated the city boundary had been built in several stages; gateways provided travellers with easy access, and five water-gates allowed the major canals to flow in and out of the city. There was no regular grid-plan in Hangchow that can be compared with that of Ch'ang-an, although the city was partly reconstructed to suit the needs of the court. The Imperial Way was built to run the length of the city from north to south, and measured some 60 metres in width; lesser roads crossed it at intervals, and a series of canals criss-crossed the suburban parts of the city on the northern, southern and eastern sides.

Conditions of overcrowding

By the middle of the thirteenth century a population of some 1,000,000 inhabitants was pressed within an area that measured less than 4 by 2 miles. To meet the current need, Chinese builders had introduced a bold innovation, in the many multi-storeyed houses which were speedily rising in timber. In the prevailing shortage of accommodation many of these houses, or parts of them, were occupied on a leasehold basis, the rents being paid either to private landlords or to officials of the state. Overcrowding resulted in an acute danger of fire, and the effects of epidemic disease were widespread. However, the society and government of the thirteenth century was sufficiently well organized to devise counter-measures of a sort. A highly developed fire-fighting organization which was run under official auspices excited the attention of a foreign traveller who visited the city after it had fallen into Mongol hands (i.e. between 1276 and 1292). This was Marco Polo, whose journey had been inspired by religious motives and the love of exploration, and whose travelogue has profoundly influenced the European conception of the Far East. Marco Polo's account was subject to exaggeration, owing to his desire to impress his audience and readers; and there is considerable repetition in a mass of detailed observation that was not particularly scrupulous or critical. Luckily, many of his statements regarding the life that was led in Lin-an or in other parts of China can be confirmed or tested by other evidence.

Public services and necessities

In addition to the public arrangements which were made to combat fire, the authorities of Lin-an provided a service for the collection of garbage. Care was taken to prevent the pollution of fresh water supplies and to maintain as high a standard of hygiene as was possible or could be imagined. Throughout the city canals were used for transport. Some of these were as wide as 30 feet, and could accommodate two laden barges riding abreast. Small craft were used to carry passengers around the city; and in a few of the city's streets, the richer residents rode on horseback or in carriages, or were borne around in sedan chairs. Marco Polo admired with envy the liberal use that had been made of stone and brick in paving the city's streets, and the large number of bridges where the city's water traffic was sometimes congested.

To feed Lin-an's population it was necessary to import several hundred tons of rice into the city daily, and to slaughter a large number of pigs. Retail shops sprang up in areas that were most convenient, e.g. the rice market was situated near the quays where rice was unloaded, and the butcher's shops lay near to the slaughter houses. Elsewhere in the city, shops were opened to facilitate a more direct distribution of goods to the residents.

The comforts of the rich
A large proportion of the inhabitants of Lin-an was engaged in providing for the luxuries of its wealthier citizens. These could dine in any one of many types of restaurant which existed to satisfy a taste for the exotic; and they could idle away their time in tavern or tea-house, or in the bath-houses which were run as commercial ventures. Parks were laid out for the open-air enjoyment of nature's beauties; and in the special centres of amusement, a man could take lessons in music, dancing or drama, or enjoy the performances of acrobats or other entertainers. Perhaps the last word on this prosperous and sophisticated city and its material excesses should be left to Marco Polo's enthusiastic if unreliable narrative:[1]

There are ten principal market-places, not to speak of innumerable local ones. These are square, being half a mile each way. In front of them lies a main thoroughfare, forty paces wide, which runs straight from one end of the city to the other. It is crossed by many bridges, carefully designed to avoid sharp inclines. And every four miles there is one of these squares, with a circumference, as stated, of two miles. Correspondingly there is a very wide canal, which runs along the side of the squares opposite to the thoroughfare. On the nearer

[1] R. E. Latham, *The Travels of Marco Polo*, Penguin Classics 1958, pp. 185f.

bank of this are constructed large stone buildings, in which all the merchants who come from India and elsewhere store their wares and merchandise, so that they may be near and handy to the market squares. And in each of these squares, three days in the week, there is a gathering of 40,000 to 50,000 people, who come to market bringing everything that could be desired to sustain life. There is always abundance of victuals, both wild game, such as roebuck, stags, harts, hares and rabbits, and of fowls, such as partridges, pheasants, francolins, quails, hens, capons, and as many ducks and geese as can be told; for so many are reared in the lake that for a silver groat of Venice you may have a brace of geese or a brace of ducks. Then there are the shambles, where they slaughter the bigger animals, such as calves, oxen, kids, and lambs, whose flesh is eaten by the rich and the upper classes. The others, the lower orders, do not scruple to eat all sorts of unclean flesh.

Among the articles regularly on sale in these squares are all sorts of vegetables and fruits, above all huge pears, weighting 10 lb. apiece, white as dough inside and very fragrant, and peaches in season, yellow and white, which are great delicacies. Grapes and wine are not produced locally; but raisins of excellent quality are imported from other ports and so too is wine, though the inhabitants do not set much store by this, being accustomed to the wine made of rice and spices. Every day a vast quantity of fish is brought upstream from the ocean, a distance of twenty-five miles. There is also abundance of lake fish, varying in kind according to the season, which affords constant employment for fishermen who have no other occupation. Thanks to the refuse from the city, these fish are plump and tasty. Seeing the quantity on sale, you would imagine they could never be disposed of. But in a few hours the whole lot has been cleared away—so vast are the numbers of those accustomed to dainty living, to the point of eating fish and meat at one meal. All the ten squares are surrounded by high buildings, and below these are shops in which every sort of craft is practised and every sort of luxury is on sale, including spices, gems, and pearls. In some shops nothing is sold but spiced rice wine, which is being made all the time, fresh and fresh, and very cheap.

Imperial Peking

The northern section of Peking still retains part of the formal layout of the thirteenth century city, which was built as a capital for the

THE GROWTH OF CITIES

Mongol emperors on a site where cities had long stood and grown in importance. The grid-plan of the Yüan builders was closely followed by the Ming emperors who rebuilt the city and renovated the Palace buildings in splendid style to suit their imperial majesty. Waggon loads of a specially chosen marble were brought a distance of 1,500 miles from Yün-nan, and this precious material was used to renew and extend the palace and to clothe the city's roads and bridges with a fresh dignity and beauty. The marble was chosen to particularly fine effect; in the summer it appears to absorb the strong sunlight and to instil brightness without glare; its rich creamy colour offsets the dull oxblood red with which many of the plaster walls of the streets were coated.

The plan of Peking and its features
The city was planned in a series of concentric rectangles. Within the main walls of the perimeter there lies the enclave of the Imperial City, bordered by its own walls and comprising ornamental lakes, parks and the Forbidden City itself. High walls and a moat protected this inner enclosure and its honoured denizen from the malicious influences of the outside world. As in the earlier examples of imperial cities, the buildings were arrayed on a symmetrical plan. The palace faced due south and included a whole range of audience halls and domestic quarters, approached through a long series of wide courts and richly decorated stairways. Throughout the Forbidden City marble balustrades and pillars lent the courts form, dignity and serenity.

Artificial lakes had been dug in the imperial city, and the soil that had been excavated was piled up to form a hillock, directly to the rear of the Forbidden City. From the summit, Peking appeared more like a vast parkland crossed by noble avenues than as an artificial creation of habitations, lanes and busy streets. The eye was struck immediately by the gay roofs of the palace buildings, fashioned in different colours and demonstrating the high standards of the Ming and Ch'ing glaziers and potters. Stupas of an earlier age; stone towers erected to house the drums and bells with which authority sounded the curfew and alarm; a high platform used for observation of the heavenly bodies; and the richly lacquered gateways that stood at the entrance of the main streets formed conspicuous features of China's last imperial capital.

Tree-lined streets were laid out on a strictly rectilinear plan, so that the principal avenues led directly to the gates of the city wall. The central artery, starting from the centre of the palace, was extended

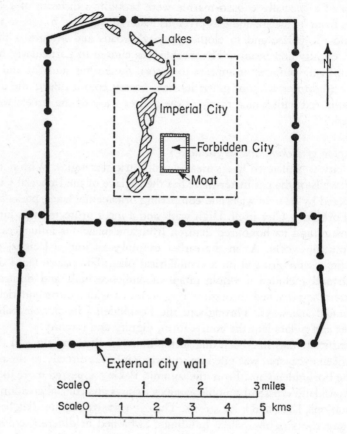

Peking; the Ming and Ch'ing cities

beyond the Imperial City and the northern section of Peking, until it reached the central gate of the furthest wall that guarded the extreme southern side of the city. Beyond the city, roads led west to the Summer Palace, which was built as a place of retreat for the Ch'ing emperors; or to the western hills whose profile can dominate the Pekinese twilight and whose folds have long provided Buddhist monasteries with tranquil refuge from the cares of the metropolitan world.

An eighteenth century observer

Lord Macartney embarked at Spithead on September 21, 1792 to undertake his mission to the Chinese court, and he arrived at the Summer Palace on August 21, 1793. He soon removed to Peking, where more suitable and comfortable quarters were put at his disposal; and before long he set out for Jehol, where the aged emperor was in residence. The main passage of Lord Macartney's journal that refers to Peking is dated on October 7, 1793:[1]

Notwithstanding what I have observed of the wonderful populousness of this country in general yet that of Pekin seems less in proportion than that of Tientsin and some other places. Though a sight so novel as that of my Embassy drew immense crowds of the inhabitants into the streets, yet I doubt whether London would be much behind hand on any great day of ceremony. I should think that when the King went to St Paul's after his illness there were more people to be seen out of doors and at the windows where he passed along than appeared in the streets of Pekin either this afternoon when I came away or the morning when I arrived. I must not, however, forget that at Pekin one scarcely meets with any but men, as the women seldom stir abroad. The houses in China are of one story only, and in general are very closely inhabited, it being no uncommon thing for a dozen people to be crowded into one small chamber that in England would be considered as a scanty accommodation for a single person. I should think that Pekin stands on at least a third less ground than London, including Westminster and Southwark, but still it is one of the largest cities in the world, and justly to be admired for its walls and gates, the distribution of its quarters, the width and allineation of its streets, the grandeur of its triumphal arches and the number and magnificence of its palaces.

[1] J. L. Cranmer-Byng, *op. cit.*, pp. 156f.

There are two streets, each of which are scarcely less than a league in length, they are near 100 feet wide and are chiefly inhabited by merchants and traders, whose shops and warehouses are most profusely decorated with every ornament that colours, gilding and varnish can bestow. The hotels of the great are mostly situated in retired, narrow streets. The one I inhabited was near the city wall, and had not been long built. It is supposed to have cost near £100,000, and was erected by a former Hoppo[1] of Canton, who has been degraded for his crimes, and has long lain under sentence in prison. As all his fortune was forfeited to the Crown, my hotel made part of the confiscation, and we were told by one of the missionaries that the wits of Pekin had been much diverted with its being allotted for our residence, and said it was but a fair retribution as the house had been built by the Hoppo out of his extortions from our countrymen at Canton.

None of the streets are paved so that in wet weather they are covered with mud and in dry weather the dust is excessively disagreeable pervading every place and everything, but what renders it intolerably offensive is the stench with which it is attended, for though proper care is taken to have all the streets cleaned very early every morning from the filth and ordures of the preceding night, yet the odour generally continues floating in the air for the greatest part of the day.

The police is singularly strict. It is indeed stretched to an extent unknown I believe in any other city, and strongly marks the jealousy of the government, and their unceasing apprehension of danger. At night all the streets are shut up by barricadoes at each end and a guard is constantly patrolling between them so that no person can pass after a certain hour without assigning satisfactory reasons or being liable to punishment if disapproved of. A number of watchmen are also stationed at short distances who carry a rattle and every two or three minutes proclaim their vigilance by the exercise of their instruments. One or two of these guardians of the peace had their stand so near to my house that I could not sleep a wink for the first three or four nights, but by degrees I became used to the noise and grew to mind it as little as the ringing of a church bell.

Ch'ang-an, Lo-yang, K'ai-feng, Lin-an and Peking, each city has in turn served as the residence of emperor and government, beckoning

[1] Superintendent of maritime customs.

to its courts his most distinguished subjects, and housing in its
palaces and temples the most illustrious treasures of his lands. To each
city has belonged its proud moments of glory and its bitter memories
of disgrace. In 626 the citizens of Ch'ang-an could have seen their young
emperor ride out alone to face the Turkish armies, and so to impress
them with his boldness and integrity that they withdrew to leave the
city unmolested. A century later another generation of Ch'ang-an's inhabitants heard with dismay of the ignominious flight of Hsüan tsung
and his handful of favourite retainers in face of the foreign rebel's
threats. When the Tartars occupied K'ai-feng in 1126, there perished
the unique collection of books and paintings that had been diligently
and expertly preserved for the Sung emperors; and Su Sung's masterpiece of clockwork was removed to northern climes as a captive, bereft
of its skilled attendants. For nearly 1,000 years the Mandate was seated
in Peking, in whose dusty climate the ceremonies of empire were
splendidly performed with that continuity that has formed so marked
a feature of Chinese civilization; but the knell of empire was already
ringing in 1860, when foreign soldiers rudely seized the contents of
the Summer Palace and set fire to its fabric, while Peking itself lay
abandoned to its fate by its Manchu masters.

TABLE NINE
CAPITAL CITIES

Full statistics are not available to illustrate the size of all of China's capital cities,
and estimates made by modern scholars vary considerably. The round figures that
are given below can be taken as no more than a general indication; exact figures
derive from Chinese sources and must be treated with reserve (for the difficulties
of handling such statistics see pp. 188 f. above).

	Indication of area	*population* (individuals)	
Ch'ang an (Han)	the perimeter measured 26 kilometres	A.D. 2	246,000
Ch'ang-an (T'ang)	nearly 10 km. east to west over 8 km. north to south	estimates for the seventh and eighth centuries vary between 1,000,000 and 2,000,000	
Lin-an (Sung)	the area is estimated at 20 sq. km.	c. 1126 below 200,000 c. 1170 below 500,000 c. 1250 over 500,000 c. 1270 over 1,000,000	
Nanking (Ming)	the perimeter measured over 30 km.	1393	1,193,620

Peking	8 km. east	1578	706,861
(Ming	to west; 10 km.	1947	1,602,234
and later)	north to south	1953	2,768,149
	(i.e. through	1964	c. 4,000,000
	both parts of		
	the city)		

The foregoing figures can be compared with the following estimates for the capital city of Japan.

Hei-an	793	laid out to	c. 1200	not more than
(also called		measure c. 4 km		100,000
Kyoto, capital		east to west, c.		
of Japan from		5½ km. north		
793 to 1868)		to south		
			c. 1200	not more than
				100,000
	1955	c. 11 km. east	1955	1,204,084
		to west, c. 17		
		km. north to		
		south		

CHAPTER NINE

RELATIONS WITH FOREIGN PEOPLES

I. THE CHINESE CONCEPT OF OTHER PEOPLES

The assumption of superiority

Chinese statements regarding foreign peoples are highly repetitive. Both in the memorials submitted to the throne and in the decrees ordering the adoption of requisite policies, foreign tribes and peoples are described in clichés which are framed to evoke suspicion, scorn or distrust, and which assume that the more fortunate Chinese are possessed of superior qualities and gifts by right. Such references are made for deliberate purposes of propaganda and frequently leave the impression that relations between Chinese authorities and their neighbours have remained basically unchanged during two millenia of imperial history.

In this way, Chinese statesmen and philosophers have often sought to foster a belief in the individual, peerless nature of the Chinese 'nation' and society, and to demonstrate that the Chinese people and culture have remained uninfluenced by foreign invasion or doctrine. However, the myth cannot be justly maintained, as the growth of more frequent and effective contacts, and the exertion of reciprocal influences between east and west, can be traced from the early to the late empires. But the official view of foreign peoples and the conduct of foreign affairs has been less conspicuously subject to change than other aspects of government, and it was only in the middle of the nineteenth century that dramatic events forced the court of Peking to reassess its attitude and to make public acknowledgement of radical changes in its diplomatic relations.

Obsolete information

Some of the responsibility for formulating a static notion of foreign peoples lies with the compilers of the Standard Histories and their methods of description. These works show small appreciation of the qualitative distinctions of China's neighbours, and there is an overriding tendency to depict such peoples as members of a single category of barabarian tribesmen. Due notice is taken of the few natural resources which are grudgingly admitted to be at their command, of the exotic products of their distant lands and of the peculiar characteristics of their uncouth customs. Such distinctive marks were noted in the early histories in a definitive way, and repeated in later compilations without check, corroboration or revision. Once a tribe had been dubbed, say by a Han writer, as a community of head-hunters, so it would remain in the compilations of a Sui, Sung or Ming historian, who would accept his predecessors' statements and append uncritically any other information that he had acquired.

The touchstone of cultural qualities

The principal considerations whereby the Chinese have distinguished themselves from other peoples have been concerned neither with race, colour nor religion. Attention has been fixed simply on the degree of civilization, as this is illustrated by a people's behaviour and mores. Han Yü, a great literary figure of the ninth century, ascribed this principle to Confucius, for, 'When he compiled the account of the Spring and Autumn period, he treated as barbarians those leaders whose way of life followed barbarian customs; but once foreign tribes had progressed to take their place under the aegis of a Chinese empire, Confucius wrote of them as if they were members of that society'.

Han Yü wished to stress the value of Confucian ideals. He reflects the traditional Confucian pride in the existence of a single governed community, ordered in accordance with an approved, formal pattern, and taking its place in the whole cosmos under the auspices of Heaven. The Confucian view of the foreigner depends partly on the stress given to the unique nature of the earthly authority delegated to the Son of Heaven. Such authority precludes the need for or the legality of other political units, and comprises a temporal power over all members of the civilized world. From this there are excluded only those who deliberately refuse to acknowledge the superior gifts of the Son of Heaven's rule, to surrender willingly to his authority or to appreciate the intellectual and cultural benefits of his society. This view is not only expressed in Chinese writings; it is noticeable in the reactions of metropolitan officials who were relegated to provincial posts in the remote regions of the south or west, which were inhabited by unassimilated tribesmen. Such men are quick to deplore the deep contrast between the delights of a sophisticated capital city and the rough manners of the countryside; the tattooed, untutored natives are regarded as objects of disgust or pity, whose form of existence is on a lower plane than that of the Emperor's subjects.

Submission to the emperor's authority

However, according to the Confucian scheme, all members of the human race can be improved by means of education and discipline, and all barbarians who can be subjected to these processes are to be included under the imperial aegis. Thus, once a barbarian people has shown itself sufficiently well educated to appreciate the benefits of Chinese authority, it qualifies to become a full member of the empire; and it follows that a tribe which is willing to serve the Son of Heaven can expect the benefit of his protection. Amenability to the discipline of civilization can be best demonstrated by the presentation of gifts to the emperor. Such gifts are chosen partly for their intrinsic material value to the Chinese but also so as to represent the most costly objects which a remote area can produce. For the Son of Heaven is entitled to receive samples of unique or rare products of those who seek his protection, even though the immediate practical use of such commodities is not great. Subject peoples can acknowledge his authority by the payment of material tribute, whose presence at court serves to enhance the emperor's majesty and to demonstrate the universal acceptance of his title to power. It is partly for this reason that the Standard Histories, which were compiled so as to assert the authority of a dynasty, list in some detail the types of valuable produced in alien lands and submitted as tributary goods to the Chinese throne.

Tribute or trade?

These principles have necessarily been modified in the light of practice, and have sometimes served as a cloak to conceal the stern dictates of reality. The tributary system has rested on the theoretical belief that the empire is self-sufficient, requiring no products from other peoples, but willing to part with its own surplus riches to assist less fortunate mortals. In practice, the conduct of a state-sponsored trade with foreign peoples has sometimes been hidden under this guise, so that a barter exchange of Chinese silks or tea for the horses of central Asia has been described as the bestowal of imperial bounties to mark the receipt of statutory tribute.

249

The falsity of the Chinese assumption
The Confucian view of foreign peoples has been hardly tenable on those occasions when the Heavenly authority of an emperor has proved to be incapable of self-defence or survival. For long periods of imperial history, Chinese dynasties were faced with the threat of invasion by the nomad or other tribes of central Asia. In the Han period these dangers emanated from the Hsiung-nu confederacies, formed by nomad horsemen, and usually identified with the Huns who later invaded Europe. And while the Hsiung-nu were frequently able to penetrate deep into Chinese territory from the north or north-west, Tungusic tribesmen were equally ready to irrupt into the Chinese plain from the north-east. The middle empires were confronted by similar dangers, from Turkish, Uighur or Tibetan tribes; and more recently these have been replaced by sovereign confederacies riding under Mongol or Manchu leadership. On a number of occasions since 311 alien confederacies of Asiatic or Tungusic extraction have not only invaded Chinese territory, but have successfully established their own regime, whose authority has remained in dominant occupation for lengthy periods. In this way the moral strength possessed or boasted by the Chinese has been of scant succour against the stronger horsemen of the uncivilized barbarian; and the value of the superior civilization claimed by Confucian thought has proved to be of little practical avail in the face of violence.

The failure of cultural superiority
In the process of restoring Chinese temporal authority after a period of foreign domination, it was often found necessary to compromise with the ideals of Confucian thought. Whereas in theory it could still be maintained that the foreigner possessed no real powers, and could be persuaded to accord with the imperial will by the mere exercise of the emperor's qualities; in practice stern measures, backed by a show of military or diplomatic strength, were necessary to prevent his renewed incursion or to woo his friendship. But despite the compelling needs of reality, it was not until after 1860 that this contradiction was fully faced and institutional changes made to accept its implications.

Meanwhile there were other reasons, which were most evident in times of dynastic strength, why a man should doubt the theory that the civilized way of Chinese life was necessarily superior to that of the barbarian. For participation in empire involved responsible obedience to authority and the acceptance of specified obligations to the state. Beyond the provinces of the northern borders there lay the intermediate lands wherein the Chinese official could not exert his full authority, but which alien horsemen could not ravage freely. The flight of deserters from Chinese armies or fugitives from justice to seek refuge in such areas testifies to the doubts of some of the emperor's subjects regarding the superiority of his regime.

The reluctant appreciation of foreign ideas and their sponsors
The arrival, propagation and acceptance of Buddhism constituted a further threat to the Confucian distinction between the civilized Chinese and the barbarian alien. For here was a faith whose lofty ideals and ethical values had arisen beyond the pale of the emperor's lands and without the support of the Chinese language or literature. Not only had this religion received a popular welcome; it also enjoyed imperial patronage; and it was as a result of Buddhist inspiration that some Chinese were actually induced to leave the confines of the empire, to seek the texts, ideals and doctrines of an alien civilization. Moreover, the acceptance of the faith implied that reliance could be placed on the intelligence and integrity of foreigners, and that due respect must be paid to their powers of intellectual leadership. It was partly thanks to Buddhism that Chinese courts admitted the value of the foreigner, and showed themselves ready to accept his teaching. In the succeeding centuries there are conspicuous examples of the services rendered to an emperor by foreign advisers, in the interests of a more efficient imperial administration.

However, foreign talents did not often supplant native counsels, and aliens were rarely employed in situations wherein the Chinese themselves could serve in adequate strength. Perhaps the most notable use of foreigners that was made by a Chinese dynasty occurred in connection with those occupations in which Chinese competition or experience was small. Soldiers from central Asia have served as generals to command Chinese forces, in a society which scorned the military profession as uncouth; scientists from Europe have placed their gifts at the disposal of emperors whose own advisers have had less formal training in such matters or have possessed less regular encouragement for scientific experiment; and it may perhaps be significant that a pronounced use of non-Chinese talent has often occurred in the times of the alien dynasties.

The compromise of the intermediate zones

In addition to the cultural distinction that has separated the Chinese and other peoples, the Chinese have been acutely conscious of occupational differences. Their own agricultural economy has frequently been contrasted with the nomadic livelihood of the northerner or the less sophisticated ways of the southern woodsmen. The distinction has been associated with a difference of quality, as it is soon clear that agriculture leads to a settled form of existence; and this in turn soon fosters the growth of a superior civilization.

Difficulties may arise in the application of this concept. While an obvious difference exists between the Chinese farming communities of the Yellow or Huai River valleys, and the roving bands of distant Mongolia, the distinction is not so clear in the intermediate areas of the borders. For such areas have been inhabited by a varied population, and form the scene of various forms of economy. They have been peopled by Chinese who have fled from the interior and who have tried to extract a living by practising their own native agriculture in unfavourable conditions of land and climate. Alongside there have been similar attempts to farm, made by those foreigners from central Asia who have tired of a wanderer's life, and have deserted the saddle for the farmstead; and such families have been ready to accept Chinese tuition in the arts of a settled existence. But both Chinese and non-Chinese have been forced to rely on other means of existence, owing to the nature of the land; and the economy has been of a mixed nature, depending both on agriculture and stock-breeding, and the controlled use of severely limited sources of water and pasture-grounds. It is only natural that in these conditions of interdependence some cultural assimilation has taken place between the Chinese and his neighbour, and neither the cultural nor the occupational distinctions between Chinese and non-Chinese are as clear here as they are elsewhere.

The intermediate zones lying between China and central Asia have frequently figured as areas where freedom of penetration has been disputed by Chinese empires or central Asian confederacies. While the exercise of full control has rarely been achieved by a Chinese government, the areas have been subject to sporadic and localized activities of Chinese officials, soldiers and merchants.

Variable attitudes

The Chinese concept of the foreigner has rested on strictly pragmatic criteria. Certain features of other peoples have been recognized as the visible marks of a particular group of foreigners and their behaviour, but Chinese writers have been less ready to formulate a theoretical or general concept of the alien. For once a man accepts the values of Chinese civilization or pursues a Chinese occupation, he no longer deserves the scorn with which the untutored, ill-disciplined barbarians are treated. It may therefore happen that there is a lack of consistency in the description of a people, depending partly on the stage reached in the relations between its leader and the Chinese court. The savage barbarian of yesterday can easily be transformed into the submissive, tribute-bearing subject of today; and he may soon become the leader of a people to whom the Son of Heaven has joyfully extended his protection, with permission and encouragement to settle in Chinese farmlands.

A further difference arises in the treatment of a tribe to which a non-Chinese dynasty traces its ancestry. The references that are made to such a people before the dynasty's establishment are not necessarily distinguishable from those made to other aliens; but, as is only to be expected, writers who served, e.g. the Mongol or Manchu emperors, would depict their forbears (actual or alleged) in very different terms, and would avoid the use of derogatory expressions in describing their characteristics.

The occasions of foreign contacts
There can be no certainty that the status of a neighbouring people will remain constant in Chinese eyes, although the criteria whereby foreigners have been assessed have remained unaltered, and the Chinese have been quick to assert the standards which have justified their condescension. Relations with other peoples have come about thanks to the initiative of both parties, and have resulted both from official sponsorship and individual enterprise. Diplomatic or military ventures started by the Chinese have tended towards imperial expansion; but as Confucian doctrine has always stressed that sovereign rule should be exercised by precept rather than force, such ventures may often be described, explained or justified as measures necessary for the defence of the Chinese peoples. When foreigners have taken the initiative in making contact with China, their purposes have been both expansionist and missionary, and their endeavours have often infringed or limited Chinese sovereignty.

Periodically, the hungry northerners have been tempted to irrupt into the Chinese plain to secure what booty they can; or travellers have set out from Europe, stimulated by the lure of commerce to search for the precious products of the Far East. Both Chinese and non-Chinese have been responsible for promoting religious contacts. The arrival of foreign Buddhist priests in China led in time to westward excursions by Chinese, seeking treasures and scriptures for the adornment of Chinese temples or the satisfaction of Chinese emperors; and representatives of Christianity have made their way to Ch'ang-an or Peking, either to seek asylum from their persecutors, or to spread their message of goodwill, as charged by Pope or parent Order.

These contacts have been tempered by three major considerations; no immediate neighbour of China has ever boasted a native civilization of comparable splendour, strength and permanence; until the nineteenth and twentieth centuries contacts with contemporary civilizations have been slow, arduous and irregular; and in the last 2,000 years the simultaneous growth of a strong central government in China and an effective confederacy of the Asian tribes has occurred only rarely and exceptionally.

II. THE EXTENSION OF CHINESE DOMINION

The ideal behaviour of the Chou kings and the danger of Ch'in's ways

The traditional account of the relations that existed between the Chinese and other peoples before the imperial age may be subject to anachronism. It was envisaged that tributary gifts of local rarities were presented to the Chinese sovereigns in the earliest days, from the extreme south of what were later to become imperial domains; and there are many reminders that the ideal kings of remote antiquity, or of the Chou kingdom, won the loyalty of uncouth tribesmen by precept, moral quality and superior standards of living. The extension of the sphere of Chou authority in this peaceful way is emphasized in contrast to the vain attempts of the first Ch'in emperor to increase his domains by means of brute force or annexation. In particular, the Ch'in attempt (214 B.C.) to occupy parts of southern China (i.e. the area lying between Kwangtung and Vietnam) is quoted as the classic example of the folly of mounting expensive punitive campaigns of conquest. Historically, the failure of the Ch'in armies can be attributed to the difficulties of terrain and climate, the weakness of communication lines and the use of insufficient forces for the task.

The pace of Han expansion

Fuller and more accurate information is available for the Han period, and it becomes possible to assess the nature and results of Chinese foreign relations more accurately. Despite later exaggeration and idealist misinterpretation, it remains true that consolidation and active expansion formed one of the principal characteristics of Han rule. For the first eighty years of the dynasty, measures were necessarily concerned with the growth of internal strength and order, while foreign policies were defensive and passive. In this period, the process of expansion took place in the steady extension of the central government's authority from the metropolitan region towards the east and the south (see Map Three); but as yet, the process was confined to lands which had formed part of the Chinese cultural sphere; there was no energy available for seeking adventures further afield.

From about 120 B.C. there began a period of diplomatic, commercial and military activity that brought the Chinese into direct relations with other peoples, in areas where the writ of a Chinese authority had never run (see Map Four). The process was one of penetration rather than conquest, and of the establishment of isolated colonial posts rather than organs of government which were capable of controlling large areas of uncharted territory. Advances were quickly made in the north, north-west, north-east and south; but although units of provincial government of the regular type were formed very shortly after the completion of a successful expedition, their degree of control was far less effective than that of their counterparts in the valleys of the Yellow River or the Huai. In many cases the process of expansion should be considered as the successful construction of a route of communications, rather than as the foundation of permanent new provinces that were held under the close grasp of the central government.

Military and economic motives

The Han governments were more pre-occupied with the problems of the northern borders than with plans for deliberate expansion in the south. For the tribesmen of the north were able not only to threaten and plunder the farms and cities of north China; they could even force their way to the very gates of Ch'ang-an. The needs of defence obliged the Chinese to devise means of preventing such incursions, and to forge diplomatic links with other peoples whose interests lay in thwarting the activities of their principal enemy, the Hsiung-nu.

But in addition to the military motive which lay behind Chinese policy, it is possible, even probable, that economic considerations played an equally important part. Since the pre-imperial days of the Chou kingdom, Chinese sovereigns had been glad to countenance the import of jades from Khotan; and in the more recent centuries before the unification, governments may have looked to central Asia to provide an adequate supply of horses for royal needs and for the armies. By 140 B.C. the major steps had been taken towards the consolidation of Han imperial rule; provincial officials were in a far better position than before to organize the collection of tax and the transport of grain on behalf of the central government. Indeed, the collection of native products had grown to such an extent that the wastage of unused stores had become unavoidable. At the same time, reports were being brought to the government of the geographical situation, material resources and political affiliations of the tribal groups who lived in the isolated oases of central Asia. This information was brought by travellers such as Chang Ch'ien, whose epic journeys of exploration to northern India have for long stirred the admiration of Chinese writers. In addition to his description of the way of life and material products of these peoples, Chang Ch'ien also brought back an account of even more distant courts of north India, where, to his great surprise, he had seen the produce of Chinese Ssu-ch'uan; and, finally, Chang Ch'ien brought reason to hope that the tribes of the oases and of the more distant regions were equally anxious to preserve themselves intact from the Hsiung-nu.

The formation of Chinese foreign policy

Chang Ch'ien returned to Ch'ang-an in *c.* 125 B.C., and presented his reports at a momentous time in Chinese history. As a further result of imperial consolidation, the central government was now able to recruit and put in the field far larger armies than hitherto. Of greater significance was the emergence at this time of statesmen who were capable of appreciating the economic needs of empire and who were anxious to control the production and transport of staple goods in the major interests of imperial government. Such men were fully capable of recognizing the simultaneous existence of a surplus of raw materials and the requirement for certain imported goods; and they were perhaps able to see the need for an effective foreign policy.

It is possible that the problems of both defence and economy were present in the minds of the statesmen of Ch'ang-an in 130–120 B.C., and that both of these motives influenced the formation of Han foreign policy. However, rigid conclusions cannot be reached, as the hindsight of 2,000 years may provoke excessively rational explanations. It could well be that the real motives of Chinese action were the result of accident or misunderstanding, and that insufficient evidence exists for full comprehension. Possibly, in these early days of imperial government, the implications of military or economic expansion could not be fully appreciated; and since there had been no opportunity as yet to practice a co-ordinated foreign policy, statesmen possessed little experience of diplomacy. But despite the pronouncements of later Confucian theorists, allowance must be made for the willingness of Chinese statesmen at this time to embark on fully sponsored commercial exchanges as well as diplomatic relations with other peoples.

Conservative and progressive views
The decision to embark on a positive foreign policy, which was taken from *c.* 130 B.C., was not reached without controversy. Conservative statesmen propounded the theoretical view which recurs throughout debates on foreign policy and which was supported by appeals to Confucian authority. They believed that campaigns to conquer other peoples were unjustifiable, however serious the provocation, however disloyal or antagonistic their behaviour had been; for the moral and spiritual powers invested in the emperor were sufficient to ensure the safety of his peoples without recourse to military compulsion. On the strictly practical level, the conservative statesmen objected that expansion was a costly affair whose material benefits would accrue slowly and insignificantly; and for this reason it would be better to pursue an unambitious policy, even at the cost of retrenchment or appeasement.

The contrary view was taken by those progressive elements who exercised a controlling influence on policies at this time, and who were about to take active measures to promote China's prosperity. They argued that security could not be maintained without undertaking positive action impressive enough to deter potential invaders; and they believed that such measures should be reinforced by the conclusion of alliances with foreign leaders, though such alliances must needs be couched in terms which denoted China's superiority. Events were soon to show that expense and administrative problems precluded the maintenance of an effective policy of expanson for long; and it seems to us today that the sole needs of defence could possibly have been met by plans that were less ambitious.

R

The Han defensive walls and lines of communication

The foreign policy that was initiated from *c.* 130 B.C. was designed to protect Chinese territory from invasion and to establish a reliable route of communication with the states of central Asia. By such a route, troops could be sent on expeditions to uphold Chinese prestige; diplomats could proceed to woo the affections of the rulers of the peoples of the oases; and caravans could ply their way between the markets of China and central Asia. In addition, the armed causeway or wall needed for these purposes would enable Chinese authorities to control the passage of civilian traffic in and out of China.

The construction of the wall was no new experiment for the Chinese. Some of the seven states of the pre-imperial age had built defensive walls not only as a means of protection from each other but also as a bulwark against the Hsiung-nu. The reorganization of the walls that had been built by the northern states and their co-ordination into a single system had been one of the successful achievements of the short-lived Ch'in dynasty, but after the collapse of that authority the Han government was preoccupied with other problems, and had lacked the resources with which to make adequate use of the neglected fortifications. With the adoption of an expansionist policy, campaigns were fought to discourage the Hsiung-nu from operating near Chinese territory; the Ch'in walls were reoccupied, repaired and efficiently manned; and the line was extended far beyond the limits reached in an earlier age. By 102 B.C. the wall had been taken through the length of the modern province of Kansu, until it reached two terminal points near Tunhuang (the Yü-men and Yang Passes). From here, communication with inner Asia was continued by means of two unprotected caravan routes, which skirted the northern and southern sides of the Taklamakan desert. These roads, which have become known as the Silk Roads, enabled travellers to proceed on their way by means of a chain of oases, and eventually converged at the western end of the desert near Kashgar.

The activities of Han soldiers

The Han wall comprised a series of connected defence posts or towers; these were built of brick or pounded earth, and were set within sight of each other, often at regular intervals. A high earthwork, erected to prevent penetration by man or beast, ran from one tower to the next. The towers were manned by small squads of one officer and about four men; they were equipped with bows mounted on the walls, supplies of arrow-shafts and arrow-heads, and necessities such as food, water and fuel. Sand and tools that were used in construction were also kept at each tower. The squads were responsible for defence against intruders and for patrolling their allotted sectors; and an established code of signals provided for the exchange of routine or emergency reports.

The well-ordered system of command which controlled these troops reflects the professional nature of contemporary military organization. This formed an integral part of the provincial administration, which co-ordinated the activities of civilian official, military officer and police. Command posts were situated to the rear of the main line of the defences, and through passage was granted to approved travellers at specified points. At these gateways or barriers (e.g. the Jade Gate, the Golden Gate), troops inspected the documents which civilians carried as a licence to permit their journeys; and a sharp watch was kept for deserters or criminals whose arrest had been ordered by the central government. At the same time the export of banned commodities (e.g. weapons of war, certain types of livestock or other goods likely to benefit a potential enemy) was prevented at the barriers. Embassies proceeding to foreign states for purposes of diplomacy and trade, and numbering several hundred members, were duly escorted through the lines into the outer world, and provided with the supplies that they needed.

The Han walls and their successors

Compared with the later defence lines, the Han walls were somewhat rudimentary. Neither their proportions nor the strength of their construction can be compared with that of the extant stone buildings of Ming construction (renovated since then). It should also be noted that different situations were chosen for the walls of the Han and the later periods.

While the Han wall was designed for the purpose of defence and communication, it did not set a limit to the area of Chinese colonial penetration. Outposts, sometimes of an agricultural nature, were established both beyond the western extremity of the line and also in colonies that were founded in Manchuria or Korea. These latter settlements existed in a state of isolation from c. 100 B.C. for two centuries or more.

Factors limiting military operations

The strength of the defences varied directly in accordance with the ability of the central government to provide sufficient forces and to supply them with their daily needs. In favourable parts of the northwest, which enjoyed a more plentiful source of water than they do at present, agricultural colonies were founded to solve some of these difficulties. These were worked by troops who were detailed for the task, and comprised small residential communities with houses and official granaries. But a forceful foreign policy which demanded active campaigning depended on the presence of resourceful military leaders of outstanding character and ability. Such men needed to acquire a local knowledge of living and fighting conditions, and they needed to be ready to risk recruiting local inhabitants into their forces and to place them under the command of the small number of Chinese officers who were available.

Very often, Chinese commanders were forced to rely on their own initiative and to take decisions of far-reaching importance in the name of the emperor. For the central government lay at too great a distance (some six weeks: see p. 216) to permit easy or speedy consultation; and it could be committed to unwise or fruitless policies by the hasty action of its commanders, who had no means of ascertaining how well they would be supported. There could be no guarantee that the reinforcements needed for a campaign, even if promised, would arrive in time for effective intervention; and as an unsuccessful campaign could lead to disgrace or impeachment, all but the bravest or foolhardy commanders would be tempted to avoid unjustified or unnecessary action.

Methods of diplomacy

From *c.* 130 B.C. to *c.* A.D. 150 Chinese military fortunes varied from notable success to abject failure. Successful campaigns, conducted over very long distances deep into Mongolia or central Asia were followed by periods of withdrawal or retrenchment. From *c.* 50 B.C. Chinese statesmen had learnt that the best means of confronting the barbarians was to profit by their divisions, and attempts were made to set one confederacy against another. These attempts were partly successful; the leader who was favoured with Chinese friendship was encouraged to settle his followers in lands close to, or even within, Chinese provinces, whence he could act as a buffer against the incursions of his rival. The mutual antagonism of certain Hsiung-nu leaders assisted the Han governments in these endeavours.

The Chinese courts had also learnt the value of arranging diplomatic marriages between the daughters of the imperial family and the tribal chieftains of the north. By this means it was hoped to arrange the succession of a leader who was partly Chinese by birth, and whose upbringing could be so ordered that his inclinations and loyalties would be directed towards Ch'ang-an. From the point of view of the alien leader, such unions were equally valuable. The acquisition of a Chinese princess served to enhance his dignity and prestige, and he thereby received a higher degree of acknowledgement from his fellows. At the same time, princesses whose tastes and comforts were sacrificed in this way to serve imperial purposes could become valuable hostages held in non-Chinese hands, sufficient to guarantee the friendship of the Chinese court and to prevent the arbitrary oppression of its officials.

Trading and other contacts of the Silk Roads
There is no means of assessing the volume of the trade that was conducted along the Silk Roads. Remnants of bales of silk that have been found in central Asia testify to its practice during the Han period; and silk, which was presumably derived eventually from China, was becoming popular in Roman society during the early empire (i.e., in the reigns of Augustus and Tiberius, 27 B.C. to A.D. 37, and later). In their own capital city, Chinese were becoming accustomed to the sight of aliens, who were ready to serve the Chinese court, sell their goods to wealthy civilians, or study the Chinese way of life at Chinese schools.

Han penetration to the south
The nature of Chinese penetration in the north and north-west is completely different from that of colonial activities in other areas where there was no need to establish static garrisons or to maintain an armed line of communications. In the south there existed no force of native horsemen ready to threaten Chinese settlements or able to penetrate to the metropolitan area; and Chinese advances were inhibited by the natural difficulties of a strange climate to which northerners were ill-accustomed and by the prevalence of tropical disease.

The early stages of Han expansion in the south derived probably from economic motives. From c. 130 B.C. it was known that rich mineral resources awaited exploitation in the south-western reaches that lay beyond Ssu-ch'uan, and that goods could possibly be transported thence by river to the region of Canton. The problems confronting Chinese explorers were those of providing adequate and safe carriage for valuable minerals or rare vegetable products to the north, and of finding a safe route through lands that were swampy, mountainous or infested by dangerous animals. Early exploration was on occasion followed by the foundation of provincial organs, but more usually by small military campaigns which were designed to impress the unassimilated natives with the might of Chinese arms and the luxuries of Chinese civilization. If possible the loyalties of such tribes were to be bought at the price of a few manufactures or silks, and their loyal co-operation should be sought, so as to free the lone Chinese settlers from molestation. By 108 B.C. Han pioneers were penetrating as far as the modern Yün-nan and Vietnam, and there is reason to show that they had reached points in Malaya about a century later. The first authenticated contact with the Roman world took place in A.D. 166, when a mission arrived at the port of P'an-yü, on the site of the later city of Canton.

Administrative concepts and arrangements

Foreign ventures and contacts forced the Han governments to take administrative measures in regard to alien peoples, and the foundations were now laid for the orthodox attitude that was to be adopted towards non-Chinese. The tributary concept, which began to take shape in Han writings, is evidenced in the institutions of government, in imperial practices and in the descriptive terms of edicts and histories.

The chief dignitary of the Han government who was responsible for foriegn relations bore the title of Grand Herald (*Ta-hung-lu*), and his duties were defined as the receipt of homage from foreign tribes who owed allegiance to the emperor. With the expansion of Han activities, new types of administrative unit were formed to suit different degrees of co-operation, loyalty or surrender. In the intermediate lands of the perimeter the obligations of native inhabitants were ill-defined, and the extent of the officials' authority was compromised by the presence of those who did not acknowledge Han dominion. Such areas could not be regarded as provinces of the normal type, that were established in the interior, and the lands were treated as protectorates or dependencies, in which the imposition of Han officials was tempered by reliance on native leadership. In some instances the loyalties of such leaders were secured by the bestowal of titles, such as king or marquis, or the seals and ribbons which were the symbols of posts in the Han civil service. In this way the Han emperor's authority was imposed nominally on 'kings' situated in Yün-nan (109 B.C.) and the Japanese Islands (A.D. 57). But another aspect of the Chinese attitude is illustrated in the descriptive terms of edict, memorial or history, where emphasis is placed on the material value of foreign lands, and their inhabitants are discussed in terms that are scornful, suspicious or pejorative.

The effects of alien overlordship
In the centuries of political disunity between the Han and T'ang empires the expansion of Chinese dominion in central Asia was necessarily brought to a halt. Nevertheless, highly important developments took place during these centuries, as the steady dissemination of Buddhism and the foundation of alien dynasties in north China resulted in significant foreign penetration of China.

Buddhist missionaries had first arrived from northern India by way of the Silk Roads (from between *c.* 100 B.C. and *c.* A.D. 50), and continued to infiltrate into China after the collapse of Han rule (A.D. 220). At the same time the faith was finding favour amongst some of the central Asiatic peoples; and by the time when such peoples came to establish dynastic rule (first quarter of the fourth century), it was possible for Chinese and non-Chinese to share some degree of religious affiliation or sympathy. There were also obvious political reasons for the co-operation of foreign conqueror and native administrator. Each side depended on the gifts of the other and came to recognize their value; and it is perhaps in these centuries that the Chinese came to accept the foreigner for his own personal qualities. The period forms a significant and necessary prelude to the readiness with which foreign traders or religious teachers were welcomed at the T'ang capital of Ch'ang-an from the seventh century.

III. THE MIDDLE EMPIRES AND THEIR NEIGHBOURS

The rise and fall of T'ang power
The re-establishment of a settled empire under the T'ang emperors in 618 was accompanied by the reassertion of Chinese military power. It was largely thanks to the personal courage and strategy of the second T'ang emperor, T'ai tsung (626–648), that China was relieved of the threats of Turkish armies, which had at times penetrated to the banks of the Wei River. For about a century and a half the Chinese government was able to pursue an active, and at times aggressive, policy, designed to increase the safety and resources of the empire. But by the middle of the eighth century the situation changed radically. The central government no longer commanded sufficient authority to

263

put an effective force into the field and to ensure its loyalty; and the rebellions of An Lu-shan and his successors (755–63) left the empire disrupted and powerless, and its institutions impaired or obsolete. At the same time the Tibetans had achieved a new degree of cohesion and strength, and by 763 had succeeded in occupying or controlling large areas to the north-west of China, including some of the regions traversed by the Silk Roads. For the second half of the T'ang dynasty, Chinese foreign policy was one of negative reaction rather than positive initiative.

The limits of Chinese advance

During the seventh century an attempt had been made to restore the land routes of the west to their earlier uses. After the collapse of Han power, the defences and communications lines had not unnaturally fallen into disrepair, except for short interludes in which they had been re-occupied by Chinese garrisons (e.g. during the Tsin and Wei dynasties). With the T'ang empire the wall was renovated with a new line of towers built according to contemporary design and situated in positions that were partly chosen afresh. But the new line was not destined to survive for long. While Chinese arms and trade were being extended towards the west, a new movement, in the form of Islamic power, had been taking place in the opposite direction. When the two sides confronted each other in battle near the Talas River (751), Chinese armies were decisively defeated. The incident not only served to check further Chinese expansion, but also allowed the cultural advance of Islam into Turkestan, and the steady process of infiltration from the west was set in motion.

Chinese loss of initiative

T'ang policy relied partly on the now traditional device of setting one barbarian to control another. However, such methods were less effective than formerly, as the situation was more complex than it had been in the Han period. By now the individual neighbours of China had achieved a greater strength and had developed a more sophisticated view of statecraft and foreign relations. Whereas the Han governments had contrived a foreign policy so as to regulate relations with a few major confederacies, and a number of small tribal groups, the T'ang governments were faced with the need to deal with a larger number of major units, whose individual powers could each affect Chinese interests.

264

There is thus a complicated story of agreements, alliances and wars, by which the Chinese were obliged to placate superior forces or to call for military assistance. The T'ang courts were engaged in relations with rival political groups in the west or north-west (the Tibetans and T'u-yü-hun), in the north-east (the Hsi peoples, the three kingdoms of Korea and that of P'o-hai) and in the south-west (Nan-chao); and in securing alliances the central government was committed to expensive obligations. A conspicuous example of China's inhibited or passive policy is seen in her relations with the Uighurs during the eighth century. The military strength of these central Asian horsemen had been one of the prime factors which enabled the T'ang government to emerge from the An Lu-shan rebellions without complete disintegration; but the high price demanded for that assistance, both in material goods and in subservience, was such that for a few years the proud government of a Chinese dynasty almost became a tributary subject of a central Asian tribe.

The dangers of employing foreign officers
By the first half of the eighth century, the T'ang government had been markedly weakened by the shortage of native military leaders. It had become necessary to recruit alien officers to take command of Chinese troops whether for action against foreign armies, or as garrisons stationed at the perimeter. In such situations alien generals could easily obtain control over large areas of Chinese territory, and could draw support from the alien peoples beond the pale, with whom they had natural affiliations. In this way there arose the conditions of separatism which split China during the ninth and tenth centuries. Several of the short-lived regimes which were established in the north between the T'ang and the Sung dynasties were founded by Asiatic families.

Foreign settlements in China
Notwithstanding the inherent weakness of Chinese foreign policy during much of the T'ang period, contacts with foreigners tended to become more brisk and fruitful than previously. The inhabitants of Ch'ang-an grew more accustomed to the sight of the foreigner who had settled in the city with his caravan of camels; and there is ample evidence to verify the import of statues, gems or ornaments that had been fashioned in the Mediterranean world. Chinese governments tolerated the establishments of foreign religions, with the result that Ch'ang-an could boast the presence of temples devoted to Nestorian,

Manichaean, Moslem or Zoroastrian cults; and in times of difficulty, such as drought, it was not unknown for the Chinese government to call on those priests to pray for succour from that particular form of heavenly dispensation to which they claimed access. Foreign trading communities were growing up at other cities, such as Canton, whose large Arab population suffered severely during the rebellion of 878 (see p. 236); as yet articles of trade were carried to and from Chinese ports in foreign vessels.

Japanese use of Chinese practices

The influence of China's civilization on her immediate neighbours can be partly measured by the attempts at imitation of this time. During the first half of the seventh century, Japan had attained a new degree of unity and nationhood, which had followed the earlier introduction of many features of cultural progress from the mainland (e.g. the Chinese system of writing, the Confucian texts, and the Buddhist religion). Shortly before the foundation of the T'ang dynasty, Japanese statesmen had learnt of the value of ordered government and the common acceptance of political forms that had long been practised in China, but which was lacking in Japanese society. Missions were sent to the Sui and T'ang Capitals of Ch'ang-an, to study the institutions of imperial government and the means of practising Confucian ideals. There soon followed an attempt to adopt Chinese political systems and to operate the provisions of Chinese government; and imitation was soon followed by adaptation and modification so as to suit local conditions in Japan. The process of imitation and acculturization was to affect much of the future social and political development of Japan, where the products of Chinese artists and authors were being appreciated no less avidly than the examples of the Chinese official and Buddhist priest.

The evidence of the Shōsōin

Examples of Chinese artistic products had long been imported into Japan, usually by way of Korea, but from the seventh century the volume of these imports increased very rapidly. An imperial collection of objects used by the Emperor Shōmu (reigned 724–48) was made and housed at Nara, and thanks to the meticulous care with which the collection has been preserved the objects are still available for examination. The collection (which is kept in a building called the *Shōsōin*) can hardly be representative of either Chinese or Japanese standards of living; but it indicates the values placed by Japanese importers on

Chinese glass, jewels, ceramics and musical instruments. The *Shōsōin* also includes figures of Middle Eastern origin, brought originally to China and re-exported thence to Japan. There are also some of the earliest administrative records of Japanese government, written in the Chinese language and cast in the form of the corresponding documents of the T'ang empire.

Material and cultural imports into China

At the same time there is considerable evidence to show that the Chinese themselves were highly appreciative of specialities imported from foreign peoples. In theory, the value of this 'tribute' lay in its demonstration of imperial superiority; in practice, Ch'ang-an's wealthier citizens were glad to buy the colourful feathers or the thick furs of foreign birds and beasts, and to show off the fineries into which these rarities had been woven. Fruits and vegetables grown in foreign climes made their way to T'ang China, together with frankincense and myrrh, minerals and jewels; and there was traffic in the holy relics and images of the Buddha, and in books of secular or religious content. Human 'tribute' was seen in slaves and hostages, or in those dancers and entertainers whose homes lay in the romantic world of central Asia or beyond. And perhaps the greatest and rarest delight that a courtier could enjoy was attendance at the court performances of the Burmese orchestra, or the musical companies who journeyed to Ch'ang-an from Java, Sumatra or Japan.

Diplomatic relations between China, Japan and the Korean States

Contacts between China and Japan had taken place largely by way of Korea, which was divided between some three independent and mutually hostile states until 675. From the Sui period, Chinese intentions in Korea had been somewhat aggressive, but military operations had proved costly and unsuccessful. Diplomatic relations between China, Japan and the three main states were complicated by the traditional systems of alliance, and when Chinese and Japanese interests conflicted, their forces had confronted one another in battle (662). But owing largely to the Japanese preference for steady peaceful conditions in which to promote cultural exchanges with the continent, friendly relations were maintained between the two courts.

Between 630 and 838 twelve diplomatic missions set out from Japan and succeeded in making contact with the Chinese capital. The missions included envoys who carried messages from their imperial masters of Nara or Hei-an (modern Kyoto); officials or junior courtiers charged with the task of studying Chinese ideals and institutions; traders bent on exploring commercial possibilities; and Buddhist priests seeking renewed inspiration for their faith. Considerable expenses were involved in despatching these missions, with their full complement of several hundred members, carried in a fleet of five to ten ships. As yet the Japanese were poor seamen, and heavy losses were exacted on the enterprises by storm and pirate. Some members of the missions returned in due course to Japan to render service in their own country; and in the eighth century, at least one senior member, whose return was hampered by shipwreck, stayed in China for the rest of his life, serving as a member of the T'ang civil service. Owing to subsequent political developments in China and Japan, 1,000 years intervened between the last Japanese diplomatic mission sent to Ch'ang-an (838–47) and the first embassy of modern times (1871).

Buddhist pilgrims
Finally, on many occasions the search for Buddhist texts and teaching promoted individual contact between Chinese and foreign peoples during the T'ang period. Of the Chinese who ventured abroad for this purpose the best known is Hsüan Tsang, who set out on the overland route to India in 629. After a series of adventures, Hsüan Tsang returned to Ch'ang-an in 645, with a large consignment of holy images, books and relics that he had collected during his travels. With his new contacts and his newly acquired knowledge, Hsüan Tsang could now embark on a full-scale project for the translation of Sanskrit texts into Chinese; and with the help of some twenty colleagues, over seventy books were translated, in order to add new force and lustre to the Buddhist cults of China. Twenty years were needed for the completion of the task.

From Japan, the Buddhist monk Ennin came to China on a similar mission, as an official member of the twelfth embassy. Ennin's visit (838–47) coincided with the great oppression of Buddhism in China (842–5), from which the religion's material prosperity was never to recover. Ennin was by no means the first Japanese monk to seek religious instruction in China, but the fortunate preservation of his diary provides a useful comment on Sino-Japanese relations and the type of contact which could be made at this time. As a result of his travels, Ennin's work constituted a major development in the propagation and future course of Buddhism in Japan.

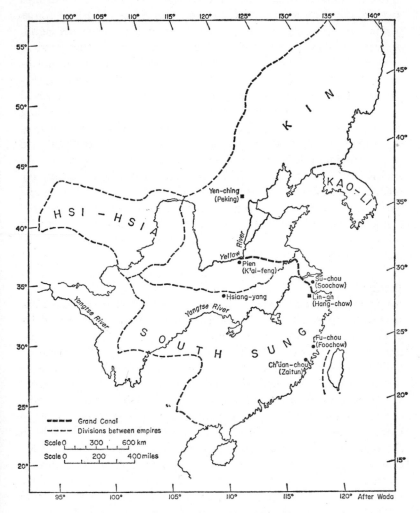

MAP 7. The Kin and Sung Empires (about 1200)

Private initiative during the Sung periods

During the Sung periods, contacts with foreigners depended more on individual initiative than official sponsorship, and diplomatic ventures were inhibited by the prevailing military weakness. The land routes to the west had been cut by Tibetan intervention during the eighth century, and these remained closed with the growth of an independent state of the Tangut, or Hsi-hsia, peoples. Both here and in the north-east the Sung court was confronted by hostile neighbours, and the expansion of the Liao and Kin empires from the north-east was achieved at the cost of Sung authority over much of northern China. The Sung government found itself obliged to bow before the superior force of the Liao and Kin houses and to pay those courts a tribute of silk and money, in increasingly large amounts fixed by treaty (e.g. in 1004 and 1042). The capture of K'ai-feng in 1126 was followed by the establishment of an alien regime over the northern part of China; and with the removal of the Sung court to the south, that government could not initiate diplomatic relations on a major scale. Contacts with other peoples were left to the private traveller and merchant rather than the diplomat or official.

Foreign trade

An important change can be noted in the conduct of foreign trade at this juncture. The technological advances of the Sung period included the application of the compass to purposes of marine navigation, and the wider introduction of the sternpost rudder. Chinese shipbuilders were now able to construct junks which could ride the high seas more safely and efficiently, and Chinese exports were now being carried in Chinese ships to foreign markets in Japan, the East Indies and the coast of Africa. Evidence of a return import of goods to China is seen in the hoards of Sung coin that have come to light in those places, and whose removal from China to pay for luxuries accentuated the treasury's shortage of copper. At the same time foreign communities were settling on the southern coast of China, where Ch'üan-chou (Marco Polo's Zaitun) and Foochow had succeeded Canton as the main centres of the Arab and Persian trading communities.

IV. RELATIONS WITH THE WEST

The modern era

Historians still face the task of assessing the full implications of the establishment of the Mongol empire, and the degree of intellectual exchange or commercial contact that took place between Asia and Europe at this time. It is however clear that from the thirteenth century a new era started in the relations between east and west, which was to be of deep significance to the more modern developments of the last few centuries. The emphasis of China's policy and contacts was shifting from her immediate neighbours to more distant countries; and the initiative of the westerner, which was but one aspect of the contemporary urge for discovery and adventure, soon resulted in the arrival in Europe of detailed and sometimes exaggerated accounts of the splendours of the Far East.

In the long centuries of the Mongol and Manchu dynasties, the Chinese had been forced to accept the dominion of the northern alien. In return they had been freed from the traditional fears of invasion, and had been able to benefit from the efficient system of communications operated by their governments not only within China but also in the peripheral lands that led the way into central Asia and thence to Europe. Different conditions applied during the Ming dynasty, whose governments were ever conscious of the northern dangers, and set up a system of garrisons and defence posts over a wide area that extended deep into Manchuria. These Chinese garrisons were conceived on a larger scale than any previous Chinese military dispositions; the Ming defences form part of the extant Great Wall of China.

Early European ventures and Christianity
The initiative of the west is seen in the despatch of travellers such as John of Plano Carpini (1245–7) or William of Rubruck (1253–4) to the Mongol court of Karakorum, or the brothers Nicolo and Maffeo Polo (c. 1260). These journeys were made by means of the land route through central Asia, and owed their origin both to political motives and a zeal for missionary activity. From now on visitors of this type were to serve Chinese courts with loyalty and wisdom as technical advisers, scientific consultants and, possibly, as members of the Chinese civil service. Foreign engineers may have assisted the Mongol armies in the siege of Hsiang-yang (1268–73); and Marco Polo (son of Nicolo) himself claimed, perhaps falsely, to have served as governor of the prosperous city of Yang-chou for three years. Representatives of the Society of Jesus and other Christian orders placed their knowledge of mathematics, astronomy and other branches of learning at the dis-

posal of the Ming and Ch'ing emperors, and succeeded in winning a few converts to their faith.

As with other foreign beliefs, the Chinese authorities were ready to tolerate the religious practices of the Christians and to permit the erection of their places of worship; for beliefs and ceremonies of a purely religious nature did not necessarily conflict with Chinese concepts of empire or manifestly threaten the basis of Chinese sovereignty. But once a foreigner ventured to question the Chinese right to exercise authority, he forfeited the toleration of the Chinese court. The classic case in which this principle was demonstrated was a famous controversy of the seventeenth and eighteenth centuries concerned with certain questions of Rites, in which the Christian representatives took opposing sides. As a result of this incident the propagation of Christianity suffered some setback.

The initiative of the Ming mariners

From the Ming period the use of the sea-route featured in the fast-growing commercial activity. At the outset of the fifteenth century the Chinese government sponsored a series of voyages of exploration, mainly to seek opportunities of trade. Convoys, which sometimes comprised over 25,000 men, carried in over sixty ships, reached points in the Persian Gulf, the African coast or India, in the hope of delivering their cargoes of silks, metal wares and porcelains, and returning to China with rare and precious luxuries that would gratify the court and the home customers.

With the passage of time and the increased demand for porcelains, the Chinese kilns undertook work specially designed for the export markets, and special shapes and patterns were devised to suit the tastes of purchasers in south-east Asia or Europe. The increased volume of trade was also to affect the development of the ceramic industry in both parts of the world. In China, the blue and white wares of the Ming factories had lacked appreciation until their value as export materials was recognized; and European potters were soon to be busily engaged in producing their own versions of Chinese designs in Delft, Meissen and Staffordshire; one of the best known examples of a pseudo-Chinese design is seen in the willow-pattern services which were first produced in Shropshire c. 1780.

Lord Macartney's mission

The official encouragement with which native voyagers were supported in the fifteenth century forms a sharp contrast with the attitude adopted towards foreign traders by the Ch'ing administration. From the seventeenth century tall ships had been arriving from the European nations to engage in trade in Far Eastern waters, and by the end of the eighteenth century the frequency of these voyages and the degree of competition had risen sharply. The purpose of Lord Macartney's mission (1793–4) to the court of the Ch'ien-lung emperor was to obtain better facilities and treatment for British traders, and to increase the volume of such enterprises. His reception shows the constancy of the traditional Chinese view of the foreign trader. He was described by the Chinese as a bearer of tribute, and was expected to behave according to the procedure prescribed for such dignitaries. The gifts which he bore to the Chinese court had scant effect on the success of the mission, which had been conceived on principles that lay at total variance with Chinese thought. Macartney's failure was due not to his own weakness, but to the basic incompatibility of the English and Chinese points of view, as can be seen from parts of a letter, graciously written by the Ch'ien-lung emperor for delivery to George III:[1]

As to the request made in your memorial, O King, to send one of your nationals to stay at the Celestial Court to take care of your country's trade with China, this is not in harmony with the state system of our dynasty and will definitely not be permitted. Traditionally people of the European nations who wished to render some service under the Celestial Court have been permitted to come to the capital. But after their arrival they are obliged to wear Chinese court costumes, are placed in a certain residence, and are never allowed to return to their own countries. . . .

Moreover the territory under the control of the Celestial Court is very large and wide. There are well-established regulations governing tributary envoys from the outer states to Peking . . . there has never been a precedent for letting them do whatever they like. . . .

The Celestial Court has pacified and possessed the territory within the four seas. Its sole aim is to do its utmost to achieve good government and to manage political affairs, attaching no value to strange jewels and precious objects. . . . As a matter of fact, the

[1] This extract is taken from Ssu-yü Teng and John K. Fairbank, *China's Response to the West*, Harvard University Press, 1954, p. 19.

S

virtue and prestige of the Celestial Dynasty having spread far and wide, the kings of the myriad nations come by land and sea with all sorts of precious things. Consequently there is nothing we lack, as your principal envoy and others have themselves observed. We have never set much store on strange or ingenious objects, nor do we need any more of your country's manufactures. . . .

The clash with European interests
In 1839 a crisis occurred in China's foreign relations. The eastward expansion of European interests was still gaining momentum, while the Chinese court persisted in its adherence to the traditional attitude of superiority over the foreigner. By now, the effective authority of the Ch'ing government had been sadly weakened, and the way lay open for Europeans to take the initiative and to enforce their requirements on the reluctant representatives of a proud empire. But in 1839, Lin Tse-hsü, the provincial governor of parts of south China, could still maintain the fiction that the empire that he served was self-sufficient and omnipotent, and that other peoples depended on Chinese products for their existence. His references to rhubarb as a Chinese export which was indispensable to the west, and to the value of European textiles betrays the prevailing Chinese ignorance of the conditions of European civilization.

Chinese acknowledgement of western strength
These boasts could not prevent the victory of British arms in the Opium War (1839–42). Twenty years later, the Chinese position had deteriorated yet further, owing partly to the devastating effects of the T'ai-p'ing (1850–65) and other rebellions. Chinese forces were defeated in the renewed fighting which broke out with European powers in 1856–60; and it became imperative to reassess the value of foreign nations in view of their ability to violate Chinese sovereign integrity. Indeed, a new respect for the technical powers of the west had already been expressed, hard after the earlier failure of imperial government. Lin Tse-hsü himself, who had been unable to defend Chinese territory by traditional means, had written (1842):[1]

The rebels' ships on the open sea came and went as they pleased, now in the south and now suddenly in the north, changing successively between morning and evening. If we tried to put up a defence

[1] From Teng and Fairbank, *op. cit.*, p. 28.

everywhere, not only would we toil and expend ourselves without limit, but also how could we recruit and transport so many troops, militia, artillery, and ammunition, and come to their support quickly? . . .

The adoption of western methods of diplomacy
But perhaps the final abandonment of the traditional Chinese attitude can be seen in the replacement of the old office responsible for the receipt of tribute, by an organ designed to treat with foreign powers on terms of equality. By the treaties of Tientsin and Peking (1858 and 1860) European powers had forced the Chinese court to concede sovereign rights over their own subjects and interests, on specified parts of Chinese soil. In addition to the preferential treatment of Europeans that was embodied in the new system of Treaty Ports, the government of China was obliged to establish the *Tsung-li ya-men* for the conduct of foreign affairs, and a new, modern stage opened in China's relations with the west. In place of arrogant superiority, Chinese ministers of state were obliged, and indeed became willing, to rely on the provisions of international law, and to acknowledge the force of diplomatic protocol. Herself impressed by the strength that these ties held among European powers, China soon showed herself equally able to respect and to obey their provisions. A new era opened with the Chinese readiness to study European cultures and languages, and to take full advantage of western investment, skills and initiative to construct railways, telegraph lines and other forms of European industry on Chinese soil.

CHAPTER TEN

HISTORICAL EVIDENCES

The place of historical writing in Chinese literature
Historical writings form one of the four major divisions in which Chinese literature has been traditionally classified. Up to the early empires, and later, Chinese scholars and men of letters saw the importance of prose literature in the motives which had inspired its composition, and the moral purposes which it could be made to serve. In this way a distinction was made in respect of the authority which an individual piece of writing came to possess, either thanks to the recognized qualities or message of the author or the educational value of his writings.

This attitude persisted in scholarly circles long after the time (T'ang period or earlier) when authors had started to write descriptive prose as a means of self-expression, or with the deliberate intention of delighting rather than instructing their readers. In the same way, poetry which could be shown to possess moralist qualities (e.g. the songs of antiquity, allegedly collected by Confucius to bring popular grievance to light, or the political propagandist ballads of the T'ang poet Po Chü-i 772–846) was to be distinguished from the recollections of emotion in tranquillity whose value was personal (e.g. much of the work of the eighth century poets Li Po and Tu Fu). The somewhat unsatisfactory classification of Chinese literature as Classical works, Histories, Philosophical works, and Collected writings has been adopted partly as a result of these principles and partly as a matter of educational convenience. As with philosophical texts, to the Chinese the value of the histories lies first and foremost in their didactic force.

The weaknesses of Chinese historical writings
The history of China has probably been described in a far greater volume of writing and with a far greater degree of continuity than that of any other civilization. However, there are many deficiencies in this material which detract from the value of its abundance. For the greater part of the imperial period there is virtually no source material which

276

can be properly described as primary, and students are forced to rely on compilations for which there is little means of corroboration or authentification.

The preponderance of chronicle over archive is accentuated by the difficulties of tracing the textual history of early works. Owing to the early invention of paper (c. A.D. 100) and application of printing (from the latter part of the T'ang period) there exists no reserve of manuscript copies of works written on parchment, comparable with those documents with which the scholars of western history can prove the authorship or trace the early transmission of their texts. A further difficulty which has frustrated historians of China is seen both in the accidental destruction of imperial libraries or governmental collections and the deliberate destruction of the sources from which many of the historical compilations were drawn. Finally, although Chinese scholars have been professionally and persistently interested in their own empires' history, much of their work has been vitiated by their outlook. Their efforts have often been directed to the clarification of academic minutiae rather than to the formulation of synthetical interpretation; and their methods have suffered from the traditional approach which has regarded the history of the last 2,000 or 3,000 years as a retrogressive process from the golden ages of a mythical past.

Epigraphical material

Few writings made originally on durable substances survive to supplement the literary sources. Apart from the oracular shells and bones of the Shang-yin period, early inscriptions are found on bronze vessels of the Shang-yin and, more extensively, the Chou periods. Important as these inscriptions are to linguists, archaeologists and historians alike, systematic handling is not always possible. Their value is strictly limited, and many can hardly be regarded as usable historical evidence.

From the Warring States period and well into the early empires wooden boards or strips were used as the regular medium for the inscription of administrative records, but only a minute quantity of this material survives. Epitaphs were cut in stone to commemorate leading personalities of the Han and subsequent empires, and can in a number of cases be related to persons, events or institutions that are mentioned in literary sources; but largely owing to their conventional form and purpose, these inscriptions are rarely of independent value to the historian.

The Book of Documents

The earliest text to be considered here is the *Shu-ching*, which is usually known in the west as *The Book of History* or *The Book of Documents*. Traditionally this text has been associated with Confucius, and for that reason it has exerted a profound, and perhaps disproportionate, influence on the historical writings of later ages. Although the work can hardly be accepted as 'history' according to the modern uses of the term, the motives attributed to its compilation recur in connection with later historical works. It was held that the book comprises certain documents selected by Confucius for transmission to posterity as a means of illustrating the ways of an ideal age whose passing was still to be regretted; and the same approach persists in later writings.

The *Book of Documents* contains the text of a number of separate speeches, solemn oaths or injunctions that were made on famous or ceremonial occasions, and which are ascribed to the kings of the Chou or earlier kingdoms; but owing to a somewhat turbulent textual history, some half of the extant text must be rejected as a spurious creation of the third century A.D. The remaining and more authentic part of the work includes material that was available (but possibly not in its present form) to writers of at least the first century B.C., and whose linguistic style bears distinct affinities to that of the bronze inscriptions of the Chou period. Such material can be regarded as genuine, provided that the association with Confucius is accepted with reserve; and considerable doubt must remain regarding the dates of origin of each of the independent passages of which the book consists. Some of the passages may well have been written long before Confucius died (479 B.C.); but little can be said for certain regarding the time or circumstances in which they were chosen for inclusion in this collection, or the processes of editorship to which they were subjected.

Thanks to its alleged associations, the *Book of Documents* has been included in the canon of sacred literature since the Han period, and has often been treated with a somewhat uncritical esteem. However, a tribute is due to a few scholars of the Sung period who cast doubt on the authenticity of the work. The content of the book has evinced historical rather than philosophical interest; and by reason of its admonishments and its sacred ascription it has played an important role in the education of statesmen, officials and scholars of the imperial age.

278

The Spring and Autumn Annals

A further work, of a very different type, but which is also associated with Confucius' editorship, has been of equal significance in formulating the Chinese treatment of history during the imperial age. The *Ch'un-ch'iu*, or 'Spring and Autumn Annals', is cast in the form of a chronicle which records selected events in strict chronological order from month to month, season to season and year to year. The book covers the period from 722 to 481 and is concerned principally with diplomatic and other incidents that affected Lu, the small state in east China where Confucius was born and where he led the life of a teacher and would-be statesman. His disciples credited him with the work of editing this chronicle and investing it with a moral tone that suited his purpose of improving the quality of government. The text itself is a dry, terse account of events whose interest is somewhat limited. Entries concern the observance of rites and sacrifices, the conduct of relations between noblemen or officials and their correct or questionable behaviour. The kingdom of Chou forms the political centre of the narrative, which includes a record of eclipses and other natural phenomena.

In this account, purposeful writing is theoretically achieved both by the selection of happenings that are deemed worthy of description and by the skilful choice of phrase to add nuance, or moral judgement, to an event; and telling criticism can be voiced by the implicit or studied omission of detail. Confucius' motive in editing this compilation was always taken to be didactic, so as to provide rulers and statesmen with examples of behaviour that was either praiseworthy or culpable. Confucius had stressed the need to obey a fixed code of behaviour in order to discipline human character, and many of the entries of the *Ch'un-ch'iu* are concerned with the upkeep of such conventions, and the need to preserve the ideal relationships of society. Whereas it is possible that records of ceremonies were kept, even from the Shang-yin period, solely for purposes of religion or ritual, in the *Spring and Autumn Annals* such motives have been replaced by those of moral exhortation.

Amplifications

Part of the importance of the *Ch'un-ch'iu* lies in its position as one of the earliest surviving examples of a record of events that was cast in exact chronological order. In addition, the somewhat enigmatic nature of the text soon provoked the production of commentaries, or explanations, in which the implied meaning of the record was clearly expounded with precise reference to the individuals or terms that were concerned. These accounts include much that is of a personal nature, and may resemble fiction more than an historian's judgment. Moreover, it is possible that the best known of the extant commentaries, the *Tso-chuan* (probably not compiled before 300 B.C.), was in fact originated quite independently of the *Ch'un-ch'iu*, and that it was only at a later stage that it was deliberately separated into short passages and used as a means of amplifying that text.

The influence of early texts

The value of these and a few similar writings of the pre-imperial age may well be brought into question by those who seek the sources of history for that period, and in view of the absence of more fruitful material or independent corroboration for these meagre texts, purists may well object that the Chou period should not be placed in the historian's province. None the less these early documents have had a profound bearing on the nature of Chinese historical writing. Like the *Book of Documents*, the *Spring and Autumn Annals*, and at times some of its amplifications, have been included in the Confucian canon of literature, and potential scholar-officials were obliged to study them with the utmost diligence, as part of the examinations' syllabus. It will be seen below that the compilation of the Standard Histories of the imperial age has rested almost exclusively in the hands of these officials, and the literary style of those histories owes much to a deep respect for that of the early documents, and a conscious desire to imitate their simplicity, directness and clarity.

II. THE STANDARD OR DYNASTIC HISTORIES

The complete series

For the imperial age, Chinese histories of a formal and uniform pattern provide students with a voluminous and somewhat bewildering mass of information. A series of twenty-six Standard Histories (*Cheng-shih*) covers the period, actually from before 221 B.C. until 1911, with an historical record that was designed to cover each dynastic period, and which is often regarded as being continuous. However, the continuity of the series is open to question. There are some periods for which a Standard History was never finished, or for which one no longer exists in entirety; for other periods, two or more such works are still extant. Moreover, the very first of the series, the *Shih-chi*, is exceptional, as it covers a period that started long before the imperial age and ended in the middle of the Western Han dynasty. Subsequent practice has usually been for a single history to be compiled for a single dynastic period, and for this reason the series is frequently, but not quite accurately, referred to as the *Dynastic Histories*. The latest work in the series, which covers the Ch'ing period (1644–1910), was published in Taipei in 1961.

The Shi-chi and its motives
The *Shih-chi*, or *Records of the Historian*, was written by Ssu-ma T'an, and after his death (*c.* 110 B.C.) by his son Ssu-ma Ch'ien. Both father and son held the office of *T'ai-shih*, or Court Astrologer, and were concerned with framing the official record of contemporary omens and their verification. However, the compilation of the *Shih-chi* was probably undertaken as a separate venture in a private capacity. It was intended as a truthful record of events from the beginning of time until the Han dynasty, and the account covers the period until shortly before the death of Ssu-ma Ch'ien in *c.* 90 B.C. The motive for the work was somewhat different from, and even contradictory to, that of the earlier texts with which Confucius was associated. The ideal of the *Shih-chi* was to present facts objectively, irrespective of moral implication, and without fear of the potential consequences for the authors. But as we shall see, despite these intentions, their view of history rested on some ineradicable pre-conceptions.

The use of earlier records
In recording events of the pre-imperial age, the authors of the *Shih-chi* relied on extant accounts or sources such as the *Book of Documents*, or the amplifications of the *Spring and Autumn Annals*. Parts of these sources were incorporated wholly into the new work, sometimes with the addition of a comment; and in some instances, an endeavour was made to simplify the archaic, and by then obsolete, language in which these ancient texts were phrased. By no means all the sources used by Ssu-ma Ch'ien and his father for this early period still survive; and we cannot identify the material on which they drew for the Han period or their procedures of compilation.

The treatment of the pre-Han regimes
For Ssu-ma T'an and Ssu-ma Ch'ien, unified empire constituted the

normal form of government and a standard against which other types of government were to be judged. This treatment is basically anachronistic. In the *Shih-chi*, the pre-imperial age is described in terms that imply a regress from a blessed state of political unity and willing human obedience to authority. Heaven had ordained the succession of the early dynasties (Hsia,[1] Yin and Chou) in accordance with the virtues, and subsequent successes, of its earthly representatives; and the collapse of Chou marked a focal point at which the Heavenly dispensation was removed from a reprobate temporal authority. Such a removal could end only in the decline of civilized standards. In their treatment of the Ch'in and Han empires, Ssu-ma T'an and his son applied the same preconceived moral judgments; the unification of Ch'in was doomed to failure owing to the inherent wickedness of the regime, and it was only natural and just that it should yield place to the benevolent rule of the Han emperors who enjoyed Heaven's blessing and protection.

The justification of contemporary government
This treatment of the earlier regimes may be regarded as vitiating the ideal of presenting a truthful record without fear of the consequences. The adoption of the principle affected the form of the *Shih-chi*, and exercised a decisive influence on the style and purpose of the later Standard Histories. For the later historians likewise portrayed a succession of political regimes so as to justify the authority of their contemporary masters. The pattern for describing dynastic changes had been fixed for all time.

The Standard History was to become an instrument of propaganda, and for this reason the last ruler of a defunct dynasty had necessarily to be portrayed as an oppressive tyrant who richly merited chastisement. In this way the contemporary dynasty could be justified in ousting its predecessor, and China's actual masters could be shown to deserve the protection of the Heavenly Mandate of government. The presentation of this theme was easier in the case of the later histories, wherein only one change of dynasty was concerned, than in the case of the *Shih-chi* which covered a period of several regimes.

Imperial Annals
The basic form of the Standard Histories consists of four parts, i.e.

[1] According to tradition this had preceded the Shang dynasty, but no archaeological or other evidence has yet been found to corroborate this account.

Imperial Annals, Tables, Treatises, and Biographies. The chapters of imperial annals are accounts of selected events arranged in chronological order, and sometimes described in the terse, pregnant style that characterizes the *Ch'un-ch'iu* of the pre-imperial age. In the Standard Histories, the Imperial Annals are devoted to recording omens or deeds attributed to Heavenly intervention; actions initiated by the emperor, or events in which he took a leading part, such as the promulgation of decrees; the appointment or dismissal of imperial consorts; the establishment of the imperial heir; the appointment or dismissal of senior officials of state; the suppression of revolts; the receipt of tribute from foreign tribes; or the initiation of punitive campaigns.

These chapters usually form the driest parts of the histories, and should rarely be taken entirely at their face value; for while major events are lucidly or accurately described, little attempt is made to provide descriptive detail or modification, or to suggest context, implication or consequence.

Tables
The Tables display the relationships of the prominent members of the imperial and noble families, or the succession of office holders in the more important posts of the civil service. In the latter case, the pages of the histories are usually divided horizontally into successive lines, each one of which is devoted to a specified office; the offices are arranged in descending order of dignity or seniority. The pages are also divided vertically into columns, usually for each year, so that entries can be made for every change of post that occurred.

To illustrate the genealogy of noble families, the opposite arrangement is usually adopted, i.e. a broad column is assigned to each family, and successive generations are named in consecutive lines that follow each other from the head to the foot of the page.

In addition to the names and dates which are usually inserted in these entries, informative detail occasionally creeps in, e.g. the circumstances in which a senior official was promoted or forced to resign; or the crimes of which statesmen and noblemen were accused and for which they were subsequently degraded or dismissed. The tables are not full records of families or office-holders, as the registers of the incumbents are usually far from complete. As the usual practice is to enter the names of eldest sons only, and to omit mention of female members of the families, the tables can hardly be used for accurate genealogical or sociological investigation.

Treatises

The treatises are narrative accounts, or dissertations on select topics of imperial government. In addition to the author's own summaries of contemporary practice and his comments, they may incorporate documents, or extracts of documents, that were drawn up for completely different purposes than those of historiography. The chapters may include memorials submitted by statesmen to suggest the solutions of administrative problems; speculations of a philosophical nature on, e.g. the phenomena of the cosmos or the uses of music; lists made out as an inventory of the imperial library; or extracts taken from the census of the empire. The following topics form the subjects of the ten treatises of the *Han-shu* (i.e. the Standard History for the Western Han dynasty, which was completed some time before *c.* A.D. 100): regulation of the calendar; rites and music; punishments of state; economic practice; sacrificial rites; astronomy; the five material elements of the cosmos; administrative units of the empire; waterways; and literary compositions. Many of these subjects recur in the later Standard Histories.

Biographies

In the biographies, leading personalities form the subject matter, and they are treated as the heroes of the story. Usually each chapter is concerned with a single individual, but sometimes a number of men are treated together within the same chapter, e.g. if they were concerned in the same series of incidents; if their careers or choice of behaviour was markedly similar; if they shared common ties of kinship; or if their achievements were of the same type. There are also chapters in this category in which the subject is formed not by an individual man, but by a foreign tribe or people.

The biographies inform the reader of a man's origin and family, the circumstances of his upbringing, education and rise to fame, and the main incidents in his career of public service. The chapters usually end with a note regarding the individual's descendants. In addition to the official subject matter, the biographies sometimes include material of a fictional or anecdotal nature, and the approach to a personality may be far from formal. Conventional epithets appear frequently, and occasion is often taken to describe the hero's reactions to a given situation of a conventional type (e.g. poverty, misrepresentation or undeserved derision) in order to demonstrate his qualities or his failings.

Throughout the Standard Histories, the treatises and biographies are compiled in a uniform style, designed to present the contents in a clear, direct and unambiguous manner. Nevertheless difficulties of interpretation or understanding have perplexed the Chinese readers from the third century, and exhaustive commentaries have happily been written to aid the students of a later age.

Variations of form

These divisions form the principal framework of the *Shih-chi* and the subsequent Standard Histories, which drew much of their inspiration form and method from Ssu-ma Ch'ien's model. Ssu-ma Ch'ien had appended personal comments, criticism or summaries at the end of most of his chapters, and the practice of presenting such an appraisal, clearly separated from the events that are described, persisted in the later compilations.

As the *Shih-chi* was concerned with matters of both the pre-imperial and imperial ages, the chapters of Annals, Tables and Biographies take as their subject the events or personalities of the 'Hsia' to the Han period; and the institutions of both the pre-imperial, and the Ch'in and Han ages are duly described in the Treatises. A formal difference between the *Shi-chi* and its successors is that the biographical chapters of the *Shih-chi* are actually split into two categories, entitled (a) the hereditary houses and (b) the biographies.

Some of the extant Standard Histories consist of parts of compilations which were made by two or more authors and which were later assembled to form a single work. There are cases in which all four elements are not present (e.g. the Tables were not always compiled). Considerable variation can be observed in the selection of topics for treatment in the treatises, and such differences reveal the growing maturity in the historians' attitude to institutions and public life. In most of the Standard Histories, a good half of the work consists of biographies.

Scissors and paste compilations

The evolution of the four-fold form of the Standard History marks a turning point in Chinese historiography. The form allowed for the inclusion of ready-made documents, with considerable benefit to posterity; but the histories are open to the criticism that they are little more than scissors and paste productions, and there are few of the twenty-six which can be entirely exempted from the charge. It has been shown that parts of earlier texts such as the *Book of Documents* were incorporated into the *Shih-chi*'s account of early history; other examples are seen in the texts of imperial decrees which were inserted after the very necessary process of editorship and simplification; in some of the extracts that appear in the treatises (see p. 284); or in passages taken from earlier Standard Histories (see p. 247 for the use of such material without acknowledgement and with subsequent anachronism).

Repetition

The four-fold form of the histories implies the inclusion of several references to the same incident, described from a different point of view or for a different purpose. For example, if a famous military commander succeeded in suppressing a rebellion, the event would be noted in the Imperial Annals, and, with greater detail, in the relevant biography of the commander. It might occur again, in the tables, if the commander's success had been rewarded by the bestowal of a title or appointment to high office; and as such an incident may have affected the institutions of government, it might also figure in one or more of the treatises. For this reason, the full information regarding a particular act may lie dispersed in a number of passages within the same history; and to trace the progress of a clan or family over a long period, it may be necessary to consult two or more of the Standard Histories to achieve full coverage.

The state's sponsorship of historical writing

The first examples of the Standard Histories were compiled, like the *Shih-chi*, as matters of private venture undertaken by individuals, or members of a single family. In these enterprises the government often lent support and encouragement; the compilers usually held official appointments, and were provided with access to some of the records of government. But a significant change took place from the T'ang period onwards, when the compilation of the histories became a task that devolved on designated officials. From now on, the state assumed responsibility for the production of the Standard Histories. A commission, which was established as part of the normal complement of the civil service, was charged with the task of presenting to the throne the finished history of the previous dynasty, and preparing a draft history of the contemporary house with a view to its publication in due course.

The dignity of this task was such that it was usual to associate one of the most senior and honoured statesmen with the project, and the appointment of such a personage as president of the commission bore considerable advantages to the government. A new dynasty could win a statesman's loyalty by charging him with so congenial and respected a duty; and his willingness to accept such an office could in turn be used to persuade junior officials to support the new regime. Moreover, the reputation of an acknowledged statesman-scholar could be used to advertise the impartiality of the work. The assumption of this responsibility by the government also marks some change of emphasis in the purposes for which the Standard Histories were compiled. They were now being written to provide guidance for officials, as well as to act as illustrations of moral precept; they were being written by bureaucrats for bureaucrats.

The process of compilation
The work of the history commissions depended on the earlier preparation of a whole series of notes, sometimes written in the form of diaries, and the perusal and editorship of a large volume of relevant material on which they were entitled to call (e.g. the reports on an official's conduct, which could be used in writing biographies). The commission selected material for inclusion in the history, and made a number of drafts, of which the final one was termed the *Veritable Record*; and as successive stages of the work were completed, the previous drafts and their sources were destroyed. Ideally the commission was free to make use of all administrative records; it was to work in seclusion, free from the fear of criticism and uninhibited by political considerations. In practice, as the members of the commission were themselves civil servants of committed political affiliations, such an ideal could rarely be achieved; and there were occasions when opposing political groups could find means of thwarting the work of the commission.

Incomplete coverage
The full series of Standard Histories is concerned with a period of over 2,000 years. The works refer to selected events throughout that period, but it cannot be claimed that they cover the period completely. There are many aspects of contemporary activities which are not mentioned, and for long intervals the Standard Histories are concerned only with matters that affected one particular reigning dynasty or a limited part of the Chinese sub-continent.

Historians and dynastic continuity
Western readers are soon struck by the peculiar Chinese concept of

historical process. Reference has been made above to the treatment of dynastic change (see pp. 281 f), and the fundamentalist concept of a golden era from which human standards have for long and inevitably been receding. There is little sense of evolution in the Standard Histories, where contemporary political, economic, social and cultural conditions are frequently taken for granted, without reference to the developments of the immediately preceding age. This deficiency is particularly noticeable in some of the later compilations, where attempts to trace causality or to interpret events in their major context are almost wholly lacking.

The Chinese view of time and the assessment of political structures is subordinated to the needs of compiling histories so as to serve the cause of contemporary dynasties. Histories were compiled to vindicate the actions or to support the authority of the compilers' own employers. In demonstrating that the unique Mandate of Heaven had been correctly and legitimately received by one regime after the collapse of another, historians were sometimes perplexed by obvious difficulties, if they had to handle the simultaneous existence of two or more dynastic houses. The compelling need to nominate those houses in which the Mandate reposed could be of particular relevance, and embarrassment, at a time when an alien house had forcibly established itself in part of Chinese territory. The portrayal of an uninterrupted line of dynasties, which successively held legitimate claim to the Mandate, has led to one of the gravest misapprehensions regarding Chinese history, to the effect that the empire has been ruled continuously for over 2,000 years.

The intervals of non-government
The practice of compiling the Standard Histories according to dynastic periods has led to considerable distortion. The different degrees of significance to be attached to particular houses have been obscured. Not only has this treatment involved the description of certain rulers in the conventional terms of tyrant, usurper or popular saviour; it has also served to conceal the existence of long periods when imperial government was only partially effective. For in the Standard Histories, dynastic events and fortunes are necessarily related to an idealist norm of continuous and controlled government, irrespective of radical changes which may have rendered such concepts completely unrealistic.

HISTORICAL EVIDENCES

Rebel or hero?

As the authors of the Standard Histories were obliged to write on behalf of their employers, the interpretation of incidents that threatened, or actually interrupted, dynastic survival varied directly in accordance with their outcome. In the case of an unsuccessful bid to establish a new regime, its leaders were described as rebels, who fully deserved their defeat and consequent punishment. But when a venture ended with the victory of the insurgents, a new dynastic regime was founded, and its protagonists were themselves anxious to employ historians to authenticate their origins. In such circumstances the struggles that had preceded foundation were portrayed as the correct solution of political difficulties.

Two examples will show the resulting inconsistency. In A.D. 9 Wang Mang established himself as emperor in place of a member of the Han house of Liu, and in 23 he was himself driven from the throne by champions who restored the Han dynasty. As these events were described after the Han restoration, Wang Mang is described as an usurper, who tried illegally to seize the throne and who met his just deserts. But with Li Shih-min, who reigned as the second of the T'ang emperors (T'ai tsung; reigned 626–648) we have an example of the opposite case. Li Shih-min's accession took place after an armed incident in which two of his brothers (including the Crown Prince) were killed and his father was forced to abdicate. His reign was long, and markedly successful, and he was duly followed by his lawful successors. Historians therefore took considerable pains to whitewash Li Shih-min's personal part in the events that preceded his accession, so that his conduct could not be brought into question. But there can be small doubt that, had the outcome of the incident been different, Li Shih-min would have been branded as a villain, and held up for general obsecration.

The expression of bias

As the compilers of the Standard Histories were trained on the basis of Confucian doctrine and were themselves members of the privileged class of scholar-officials, it is not surprising that their works are biassed against potentially rival groups or other types of state servant. Only rarely will a Standard History admit the virtues of a eunuch, or will it be able to shake free of political prejudice. Historians could easily show their bias in the choice of subjects for inclusion in the biographies. If expediency so demanded, a name could be entirely omitted from the select list. Alternatively, a moral judgment could be clearly expressed

T

by grouping a man with those who had earned admiration or notoriety. A man's reputation could be made for ever, if he was included in the chapter that described the lives of 'Notable scholars'; and it could be damned beyond redemption by inclusion among the 'Oppressive officials'.

The choice of subject matter

In laying emphasis on certain aspects of public or official life, the Standard Histories may appear to lack a due sense of proportion. To the Chinese court and palace, the exact observances of the ceremonies prescribed for the emperor were matters of far greater significance than they are to modern students of history; and in the Standard Histories, such events are selected for description in terms that will satisfy the standpoint of the emperor and his officials. By contrast, a modern historian may look in vain for reference to some of the major subjects that excite his attention. In the biographies, the actions of an individual are mentioned, provided that they have some bearing on his work as an official; personal details that shed light on the character of a man, or his intellectual or emotional development, may well be excluded as lacking relevance; and for that reason, very little is known of the private life or personal leanings of most of the personages who appear on the pages of Chinese history.

Similarly, the compilation of the histories was directed to recording the activities of the small class of the privileged élite, and was not primarily concerned with the destinies, or livelihood of the great majority of the population. For this reason, selected chapters or passages, if presented out of context, can easily give rise to a highly false impression of the constitution of Chinese society or the way of life of its peoples. Developments of major importance that concerned, e.g. economic practice, scientific discovery or technological advance are rarely mentioned for their intrinsic value; they feature only as incidents that derive from imperial initiative or provoke official reaction.

The ideal view of institutions

A further cause of misapprehension may result from the esteem with which official institutions are treated. The organs established by the state are described in considerable detail, acccording to a perfect scheme which provides for ideal government, a fair distribution of authority and the faultless implementation of superior orders. There is little or no suggestion of an underlying difference between theory and practice, or of the effect of human failings and misdemeanour in weakening such systems or vitiating their operation.

The difficulty of corroboration

The Standard Histories are annalistic compilations removed by several stages from the events that they record and their contemporary evidence. And although many stages of compilation intervened between the initiation of the first drafts and the completion of the final work, the documents that resulted from such intermediate processes have been deliberately destroyed, almost in entirety. There was no certainty that complete or relevant records of administration would be made available to the history office, and there can have been few opportunities for the members of the commission to seek corroboratory evidence, even had they been anxious to do so. For the earlier periods of history, the modern reader is rarely able to confirm the statements of the histories by means of independent controls, and it is only from the T'ang or Sung periods onwards that the great wealth of Chinese writings can be used effectively to illustrate and supplement the assertions or theories of the Standard Histories.

However, the major, and voluminous, sources of information which can be used in this way may sometimes be difficult to handle or to evaluate; and the welcome corroboration that is provided in contemporary diaries or travelogues, short stories or dramas, or the long novels of the Ming period and later cannot be expected to be of a uniform or comprehensive nature. The importance of these works lies partly in their casual acceptance of established practices and the mundane context in which they place the idealist theories of the state historian.

III. THE BEGINNINGS OF CRITICISM

The shortcomings of the history commission

The difficulties of working as a member of the history commission soon led to the beginnings of criticism. Liu Chih-chi (661–721), who had worked for two years in that office, was moved by his experiences and frustrations to write the Shih-t'ung, or 'Generalities on History' (completed in 710) in which he endeavoured to describe the difficulties of the system and to suggest solutions. Liu complained of the difficulty of reaching a decision within the commission, as compromise was continually necessary so as to satisfy all members. He noted that there was in fact no assured access to official documents, and that the seclusion of the commission within the palace was in practice intimidating rather than protective. In addition, contradictory instructions were sometimes given by different editors, and the work of the commission was marked by inconsistency; and there was no sure or efficient means of fairly allocating tasks between different members.

Suggestions for change

Liu Chih-chi was bold enough to adopt a radical approach to the problems of historiography. He wrote that the accepted authority of the acknowledged masters of Chinese thought must be brought into question, and that an uncritical respect for the classical texts of the Confucian tradition must be rejected. He scorned the use that had been made of legend or myth to establish an historical tradition, or the genealogical claims lodged on behalf of imperial ancestors; and he suggested ways for improving the arrangement and content of the Standard Histories. He hoped that these could be framed to suit the practical needs of government in a more rational way; that material included improperly in the past (e.g. bibliographical catalogues of imperial collections, or lists of natural phenomena such as eclipses) would be excluded in future; that the commission would stop using literary conventions which could give a misleading impression of personalities; and that it would concentrate its energies on preparing a more direct record of actual events or speeches. Liu Chih-chi was suggesting the abandonment of the traditional devices of concealment or distortion, that could be traced back to the Ch'un-ch'iu and which had been used to lend bias to the historians' work; he sought to encourage historians to write accurate accounts of the truth, irrespective of consequence.

Ssu-ma Kuang's achievement

Liu Chih-chi is one of the earliest exponents of a critical approach to historiography, and his ideas presaged the practical undertakings of a later generation. These are seen conspicuously in the work of Ssu-ma Kuang (1019–86), whose view combined Liu Chih-chi's dislike of periodization in dynastic terms with a search for corroboration and consistency. The resulting work, 'The Comprehensive Mirror for aid in government' has sometimes been described as the most manageable account of Chinese history; it can be read with greater ease and comprehension than the Standard Histories.

The Comprehensive Mirror

Ssu-ma Kuang had embarked on an official career at a time when the bureaucratic profession had reached a new height of prestige. He had become one of the leading conservative statesmen, and was deeply opposed to the current suggestions of political, economic and social reform which were being voiced by Wang An-shih (see pp. 206 f.). With the ascendancy of the latter's views, Ssu-ma Kuang retired from active politics (1070) and devoted himself to historical research. In this field his views were markedly different from his political opinions, and his radical approach was soon to be illustrated in his writings. For he organized a project for the compilation of a new historical account of China, which was finally entitled the *Tẓu-chih-t'ung-chien*, or 'Comprehensive Mirror for aid in government'. The title was in fact bestowed by the emperor, and perhaps betrays a desire to maintain association with the traditional Confucian theory of presenting history as a means of moral uplift.

Ssu-ma Kuang's project was organized as a private venture which enjoyed some measure of official support; and the work involved the recruitment of a team of writers, and the evolution of new procedures for drafting and compilation. Thanks to his motive, Ssu-ma Kuang and his colleagues adopted somewhat different working methods from those of the official history commission. The compilation was based not on diaries or court records such as had been available to the compilers of the Standard Histories, but mainly on those histories themselves. For the earlier period, Ssu-ma Kuang and his team had scant means of corroboration but for the more recent centuries he was more fortunate.

The faults of the Standard Histories

The *Comprehensive Mirror* had been inspired by dissatisfaction with the Standard Histories. Ssu-ma Kuang was well aware of the internal inconsistencies between different parts of one and the same history, and of the textual inaccuracies that were brought to light by the comparison of different passages; and in seeking to make such comparisons, he had found that the form of the Standard Histories was unwieldy, and precluded easy access to all the information relevant to a particular time or incident. Above all, Ssu-ma Kuang felt that the division of time by dynastic periods was misleading, and that it led to a false view of imperial, human and social development.

Ssu-ma Kuang's treatment of events

In the *Comprehensive Mirror* steps were taken to eliminate these artificial distinctions. History was to be presented in consecutive, logical fashion, without the shackles of the four-fold division of the Standard Histories or their other limitations. Passages were therefore taken from all parts of those works, and the text was recast in such a way that all the details of an incident were recorded in one place. The resulting chronicle comprised much of the original text of the Standard Histories, with as little alteration as possible. It was arranged in strict chronological order, under annual headings, and covered the period from 403 B.C. to A.D. 959. The *Mirror* recorded the fortunes of co-existent dynasties in north and south, whether they had qualified to become the legitimate holders of the Mandate, or were regarded as usurpers of the throne.

This history could hardly cover the years of the contemporary Sung dynasty, and the *Comprehensive Mirror* closes just before its foundation in A.D. 959. But the choice of 403 B.C. as the point of origin is not without interest, as the year was chosen for its historical significance. It marks the dissolution of Tsin, a major state of the Spring and Autumn period, and its replacement by the three smaller units (Han, Wei and Chao) of the Warring Kingdoms. Ssu-ma Kuang's radical approach is seen in the choice of this year rather than 480 as his *terminus a quo*. For the *Spring and Autumn Annals*, whose compilation was ascribed to Confucius, concluded with the events of 481; and traditionalists could well claim that that date would form a more appropriate beginning. However, Ssu-ma Kuang preferred to start at a point where he discerned historical change, rather than adopt a slavish compliance with a tradition that implied arbitrary periodization.

Ssu-ma Kuang's use of different sources
The textual inconsistencies between different parts of the Standard Histories sometimes forced the compilers of the *Comprehensive Mirror* to choose between several conflicting versions, and in such cases they were obliged to exercise a personal judgment so as to present the more probable account. Where possible, other evidence was consulted, e.g. from surviving fragments of the Veritable Records or other drafts that had preceded the publication of the Standard Histories; from inscriptions; or from non-historical sources such as literary collections or even anecdotes. To explain or justify a choice that had been made between different versions, or to cite the sources of corroboratory information, a set of notes was afterwards compiled, so that readers of the *Mirror* could themselves assess the conclusions of the authors. In the

Comprehensive Mirror itself, Ssu-ma Kuang's highly pertinent comments on the significance of particular events appear occasionally, clearly separated from the main narrative.

Textual criticism of the Ch'ing period

The next major advance in historiography took place in the eighteenth century. In the intervening period there had occurred highly important intellectual developments, including the metaphysical speculations that are associated with the Neo-Confucian thinkers. There had been long periods of alien rule, in which philosophers and scholars had been tempted to retire from the active world of the metropolis to re-assess fundamental concepts. At the collapse of the Ming dynasty in 1644, several leading intellectuals could not bring themselves to sever their loyalties to the defunct house, whose weaknesses they ascribed partly to intellectual failure. They felt that excessive attention had been paid to philosophical speculation, and that the practical problems of statesmen required deeper investigation. In reviewing historical events and political theory, they had written a few outstanding, and highly realistic, essays on subjects such as the scope of imperial authority, the abuse of privilege and its relation to dynastic decline, or the proper use of the resources of empire.

At the same time, the official policy of the new Ch'ing dynasty was influencing intellectual effort. The government was emulating the achievements of its predecessors by patronising scholarship; there were imperial projects to preserve rare literature and to propagate the message of the classical texts; and the academic world was being pressed into imperial service, to provide commentaries that could be accepted as orthodox. The new school of Ch'ing scholars not unnaturally reacted against the metaphysics of their predecessors of the Sung and Ming periods, and there was growing up a new school of textual critics, who were endeavouring to elucidate the Confucian texts, according to a rigorous canon of philological analysis. Similar attention was being paid to the texts of the Standard Histories. In a new print of these works which was made at official behest in 1739, a section of notes formed a regular feature at the end of each chapter. These notes were compiled so as to remind the reader of parallel passages; to explain expressions that had long been obsolete; and to solve his difficulties of interpretation. Like Ssu-ma Kuang and his colleagues, the editors called on any other relevant evidence that they thought suitable, and a new value was placed on the importance of inscriptions.

The reaction against the scholastic approach

The new edition of the Standard Histories was a major contribution of the Ch'ing scholars to contemporary literary activity, and new standards were reached in evolving a critical discipline and methods of academic research. But the current trend was itself criticized. Chang Hsüeh-ch'eng (1738–1801), who lived at a time when Ch'ing scholarship was reaching its height, thought that the academic world was concentrating unduly on scholastic minutiae. He felt that historical evidences were being considered piecemeal in isolation, and that the existence of major problems or implications was passing unnoticed; and owing to the disproportionately deep researches in textual matters, no attempt was being made at historical synthesis. In the prevailing intellectual climate, Chang Hsüeh-ch'eng was bold enough to assert that it was more important to study history so as to improve the human lot than to con Confucian texts for their inherent moral lessons; and that such texts should themselves be treated first and foremost as historical evidences. Chang's independence of mind is seen in his criticism of the traditional methods of historical compilation. He saw the need for the selection of material, its evaluation and treatment in a synthetical way; and he believed that a subjective approach could, and should, be adopted without distorting the facts presented by the evidence.

IV. SUPPLEMENTARY SOURCES

The major encyclopaedias

The anthology had come into being as a genre of literature long before the T'ang period. Scholars had carefully and devotedly selected choice passages from literary works, either to set out examples of different styles of prose and poetry, or to illustrate the teachings of a particular school of philosophy. Similar collections of purple passages or phrases were sometimes made to assist students who were preparing for the examinations by seeking familiarity with literary elegance; and from the ninth century, collections or encyclopaedias were being compiled deliberately to assist civil servants in the execution of their duties. As the information which would be of greatest use to civil servants concerned the institutions and operation of government, or precedents which could act as authority for an administrative decision, such works also provide a useful source of knowledge for latter day historians.

These encyclopaedias are usually divided into large sections which correspond with major aspects of government (e.g. economic practice, the system of recruiting officials, the functions of the civil service, the rites, music, the armed forces, state punishments, administrative geography, and frontier defences); these are further sub-divided chronologically, and describe practice from the earliest period up to the time of the compiler. The early encyclopaedists drew their copy both from works which still survive, including the Standard Histories, and from other material which is now lost; and they were glad to append a few paragraphs of their own composition, in which contemporary practice could be explained or the stark facts of institution amplified. At their best, the encyclopaedias could enable an original thinker to communicate his own personal comment on matters of the past, as he was bound neither by the set form of the Standard Histories nor the inhibitions of working in the History Office. At their worst, these works were yet a further type of blind and uncritical scissors and paste compilation. They are of greatest use with reference to the T'ang and subsequent periods.

The Hui-yao *and the local histories*
Following the major encyclopaedias, there are shorter works of the same type which concern a single dynastic period (the *Hui-yao*), and which are also arranged according to different aspects of government. In addition Chinese scholars have compiled a large number of works which refer only to specified localities. These gazeteers, or local histories, draw on a wider range of evidence than other works considered here, and provide varied types of information, such as the extent of local mineral resources, the main lines of communication, prominent buildings or other features. Local myth or folklore is sometimes included in the gazeteers, which also contain biographical accounts of distinguished individuals or families.

Accounts written by foreigners
One of the earliest surviving descriptions of China written by a foreign traveller is the diary kept by Ennin during his visit of the ninth century (see p. 268). Many descriptive accounts have since appeared, principally from the pens of western observers. Reference has been made above (p. 238) to the account of Marco Polo; and since then China has figured in the reports of missionaries (of the Jesuit and other orders, from the sixteenth century), diplomats (e.g. Lord Macartney's journal,

1793–4; and Lord Amherst's despatches, 1816) and, more recently, prospectors, press correspondents or businessmen. With so great a diversity of writers, the type and value of these accounts varies considerably. While Ennin was mostly interested in the manner of Buddhist worship and the opportunities for seeking true doctrine, Marco Polo was anxious to impress his audience with the tales of the splendours that he had witnessed; and while Lord Macartney possessed shrewd powers of observation, his assessment of Ch'ien-lung's court and empire was limited by unfamiliarity with the Chinese language, and by his involuntary view of China from the standpoint of the eighteenth century European. The value of the foreigners' reports lies in the corrective that they can give to the official Chinese view; but as the foreign writers were themselves sometimes guilty of special pleading, their own accounts may stand in similar need of rectification. It is only rarely, and comparatively recently, that there have been forthcoming simultaneous accounts written by foreign observers of antagonistic persuasions.

Records of administrative action
Finally, it may be justly asked what material exists in archive to record the transactions that took place between officials and the members of the public; for it is by such records that the extent or success of government can be measured. It can be surmised that the Chinese bureaucracy produced a veritable mountain of administrative documents; of reports forwarded from one level of government to the next, with appropriate recommendation added at every stage; of instructions transmitted from the highest in the land to the most humble servant of the community, with precise orders for implementation; or of receipts with which civilians could prove themselves quit of their obligations or entitled to receive privileged treatment.

For the first 1,000 years of imperial government a mere handful of fragments survives from so rich a store of historical evidence. The administration of the Han officials is verified by a few strips of wooden document found in central Asia; the same region yields valuable, and more sizeable, scraps of paper, which prove, among other things, that the officials of T'ang China did in practice allocate the land according to the theoretical provisions of the state. For the Sung and subsequent periods, a greater volume of archive material becomes available, and statistical information can be used for limited purposes; and students of the Ch'ing dynasty are faced with far more material than they can easily handle. But for the greater part of the imperial period, the complexity and efficiency of the administration cannot be directly evidenced by a correspondingly rich supply of documentary proof.

CONCLUSION

Reliance on political and dynastic change as the sole means of marking China's historical development is now happily passing out of fashion and giving place to an assessment in the light of cultural, social and economic evolution. These dynamic processes are of their very nature steady rather than sudden, inconspicuous rather than dramatic, and it is often difficult to designate particular years or events by which their pace can be measured. But in reviewing the practices of the early, middle and later empires, it frequently comes about that the brilliant age of Sung China, of the eleventh to thirteenth centuries, forms a convenient epoch for discerning the onset of radical transformations.

Up to the T'ang age the emphasis of China's economy was situated in the north, but from the latter part of the Sung dynasty the south had acquired a greater significance. Numerous dynasties arose in northern China both before and after 1126; but up to the tenth century they ruled from the north-west, thereafter from the north-east. Before Sung, Chinese towns had come into being largely in response to official urges; from the eleventh and twelfth centuries richer and larger cities arose to suit the growing commercial prosperity of a new age, whose transactions now depended on paper money.

Before Sung, the ranks of officialdom had usually been filled by members of a distinct and highly select circle. By the Ming period the prosperous merchant of the south was fast acquiring social predominance; and entreé to the élite class had been opened to men whose origins and interests, training and experience would not satisfy the orthodox standards of the previous age.

From the Sung period—or perhaps earlier—there can be traced the beginnings of a lively drama and literature suited to vulgar taste rather than formal approbation. Intellectually the approaches of the scholar-officials of the Han and T'ang dynasties form a conspicuous contrast with the exercises in metaphysics of the Sung and Ming thinkers; and the spirit of academic enquiry was to lead Sung scholars and scientists to new methods of research and criticism, to new adventures in experiment and technology. When the re-assessment or man's place in the world and society, that had been propounded by some of the Sung philosophers, was itself outmoded or stale, there arose a new school of critical and scientific research, which imparted fresh and rigorous canons to the intellectual achievements of the seventeenth and eighteenth centuries.

If, for practical purposes, it is necessary to divide the history of imperial China into periods, such divisions must recognize the importance of the Sung era as a watershed that separates two different types of Chinese culture, society and economy. Historians may recognize different subdivisions, according to their particular interests in different aspects of China's history. In dynastic terms, the establishment of an alien dynasty in 317 and the re-establishment of native houses in 618 and 1368 can perhaps claim to be events of crucial importance. Economists may prefer to fasten on the completion of the first and second Grand Canals, in about 600 and 1300, or the attempts at financial reform of the eighth and sixteenth centuries. In cultural terms, the acceptance of Buddhism as an integral part of Chinese culture marks a vital change in the first 1,000 years of Chinese empire; and the arrival of the westerner in the sixteenth century, though not conspicuously influential for some time, heralded the dawn of a new era in which the established traditions of the old China were to be questioned, scorned and rejected.

APPENDIX

(1) GUIDE TO PRONUNCIATION

The pronunciation of Chinese words and names has sometimes been un-necessarily complicated by the adoption of unsystematic or unsatisfactory methods of Romanization, or by the inconsistent reference to different spoken dialects. The system that is used most regularly in English books which are concerned with Chinese cultural subjects is the one that was first evolved by Sir Thomas Wade, from 1859, and later modified by H. A. Giles; despite its shortcomings it has been retained for use here.

Traditionally, Chinese scholars have distinguished between three ele-ments of which their monosyllabic words are composed; (a) an initial con-sonant or a null; (b) a final element, being either a simple vowel, a diphthong or triphthong, and ending sometimes with sounds that are represented in the Wade-Giles system as *n* or *ng*; and (c) a tone, i.e. the variation of distinctive pitch with which the syllable is pronounced. The most important feature of simplification introduced into the modified Wade-Giles system that is in general use is the omission of diacritical marks that were adopted originally to designate the tones.

The following list of approximate equivalent sounds has been drawn up on a non-technical basis, to provide immediate guidance only. It refers to the linguistic form which has been known variously under the terms *Kuan-hua* (Mandarin), *Kuo-yü* (National Language) or, more recently, *P'u-t'ung-hua* (Common Speech). This is mainly based on the dialect of Peking, but it also contains features of other Northern Chinese dialects; and it is used in the semi-formal conversations of educated people. For a systematic con-sideration of the subject, with equivalent sounds rendered according to the International Phonetic Alphabet, see W. Simon and C. H. Lu, *Chinese Sentence Series* (London, 1942); and for a recent attempt at practical guidance see John de Francis, *Beginning Chinese* (Revised edition, Yale University Press, New Haven and London, 1963).

If all the initial and final elements were used in combination, and if each combination were pronounced in each of the four tones of this dialect, the potential total of different monosyllabic words would be around 3,500. In practice, only about 400 combinations of initial and final elements occur, and these are not all pronounced in all four tones. The total number of different syllables actually in use in this dialect is thus about 1,500. It should be noted that the list of initial and final elements that is given here derives from the conventions of the Wade-Giles spelling, and does not entirely or necessarily represent the distinctions drawn by Chinese traditional scholars or modern phoneticians. Two examples are given in the Tables where possible.

(a) Initial elements

Initial element	Complete Chinese word	Approximate English equivalent	Initial element	Complete Chinese word	Approximate English equivalent
ch	Chin	gin	s	sang	sung
	Chou	Joe		se	sir
ch'	Ch'i	cheese	sh	shai	shy
	Ch'in	chin		shou	show
f	fan	fun	ss (or sz)	ssu	release
	fei	failure		szu	peace
h	ho	her	t	tang	dung
	hang	hung		te	dirt
hs	hsi	sheet	t'	T'ang	tongue
	hsing	Cingalese		t'ou	toe
j	jao	row (i.e. quarrel)	ts	tsai	Clydeside
	ju	rue			
k	kai	guy	ts'	ts'en	Watson
	kan	gun	tz	tzu	cheese, Windsor
k'	k'ao	cow	tz'	tz'u	Whitsun
	k'uai	quite			
l	lao	loud	w	wan	wonder
	liu	lewd		wei	way
m	mai	my	y	yang	young
	mei	may			
n	nan	nun			
	nai	night			
p	pang	bung			
	pi	bee			
p'	p'an	pun			
	p'in	pin			

(b) Final elements

Final element	Pronounce as in	Notes
a	past; father	
ai	guy; my	
an	fun; gun	
ang	tongue; bung	
ao	cow; loud	
e	sir; dirt	More strictly written ê. After h, k, and k', written o.
ei	failure; may	
en	orphan; woman	
eng	organ-grinder; ocean-going	
erh	journey; cur	
i	sheet; bee	
ia	deeply under[1]	
iai	Holy Island[1]	
iang	young	
iao	twenty owls[1]	

[1] As in rapid speech.

Final element	Pronounce as in	Notes
ieh	collegiate; yes	
ien	quickly entering[1]	
ih	lozenge	After ch, ch', sh and j
in	chin; pin	
ing	ring; ling	
iu	lewd; view	
iung	Dominion grade; how does the tune go?	
o	her; girl	after h, k and k' only
	paw; law	after other initials
ou	Joe; toe	
u	release; piece	More strictly written ŭ; after ss, sz, tz, tz' only
	yeoman	after y
	do; two	after other initials
ua	Guam	
uai	quite; white	
uan	one	
uang	one goal[1]	
ui	sway; wane	written uei after k and k'
un	town	
ung	(German) Achtung	
uo	walk	
ü	(French) une	
üan	(French) Tu Anne	
üeh	ewer	
ün	(French) une	

[1] As in rapid speech.

(2) NOTES FOR FURTHER READING

The following list of books has been compiled to provide initial guidance for readers who wish to pursue an interest in the subjects that have been mentioned above. It has deliberately been restricted to a few select works written in European languages that are available with comparative ease.

One of the main difficulties facing students of traditional China is the lack of usable interpretative editions or versions of original source material, and of text book histories that cover specific periods. Much of the secondary writing is perforce of a technical nature, and must still be characterized by the philologists' approach rather than the historians' use and evaluation of evidence. In selecting titles for inclusion below, I have been well aware that it is impossible to be comprehensive, up-to-date or impartial, or to satisfy the interests of all types of reader. The literature of the subject is increasing yearly. Specialized lists appear in many of the books that are listed here; and short descriptive notes to many titles will be found in C. O. Hucker; *China A Critical Bibliography* (Tucson, Arizona, 1962). See also the *Revue Biblio-*

graphique de Sinologie (Mouton, Paris) for English and French abstracts of specialist publications on Chinese subjects (this series covers the most important books and articles written in European and Oriental languages since 1955).

1. *General histories and books of general significance*
The most recent, and perhaps the most comprehensive, of the general histories is *East Asia, The Great Tradition*, by E. O. Reischauer and J. K. Fairbank (London, 1960), and its companion volume that concerns the modern period (*East Asia, The Modern Transformation*, by J. K. Fairbank, E. O. Reischauer and A. Craig, 1965). For a useful short account, see L. C. Goodrich, *A Short History of the Chinese People* (London, second edition 1958; third impression 1962); and for a sociologist's interpretation, W. Eberhard, *A History of China* (London, 1950). For the development of China's cultural characteristics, see H. Maspero and J. Escarra, *Les Institutions de la Chine* (Paris, 1952); and a short introductory survey, by A. F. P. Hulsewé, extending from the earliest times to the Han period, has been included under the title *China im Altertum* in *Propyläen-Weltgeschichte* II pp. 479–571 (Berlin, 1962). A recent appreciation of various aspects of Chinese civilization has been published as *The Legacy of China*, edited by R. Dawson (Oxford, 1964).

2. *Monographs etc. concerning particular subjects*
The following works have been arranged as far as possible so as to correspond with the order of the subjects that are discussed in the foregoing chapters. Where a subject overlaps between different chapters, only one entry has usually been made.

Chapter One
The physical characteristics of China itself and the neighbouring parts of Asia are shown very clearly in *The Reader's Digest Great World Atlas* (London, 1962); for the development of kingdoms and empires, see A. Herrmann, *Historical and Commercial Atlas of China* (Cambridge, Massachusetts; the original edition, in colour, of 1935 is now out of print, and has been followed by an impression in black and white, undated, *c.* 1961; a reprint in colour has been produced recently in Taipei, Formosa). In *China's Geographic Foundations* (New York, 1934) G. B. Cressey provides a modern geographer's survey, with due attention to varieties of climate, natural resources, communications and economic practice (see also the same author's *Land of the 500 Million*, New York, 1955). In *Key Economic Areas in Chinese History* (London, 1936; reprinted, New York, 1963), Chi Ch'ao-ting produced one of the first attempts to examine the effect of geographical and economic factors on the growth of political units. See also O. Lattimore,

APPENDIX

Inner Asian Frontiers of China (Second edition, New York, 1951; paper-back, Boston, 1962).

Chapter Two

A standard account of China's pre-history and the initial development of communal life as evidenced by material finds is provided by T. K. Cheng in *Archaeology in China* (Cambridge, 1959–); for a briefer account, see W. Watson, *China before the Han Dynasty* (London, 1961). An account of the political history and institutions of the pre-imperial age, which is based on early Chinese writings, is given by H. Maspero in *La Chine Antique* (re-vised edition, Paris, 1955). The stages whereby dynasties were founded and organized are described by D. Bodde in *China's First Unifier, a Study of the Ch'in Dynasty as seen in the life of Li Ssu* (Leiden, 1938); and by W. Bing-ham, in *The Founding of the T'ang Dynasty, The Fall of Sui and Rise of T'ang, a Preliminary Survey* (Baltimore, 1941). A case history of a rebellion against imperial authority, where economic, political and military factors are analyzed, is studied by E. G. Pulleyblank, in *The Background of the Rebellion of An Lu-shan* (London, 1955). For an example of the rise of a dynasty of foreign origin, see F. Michael, *The Origin of Manchu Rule in China* (Baltimore, 1942).

Chapter Three

The short list of renderings of a few Chinese philosophical works that is given in Table Three (p. 91) can be supplemented by A. Waley's *Three Ways of Thought in Ancient China* (London, fourth impression, 1964), and more extensively in *Sources of the Chinese Tradition*, compiled by W. T. de Bary, Chan Wing-tsit and Burton Watson (New York, 1960); this volume includes translations of basic source material, so as to illustrate the history of Chinese thought from earliest times to the present age. Interpretative studies of Chinese philosophical works are given in Fung Yu-lan, *A Short History of Chinese Philosophy* (New York, 1948), and more briefly by H. Creel in *Chinese Thought from Confucius to Mao Tse-tung* (Chicago, 1953; paper-back, New York, 1960). The following volumes have been produced as a result of a series of conferences concerning the development of Chinese thought and comprise specialist articles by a large number of contributors (titles are preceded by the names of the editors): A. Wright, *Studies in Chinese Thought* (Chicago, 1953); J. K. Fairbank, *Chinese Thought and Institutions* (Chicago, 1957); D. Nivison and A. Wright, *Confucianism in Action* (Stanford, 1959); A. Wright, *The Confucian Persuasion* (Stanford, 1960); and D. Twitchett and A. Wright, *Confucian Personalities* (Stanford, 1962).

Chapter Four

For introductory volumes to the arts of China, see L. Sickman and A. Soper,

The Art and Architecture of China (London, 1956); W. Willets, *Chinese Art* (London, 1958); and M. Sullivan, *An Introduction to Chinese Art* (London, 1961). English translations of the earliest collections of Chinese poetry are to be found in A. Waley, *The Book of Songs* (London, second impression, 1950) and D. Hawkes, *Ch'u Tẓ'u, The Songs of the South* (Oxford, 1959). Chinese poems of the imperial period are included in A. Waley, *Chinese Poems* (London, 1946 and 1956, and paper-back 1964); and in *The Penguin Book of Chinese Verse* (ed. A. R. Davis; London, 1962). For prose writings, see E. Edwards, *Chinese Prose Literature of the T'ang Period* (London, Probsthain, 1937–8). English versions of Chinese works of fiction are available as *All Men are Brothers* (trs. Pearl Buck; New York, 1937, reprinted, 1957); *Monkey* (trs. A. Waley; London, sixth impression, 1953), and *Dream of the Red Chamber* (trs. Wang Chi-chen; New York, 1958). Six short stories are translated by C. Birch, in *Stories from a Ming Collection* (London, 1958); see also C. C. Wang, *Traditional Chinese Tales* (New York, 1944).

An informative textbook of the history of literature, without citations from the original sources, which was written by Nagasawa Kikuya, has been enlarged and translated by P. Eugen Feifel, as *Geschichte der Chinesischen Literatur* (Darmstadt, 1959). In *Early Chinese Literature* (New York, 1962); Burton Watson treats the same subject, as far as the Han period, under the main headings of history, philosophy and poetry; translations of select passages are included.

The place taken by Buddhism in China's cultural evolution has been described by A. Wright in *Buddhism in Chinese History* (Stanford, 1959). For the Chinese language, see B. Karlgren, *Sound and Symbol in Chinese* (London, 1923 and 1946; paper-back by Hong Kong University Press, 1962). The early production of Chinese manuscript texts, and the development of printing are described in T. H. Tsien, *Written on Bamboo and Silk* (Chicago, 1962), and T. F. Carter, *The Invention of Printing in China and its Spread Westward* (Second edition, revised by L. C. Goodrich, New York, 1955). For the history of science in China, see J. Needham, *Science and Civilization in China* (Cambridge, 1954– ; this comprehensive work is scheduled to comprise seven volumes). In *Heavenly Clockwork* (Cambridge, 1960), the same author describes Su Sung's astronomical clock and discusses its historical context. For a brief statement regarding the growth of scientific thought, see J. Needham, *Poverties and Triumphs of the Chinese Scientific Tradition* (in *Scientific Change*, pp. 117 f; London, 1963).

For the way of life and achievements of a few members of the élite cultured class, see Lin Yutang, *The Gay Genius* (London, 1948); A. Waley, *The Poetry and Career of Li Po, The Life and Times of Po Chü-i*, and *Yüan Mei, Eighteenth-Century Chinese Poet* (London, 1949, 1951 and 1956); and F. W. Mote, *The Poet Kao Chi, 1336–74* (Princetown, 1962).

APPENDIX

Chapter Five

Owing to the paucity of suitable evidence for the earlier periods, most studies that are concerned with social structure have been directed to investigating the conditions of later rather than earlier China. In *The Chinese Gentry, Studies on their Role in Nineteenth-century Chinese Society* (Seattle, 1955), Chang Chung-li has analysed the various aspects of the élite class that dominated Chinese society, and the same topic is treated by Ping-ti Ho in *The Ladder of Success in Imperial China, Aspects of Social Mobility, 1368–1911* (New York, 1962). For a description of the traditional family system, see Olga Lang, *Chinese Family and Society* (New Haven, 1946). In *Lineage Organization in South-eastern China* (London, 1958), M. Freedman studies a case history of social relationships in southern China. Aspects of the relationship between the organization of government and the methods of recruitment to the civil service are considered by E. A. Kracke in *Civil Service in Early Sung China 960–1067* (Cambridge, Massachusetts, 1953). *Chinese Social History*, by E-tu Zen Sun and J. de Francis (Washington, 1956) consists of translations of twenty-five selected studies written by Chinese scholars from about 1930, concerning social or economic topics and problems from the earliest times to the nineteenth century.

Chapter Six

A clear account of the institutions of government is given in C. O. Hucker, *The Traditional Chinese State in Ming Times (1368–1644)* (Tucson, Arizona, 1961). Longer studies, which comprise introductions and annotated translations of certain chapters of one of the Chinese Standard histories of the T'ang dynasty, and which describe the system of government as this was envisaged ideally, are available in R. des Rotours *Le Traité des Examens* (Paris, 1932), and *Traité des Fonctionnaires et Traité de L'armée* (Leiden, 1947–8). For the practical implementation of the administration, see Ch'ü T'ung-tsu, *Local Administration in China under the Ch'ing* (Cambridge, Massachusetts, 1962), and S. van der Sprenkel, *Legal Institutions in Manchu China* (London, 1962).

Chapter Seven

Money and Credit in China, by Lien-sheng Yang (Cambridge, Massachusetts, 1952), covers the development of systems of coinage and banking from the earliest times. In *Food and Money in Ancient China* (Princetown, 1950), Nancy Lee Swann provides an annotated translation of chapters of the Standard Han History. Her introduction ranges over many aspects of social, political and economic practice of the Han period. For a short account of the conditions of land-ownership, see D. C. Twitchett, *Land Tenure and the Social Order in T'ang and Sung China* (London, School of Oriental and African Studies, 1962); and in *Financial Administration under the T'ang Dynasty*

(Cambridge, 1963), the same author examines the financial and other economic difficulties which faced the T'ang governments and their attempts at solution. Some technical studies are included in *Chinese Social History* (see under Chapter Five). See also E. Balazs, *Chinese Civilization and Bureaucracy* (New Haven and London, 1964).

Chapter Eight

A. Waley's *The Life and Times of Po Chü-i* (London, 1951), gives an insight into official life at the T'ang capital city in the early part of the ninth century. The more seamy side is illustrated in some of the short stories that are included in C. C. Wang, *Traditional Chinese Tales* (New York, 1944). Marco Polo's descriptive but fanciful account of Chinese cities of the thirteenth century can be read in R. E. Latham's edition of his writings (*The Travels of Marco Polo*, London, 1958); and this can be set against the more critical *Daily Life in China on the Eve of the Mongol Invasion 1250–1276* (by J. Gernet; original edition by Hachette, Paris, 1959, as *La Vie Quotidienne en Chine à la Veille de L'invasion Mongole 1250–1276*; English translation, with title as given above, by H. M. Wright, London, 1962). For descriptions of palace life in Peking during the Ch'ing dynasty, see E. Backhouse and J. O. P. Bland, *Annals and Memoirs of the Court of Peking* (London, 1914); J. O. P. Bland and E. Backhouse, *China under the Empress Dowager* (revised edition, London, 1939); and H. McAleavy, *A Dream of Tartary* (London, 1963).

Chapter Nine

O. Lattimore's *Inner Asian Frontiers of China* (Second edition, New York, 1951; paper-back, Boston, 1962), constitutes a standard work which considers China as part of Asia and in relation to her Asiatic neighbours, with full attention to the social and economic implications. For a brief account of the expansion of the Han empire, see M. Loewe, *Military Operations of the Han Period* (The China Society, London, 1961). The importance of China's foreign trading interests during the T'ang dynasty is illustrated in *The Golden Peaches of Samarkand*, by E. H. Schafer (Berkeley, 1963). In *China's Discovery of Africa* (London, 1949), J. J. L. Duyvendak summarized the circumstances attending some of the Chinese maritime expeditions of the early part of the fifteenth century. The development of Chinese relations with western nations can be studied in Lord Macartney's account of his mission to the Chinese court in 1793–4 (edited by J. L. Cranmer-Byng, under the title *An Embassy to China* (London, 1962), and in *China's Response to the West* (Cambridge, Massachusetts, 1954), where Teng Ssu-yü and J. K. Fairbank introduce some of the more important documentary evidence. Other aspects of China's early attitude to foreign lands can be seen in the accounts of two travellers, i.e. *The Real Tripitaka* (London, 1952), where A. Waley records the adventures of a Chinese pilgrim who visited India in

APPENDIX

the seventh century; and *Ennin's Travels in T'ang China* (New York, 1955), where E. Reischauer provides explanatory comment on the diary kept by a Japanese Buddhist priest who travelled in China during the ninth century.

Chapter Ten

The methods of Chinese historians are described by C. S. Gardner in *Chinese Traditional Historiography* (Cambridge, Massachusetts, 1938; second edition, 1961), and a number of the problems are discussed more fully in *Historians of China and Japan*, edited by W. G. Beasley and E. G. Pulleyblank (London, 1961). H. H. Frankel's *Catalogue of Translations from the Chinese Dynastic Histories for the Period 220–960* (Berkeley, 1957), is a valuable list, but many of the entries may not be easily accessible outside specialist libraries.

Of all the Standard Histories, the earliest, i.e. the *Shih-chi* has been made most easily available to western readers. A critical translation of forty-seven chapters ,which has yet to be bettered, was produced by E. Chavannes as *Les Mémoires Historiques de Se-ma Tsien* (Paris, 1895–1905). In *Records of the Grand Historian* (New York, 1961). B. Watson has translated those chapters of the work which refer to the Han period. In an earlier study (*Ssu-ma Ch'ien Grand Historian of China*; New York, 1958), the same author has provided an account of the literary and historical context of Ssu-ma Ch'ien's writings.

3. *The modern period*

The continuing pressure of academic interest in modern China has resulted in an overwhelming increase in the volume of writings on this subject during the last decade. For the place of China as it is being evolved in modern times, see F. H. Michael and G. E. Taylor, *The Far East in the Modern World* (New York, 1956), or H. M. Vinacke, *A History of the Far East in Modern Times* (Sixth edition, New York, 1959). Li Chien-nung's *The Political History of China 1840–1928* (translated by Teng Ssu-yü and J. Ingalls; Princeton, 1956), forms a useful straight narrative history, and can be supplemented by the forthcoming volume by J. K. Fairbank, E. O. Reischauer and A. Craig (details on p. 304 above). Three books are chosen for mention here by way of illustrating the transition from traditional to modern China; A. Waley, *The Opium War through Chinese Eyes* (London, 1958); M. Wright, *The Last Stand of Chinese Conservatism, the T'ung-chih Restoration 1862–74* (Stanford, 1957); and Jerome Ch'en, *Yüan Shih K'ai 1859–1916* (London, 1961). For a brief summary of China's place in the modern world, see J. K. Fairbank, *The United States and China* (New York, second edition, 1958).

INDEX

Only the more important references are given here for the names of dynasties or other terms which recur throughout the book.

INDEX

INDEX

INDEX

legal status, 176
Legalists, school of, *see* Authoritarian theory
Legists, *see* Legalists
legitimacy, of dynasties, 84 f
lesser treasury, the, 157
Lhasa (town), 41
li (conventional propriety), 96, *see* ceremonial
Liang (dynasty; 502–556), 69
  (Han kingdom), Map 3
Liao (dynasty; 937–1125), 62, 69, 270
Liao-ning (province), 41
Lieh-tzu (philosophical text), 92
Lieh Yü-k'ou (legendary philosopher), 92
Lin-an (town), 62, 226, 237 f, 244–5, Map 7, *see* Hangchow
Ling-nan (circuit), Map 6
Lin Tse-hsü (provincial governor), 274
Lin-tzu (town), 223, Map 4
Li Po (poet), 276
li-pu (board of civil appointments), 157
li-pu (board of rites), 158
liquor, state monopoly of, 211
Li Shih-min (T'ang emperor), 289
literacy, 98
literary composition, 97
literature, 98, 105, 276
litigation, 179
liturgies, of Buddhism, 101
Liu, imperial house of, 289
Liu Chih-chi (historian), 291
Liu Pang (first Han emperor), 68
liu-pu (the six boards), 157
local government, 222
  histories, 297
loess deposits, 36, Map 2
logical compounds, in Chinese writing, 116, 119
lower Yangtse valley, 33 f, 39, 216, etc.
loyalties, conflict of, 90
Lo-yang (town), 28, 41, 61, 64, 217, 223, 244, Maps 2, 4, 5, 6
  as capital city and religious centre, 222, 231 f
  fall of, 58, 192

Lu (pre-imperial state), 279
Lu-chou (town), 41
Lung-chiang *see* Tsitsihar
Lung-hsi (commandery), Map 3
Lung-shan (neolithic culture), 44
Lung-yu (circuit), Map 6
Lun-yü (Confucian Analects), 91
luxury goods, 73, 99, 212, 239

Macartney, Lord, 108, 236, 243, 272 f, 297
magistrates, 170, 178
  and justice, 181
  staff of, 178
mail, delivery of, 216
maize, 36
'major' dynasties, 57
Malaya, 22, 262
Manchu dynasty, *see* Ch'ing
  leadership, 250
  officials, 162
Manchuria, 21, 23, 25, 41, 175, 221, 223, 259 etc., Maps 1, 2
Mandarin, speech-form, 301
Mandate of Heaven, 84, 90, 185, 282, 288, etc.
Manichaean religion, 266
man-power, 35, 73, 95, 105, 133, 220
manufacture, of equipment, 160
marble, 241
Marco Polo *see* Polo
markets, 208, 212
marquises, of Han period, 134, 167
marriage arrangements, 123, 147, 149
masters of writing, 154, 165
medical care, by Buddhists, 101
  of emperor, 157
Mediterranean world, 26, 265
Meissen, 272
Mekong (River), Map 1
melons, price of, 198
memorials to the throne, 82, 161, 176
men-hsia-sheng (imperial chancellery), 154 f, 157
Mencius (philosopher), 91, 98, 202
Meng K'o *see* Mencius
Meng-tzu (philosophical text), 91

317

INDEX

INDEX

INDEX

ta-ssu-nung (Grand Controller of Agriculture), 154, 157
taxable units, 191
taxation, 145, 154, 170, 186 etc.
  collection of, 143, 158
  in kind, 206–7, 220
  quota system, 205
  systems of land taxation, 198 f
tea, 36, 188, 249
  monopoly of, 211
  price of, 198
  trade in, 207, 214
technology, 94, 107, 109, 299
telegraph lines, 275
temples (Buddhist), 101
tenancy of land, 201
Ten kingdoms, the, (907–979), 69
T'eng-yüeh (town), 26, Map 1
terraced farming, 35
textiles, 38
textual criticism, 295
Three Consultants, the, 157
Three Departments, the, 154 f, 157
Three Kingdoms, the, (220–280), 68, Map 5
throne, power of, 156
Ti, veneration of, 74
Tibet, 21, 22, 26, 41, 175, Maps 1, 2
Tibetan peoples, 24, 250, 265
T'ien (Heaven), 74 *see* Mandate of Heaven, Son of Heaven
T'ien-chin *see* Tientsin
T'ien shan (mountains), 26, Map 1
Tientsin (port), 41, 223, Map 8
T'ien-tzu see Son of Heaven
Ti-hua (town), 41
timber, 39, 188, 238
time-keeping, 112
t'ing-wei (Commandant of justice), 157
titles, of officials, 153 f
  sale of, 208
tones, in Chinese language, 301
tools, as currency, 194
torture, 165, 181
townsmen, occupations of, 145
trade, 222, 227, 239, 249, 261 *see* commerce, merchants

convoys, 272
development of, 212 f
foreign, 210
maritime, 22, 272
traditions, breakdown of, 300
transport, 176, 186, 201, 220
  for emperor, 153
treaties of Tientsin and Peking, 275
treatises (in histories), 284
treaty ports, 223, 275
tribute, 249, 267
  grain, 207
Ts'ao Ts'ao (military leader), 204
Tsin (pre-imperial state), 294
Tsin (dynasties; western Tsin 265–316, eastern Tsin 317–419), 13, 58, 63, 68
Tsinan (town), 41
Tsingtao (town), 41
Tsitsihar (town), 41
Tso-chuan (historical text), 280
tsung-cheng (Director of the Ancestral Clan), 157
tsung-li-ya-men (organ of government), 275
tu-ch'a-yüan (censorate), 160
Tu Fu (poet), 276
Tung-t'ing lake, 29, Map 2
Tungus tribes, 24
Tun-huang (place-name), 28, 41, 258, Maps 2, 4
T'u-yü-hun tribes, 265
Turkestan, 21, 25, 41, 175, 264, Maps 1, 2
Turkish armies, 263
  peoples, 24, 250
typhoons, 218
Tzu-chih-t'ung-chien (historical compilation), 293

Uighur peoples, 250, 265
umbrellas, price of, 198
unassimilated tribesmen, 176
unofficial organs of government, 154
unplanned towns, 224
upper Yangtse valley, 29, 34 f, 215 etc.
Urumchi (town), 41

323

INDEX

DATE DUE